Competitive Programming in Python

Want to kill it at your job interview in the tech industry? Want to win that coding competition? Learn all the algorithmic techniques and programming skills you need from two experienced coaches, problem-setters, and judges for coding competitions. The authors highlight the versatility of each algorithm by considering a variety of problems and show how to implement algorithms in simple and efficient code. What to expect:

* Master 128 algorithms in Python.
* Discover the right way to tackle a problem and quickly implement a solution of low complexity.
* Understand classic problems like Dijkstra's shortest path algorithm and Knuth–Morris–Pratt's string matching algorithm, plus lesser-known data structures like Fenwick trees and Knuth's dancing links.
* Develop a framework to tackle algorithmic problem solving, including: Definition, Complexity, Applications, Algorithm, Key Information, Implementation, Variants, In Practice, and Problems.
* Python code included in the book and on the companion website.

Christoph Dürr is a senior researcher at the French National Center for Scientific Research (CNRS), affiliated with the Sorbonne University in Paris. After a PhD in 1996 at Paris-Sud University, he worked for one year as a postdoctoral researcher at the International Computer Science Institute in Berkeley and one year in the School of Computer Science and Engineering in the Hebrew University of Jerusalem in Israel. He has worked in the fields of quantum computation, discrete tomography and algorithmic game theory, and his current research activity focuses on algorithms and optimisation. From 2007 to 2014, he taught a preparation course for programming contests at the engineering school École Polytechnique, and acts regularly as a problem setter, trainer, or competitor for various coding competitions. In addition, he loves carrot cake.

Jill-Jênn Vie is a research scientist at Inria in machine learning. He is an alumnus from École normale supérieure Paris-Saclay, where he founded the algorithmic club of Paris-Saclay (CAPS) and coached several teams for the International Collegiate Programming Contest (ICPC). He published a book in theoretical computer science to help students prepare for prestigious French competitive exams such as *Grandes Écoles* or *agrégation*, and directed a television show "Blame the Algorithm" about the algorithms that govern our lives. He is part of the advisory board of the French Computer Science Society (SIF), itself a member of the International Federation for Information Processing (IFIP).

Competitive Programming in Python

128 Algorithms to Develop Your Coding Skills

CHRISTOPH DÜRR

CNRS, Sorbonne University

JILL-JÊNN VIE

Inria

Translated by Greg Gibbons and Danièle Gibbons

CAMBRIDGE
UNIVERSITY PRESS

CAMBRIDGE
UNIVERSITY PRESS

University Printing House, Cambridge CB2 8BS, United Kingdom

One Liberty Plaza, 20th Floor, New York, NY 10006, USA

477 Williamstown Road, Port Melbourne, VIC 3207, Australia

314–321, 3rd Floor, Plot 3, Splendor Forum, Jasola District Centre, New Delhi – 110025, India

79 Anson Road, #06–04/06, Singapore 079906

Cambridge University Press is part of the University of Cambridge.

It furthers the University's mission by disseminating knowledge in the pursuit of
education, learning, and research at the highest international levels of excellence.

www.cambridge.org
Information on this title: www.cambridge.org/9781108716826
DOI: 10.1017/9781108591928

© Cambridge University Press 2021

Translation from the French language edition:
Programmation efficace - 128 algorithmes qu'il faut avoir compris et codés en Python au cour de sa vie
By Christoph Dürr & Jill-Jênn Vie
Copyright © 2016 Edition Marketing S.A.
www.editions-ellipses.fr
All Rights Reserved

First published 2021

Printed in the United Kingdom by TJ Books Limited, Padstow Cornwall

A catalogue record for this publication is available from the British Library.

Library of Congress Cataloging-in-Publication Data
Names: Dürr, Christoph, 1969– author. | Vie, Jill-Jênn, 1990– author. |
    Gibbons, Greg, translator. | Gibbons, Danièle, translator.
Title: Competitive programming in Python : 128 algorithms to develop your
    coding skills / Christoph Dürr, Jill-Jênn Vie ; translated by Greg
    Gibbons, Danièle Gibbons.
Other titles: Programmation efficace. English
Description: First edition. | New York : Cambridge University Press, 2020.
    | Includes bibliographical references and index.
Identifiers: LCCN 2020022774 (print) | LCCN 2020022775 (ebook) |
    ISBN 9781108716826 (paperback) | ISBN 9781108591928 (epub)
Subjects: LCSH: Python (Computer program language) | Algorithms.
Classification: LCC QA76.73.P98 D8713 2020 (print) | LCC QA76.73.P98
    (ebook) | DDC 005.13/3–dc23
LC record available at https://lccn.loc.gov/2020022774
LC ebook record available at https://lccn.loc.gov/2020022775

ISBN 978-1-108-71682-6 Paperback

Contents

Preface

Algorithms play an important role in our society, solving numerous mathematical problems which appear in a broad spectrum of situations. To give a few examples, think of planning taxi routes given a set of reservations (see Section 9.12); assigning students to schools in a large urban school district, such as New York (see Section 9.4); or identifying a bottleneck in a transportation network (see Section 9.8). This is why job interviews in the IT (Information Technology) industry test candidates for their problem-solving skills. Many programming contests are organised by companies such as Google, Facebook and Microsoft to spot gifted candidates and then send them job offers. This book will help students to develop a culture of algorithms and data structures, so that they know how to apply them properly when faced with new mathematical problems.

Designing the right algorithm to solve a given problem is only half of the work; to complete the job, the algorithm needs to be implemented efficiently. This is why this book also emphasises implementation issues, and provides full source code for most of the algorithms presented. We have chosen Python for these implementations. What makes this language so enticing is that it allows a particularly clear and refined expression, illustrating the essential steps of the algorithm, without obscuring things behind burdensome notations describing data structures. Surprisingly, it is actually possible to re-read code written several months ago and even understand it!

We have collected here 128 algorithmic problems, indexed by theme rather than by technique. Many are classic, whereas certain are atypical. This work should prove itself useful when preparing to solve the wide variety of problems posed in programming contests such as ICPC, Google Code Jam, Facebook Hacker Cup, Prologin, France-ioi, etc. We hope that it could serve as a basis for an advanced course in programming and algorithms, where even certain candidates for the 'agrégation de mathématiques option informatique' (French competitive exam for the highest teacher's certification) will find a few original developments. The website tryalgo.org, maintained by the authors, contains links to the code of this book, as well as to selected problems at various online contests. This allows readers to verify their freshly acquired skills.

This book would never have seen the light of day without the support of the authors' life partners. Danke, Hương. Merci, 智子. The authors would also like to thank the students of the École polytechnique and the École normale supérieure of Paris-Saclay, whose practice, often nocturnal, generated a major portion of the material of this text. Thanks to all those who proofread the manuscript, especially René Adad, Evripidis Bampis, Binh-Minh Bui-Xuan, Stéphane Henriot, Lê Thành Dũng Nguyễn, Alexandre Nolin and Antoine Pietri. Thanks to all those who improved the programs on GitHub: Louis Abraham, Lilian Besson, Ryan Lahfa, Olivier Marty, Samuel Tardieu and Xavier Carcelle. One of the authors would especially like to thank his past teacher at the Lycée Thiers, Monsieur Yves Lemaire, for having introduced him to the admirable gem of Section 2.5 on page 52.

We hope that the reader will pass many long hours tackling algorithmic problems that at first glance appear insurmountable, and in the end feel the profound joy when a solution, especially an elegant solution, suddenly becomes apparent.

Finally, we would like to thank Danièle and Greg Gibbons for their translation of this work, even of this very phrase.

Attention, it's all systems go!

1 Introduction

> You, my young friend, are going to learn to program the algorithms of this book, and then go on to win programming contests, sparkle during your job interviews, and finally roll up your sleeves, get to work, and greatly improve the gross national product!

Mistakenly, computer scientists are still often considered the magicians of modern times. Computers have slowly crept into our businesses, our homes and our machines, and have become important enablers in the functioning of our world. However, there are many that use these devices without really mastering them, and hence, they do not fully enjoy their benefits. Knowing how to program provides the ability to fully exploit their potential to solve problems in an efficient manner. Algorithms and programming techniques have become a necessary background for many professions. Their mastery allows the development of creative and efficient computer-based solutions to problems encountered every day.

This text presents a variety of algorithmic techniques to solve a number of classic problems. It describes practical situations where these problems arise, and presents simple implementations written in the programming language Python. Correctly implementing an algorithm is not always easy: there are numerous traps to avoid and techniques to apply to guarantee the announced running times. The examples in the text are embellished with explanations of important implementation details which must be respected.

For the last several decades, programming competitions have sprung up at every level all over the world, in order to promote a broad culture of algorithms. The problems proposed in these contests are often variants of classic algorithmic problems, presented as frustrating enigmas that will never let you give up until you solve them!

1.1   Programming Competitions

In a programming competition, the candidates must solve several problems in a fixed time. The problems are often variants of classic problems, such as those addressed in this book, dressed up with a short story. The inputs to the problems are called *instances*. An instance can be, for example, the adjacency matrix of a graph for a shortest path problem. In general, a small example of an instance is provided, along with its solution. The source code of a solution can be uploaded to a server via a web interface, where it is compiled and tested against instances hidden from the public. For some problems the code is called for each instance, whereas for others the input begins with an integer indicating the number of instances occurring in the input. In the latter case, the program must then loop over each instance, solve it and display the results. A submission is accepted if it gives correct results in a limited time, on the order of a few seconds.

Figure 1.1 The logo of the ICPC nicely shows the steps in the resolution of a problem. A helium balloon is presented to the team for each problem solved.

To give here a list of all the programming competitions and training sites is quite impossible, and such a list would quickly become obsolete. Nevertheless, we will review some of the most important ones.

ICPC   The oldest of these competitions was founded by the *Association for Computing Machinery* in 1977 and supported by them up until 2017. This contest, known as the ICPC, for *International Collegiate Programming Contest*, is organised in the form of a tournament. The starting point is one of the regional competitions, such as the *South-West European Regional Contest* (SWERC), where the two best teams qualify for the worldwide final. The particularity of this contest is that each three-person team has only a single computer at their disposal. They have only 5 hours to solve a maximum number of problems among the 10 proposed. The first ranking criterion is the number of submitted solutions accepted (i.e. tested successfully against a set of unknown instances). The next criterion is the sum over the submitted problems of the time between the start of the contest and the moment of the accepted submission. For each erroneous submission, a penalty of 20 minutes is added.

There are several competing theories on what the ideal composition of a team is. In general, a good programmer and someone familiar with algorithms is required, along with a specialist in different domains such as graph theory, dynamic programming, etc. And, of course, the team members need to get along together, even in stressful situations!

For the contest, each team can bring 25 pages of reference code printed in an 8-point font. They can also access the online documentation of the Java API and the C++ standard library.

Google Code Jam   In contrast with the ICPC contest, which is limited to students up to a Master's level, the Google Code Jam is open to everyone. This more recent annual competition is for individual contestants. Each problem comes in general with a deck of small instances whose resolution wins a few points, and a set of enormous instances for which it is truly important to find a solution with the appropriate algorithmic complexity. The contestants are informed of the acceptance of their solution for the large instances only at the end of the contest. However, its true strong point is the possibility to access the solutions submitted by all of the participants, which is extremely instructive.

The competition *Facebook Hacker Cup* is of a similar nature.

Prologin   The French association Prologin organises each year a competition targeted at students up to twenty years old. Their capability to solve algorithmic problems is put to test in three stages: an online selection, then regional competitions and concluding with a national final. The final is atypically an endurance test of 36 hours, during which the participants are confronted with a problem in Artificial Intelligence. Each candidate must program a "champion" to play a game whose rules are defined by the organisers. At the end of the day, the champions are thrown in the ring against each other in a tournament to determine the final winner.

The website `https://prologin.org` includes complete archives of past problems, with the ability to submit algorithms online to test the solutions.

France-IOI   Each year, the organisation France-IOI prepares junior and senior high school students for the International Olympiad in Informatics. Since 2011, they have organised the 'Castor Informatique' competition, addressed at students from Grade 4 to Grade 12 (675,000 participants in 2018). Their website `http://france-ioi.org` hosts a large number of algorithmic problems (more than 1,000).

Numerous programming contests organised with the goal of selecting candidates for job offers also exist. The web site `www.topcoder.com`, for example, also includes tutorials on algorithms, often very well written.

For training, we particularly recommend `https://codeforces.com`, a well-respected web site in the community of programming competitions, as it proposes clear and well-prepared problems.

1.1.1   Training Sites

A number of websites propose problems taken from the annals of competitions, with the possibility to test solutions as a training exercise. This is notably the case for Google Code Jam and Prologin (in French). The collections of the annals of the ICPC contests can be found in various locations.

Traditional online judges   The following sites contain, among others, many problems derived from the ICPC contests.

uva   `http://uva.onlinejudge.org`
icpcarchive   `http://icpcarchive.ecs.baylor.edu`,   `http://livearchive
.onlinejudge.org`

Chinese online judges Several training sites now exist in China. They tend to have a purer and more refined interface than the traditional judges. Nevertheless, sporadic failures have been observed.

poj `http://poj.org`
tju `http://acm.tju.edu.cn` (Shut down since 2017)
zju `http://acm.zju.edu.cn`

Modern online judges Sphere Online Judge `http://spoj.com` and Kattis `http://open.kattis.com` have the advantage of accepting the submission of solutions in a variety of languages, including Python.

spoj `http://spoj.com`
kattis `http://open.kattis.com`
zju `http://acm.zju.edu.cn`

Other sites

codechef `http://codechef.com`
codility `http://codility.com`
gcj `http://code.google.com/codejam`
prologin `http://prologin.org`
slpc `http://cs.stanford.edu/group/acm`

Throughout this text, problems are proposed at the end of each section in relation to the topic presented. They are accompanied with their identifiers to a judge site; for example [spoj:CMPLS] refers to the problem '*Complete the Sequence!*' at the URL `www.spoj.com/problems/CMPLS/`. The site `http://tryalgo.org` contains links to all of these problems. The reader thus has the possibility to put into practice the algorithms described in this book, testing an implementation against an online judge.

The languages used for programming competitions are principally C++ and Java. The SPOJ judge also accepts Python, while the Google Code Jam contest accepts many of the most common languages. To compensate for the differences in execution speed due to the choice of language, the online judges generally adapt the time limit to the language used. However, this adaptation is not always done carefully, and it is sometimes difficult to have a solution in Python accepted, even if it is correctly written. We hope that this situation will be improved in the years to come. Also, certain judges work with an ancient version of Java, in which such useful classes as `Scanner` are not available.

1.1.2 Responses of the Judges

When some code for a problem is submitted to an online judge, it is evaluated via a set of private tests and a particularly succinct response is returned. The principal response codes are the following:

Accepted Your program provides the correct output in the allotted time. Congratulations!

Presentation Error Your program is almost accepted, but the output contains extraneous or missing blanks or end-of-lines. This message occurs rarely.

Compilation Error The compilation of your program generates errors. Often, clicking on this message will provide the nature of the error. Be sure to compare the version of the compiler used by the judge with your own.

Wrong Answer Re-read the problem statement, a detail must have been overlooked. Are you sure to have tested all the limit cases? Might you have left debugging statements in your code?

Time Limit Exceeded You have probably not implemented the most efficient algorithm for this problem, or perhaps have an infinite loop somewhere. Test your loop invariants to ensure loop termination. Generate a large input instance and test locally the performance of your code.

Runtime Error In general, this could be a division by zero, an access beyond the limits of an array, or a `pop()` on an empty stack. However, other situations can also generate this message, such as the use of `assert` in Java, which is often not accepted.

The taciturn behaviour of the judges nevertheless allows certain information to be gleaned from the instances. Here is a trick that was used during an ICPC / SWERC contest. In a problem concerning graphs, the statement indicated that the input consisted of connected graphs. One of the teams doubted this, and wrote a connectivity test. In the positive case, the program entered into an infinite loop, while in the negative case, it caused a division by zero. The error code generated by the judge (Time Limit Exceeded ou Runtime Error) allowed the team to detect that certain graphs in the input were not connected.

1.2 Python in a Few Words

The programming language Python was chosen for this book, for its readability and ease of use. In September 2017, Python was identified by the website `https://stackoverflow.com` as the programming language with the greatest growth in high-income countries, in terms of the number of questions seen on the website, notably thanks to the popularity of machine learning.[1] Python is also the language retained for such important projects as the formal calculation system SageMath, whose critical portions are nonetheless implemented in more efficient languages such as C++ or C.

Here are a few details on this language. This chapter is a short introduction to Python and does not claim to be exhaustive or very formal. For the neophyte reader we recommend the site `python.org`, which contains a high-quality introduction as well as exceptional documentation. A reader already familiar with Python can profit

---

[1] `https://stackoverflow.blog/2017/09/06/incredible-growth-python/`

enormously by studying the programs of David Eppstein, which are very elegant and highly readable. Search for the keywords Eppstein PADS.

Python is an interpreted language. Variable types do not have to be declared, they are simply inferred at the time of assignment. There are neither keywords begin/end nor brackets to group instructions, for example in the blocks of a function or a loop. The organisation in blocks is simply based on indentation! A typical error, difficult to identify, is an erroneous indentation due to spaces used in some lines and tabs in others.

Basic Data Types

In Python, essentially four basic data types exist: Booleans, integers, floating-point numbers and character strings. In contrast with most other programming languages, the integers are not limited to a fixed number of bits (typically 64), but use an arbitrary precision representation. The functions—more precisely the *constructors*: bool, int, float, str—allow the conversion of an object to one of these basic types. For example, to access the digits of a specific integer given its decimal representation, it can be first transformed into a string, and then the characters of the string can be accessed. However, in contrast with languages such as C, it is not possible to directly modify a character of a string: strings are *immutable*. It is first necessary to convert to a list representation of the characters; see below.

Data Structures

The principal complex data structures are dictionaries, sets, lists and n-tuples. These structures are called *containers*, as they contain several objects in a structured manner. Once again, there are functions dict, set, list and tuple that allow the conversion of an object into one of these structures. For example, for a string s, the function list(s) returns a list L composed of the characters of the string. We could then, for example, replace certain elements of the list L and then recreate a string by concatenating the elements of L with the expression ''.join(L). Here, the empty string could be replaced by a separator: for example, '-'.join(['A','B','C']) returns the string "A-B-C".

1.2.1   Manipulation of Lists, *n*-tuples, Dictionaries

Note that lists in Python are not linked lists of cells, each with a pointer to its successor in the list, as is the case in many other languages. Instead, lists are arrays of elements that can be accessed and modified using their index into the array. A list is written by enumerating its elements between square brackets [and], with the elements separated by commas.

> **Lists**   The indices of a list start with 0. The last element can also be accessed with the index −1, the second last with −2 and so on. Here are some examples of operations to extract elements or sublists of a list. This mechanism is known as *slicing*, and is also available for strings.

The following expressions have a complexity linear in the length of L, with the exception of the first, which is in constant time.

L[i]	the ith element of L
L[i:j]	the list of elements with indices starting at i and up to (but not including) j
L[:j]	the first j elements
L[i:]	all the elements from the ith onwards
L[-3:]	the last three elements of L
L[i:j:k]	elements from the ith up to (but not including) the jth, taking only every kth element
L[::2]	the elements of L with even indices
L[::-1]	a reverse copy of L

The most important methods of a list for our usage are listed below. Their complexity is expressed in terms of n, the length of the list L. A function has *constant amortised complexity* if, for several successive calls to it, the average complexity is constant, even if some of these calls take a time linear in n.

len(L)	returns the number of elements of the list L	$O(1)$
sorted(L)	returns a sorted copy of the list L	$O(n \log n)$
L.sort()	sorts L in place	$O(n \log n)$
L.count(c)	the number of occurrences of c in L	$O(n)$
c in L	is the element c found in L?	$O(n)$
L.append(c)	append c to the end of L	amortised $O(1)$
L.pop()	extracts and returns the last element of L	amortised $O(1)$

Thus a list has all the functionality of a stack, defined in Section 1.5.1 on page 20.

n-tuple An n-tuple behaves much like a list, with a difference in the usage of parentheses to describe it, as in (1, 2) or (left, 'X', right). A 1-tuple, composed of only one element, requires the usage of a comma, as in (2,). A 0-tuple, empty, can be written as (), or as tuple(), no doubt more readable. The main difference with lists is that n-tuples are immutable, just like strings. This is why an n-tuple can serve as a key in a dictionary.

Dictionaries Dictionaries are used to associate objects with values, for example the words of a text with their frequency. A dictionary is constructed as comma-separated key:value pairs between curly brackets, such as {'the': 4, 'bread': 1, 'is': 6}, where the keys and values are separated by a colon. An empty dictionary is obtained with {}. A membership test of a key x in a dictionary dic is written x in dic. Behind a dictionary there is a hash table, hence the complexity of the expressions x in dic, dic[x], dic[x] = 42 is in practice constant time, even if the worst-case complexity is linear, a case obtained in the improbable event of all keys having the same hash value.

If the keys of a dictionary are all the integers between 0 and $n - 1$, the use of a list is much more efficient.

A loop in Python is written either with the keyword `for` or with `while`. The notation for the loop `for` is `for x in S:`, where the variable x successively takes on the values of the container S, or of the keys of S in the case of a dictionary. In contrast, `while L:` will loop as long as the list L is non-empty. Here, an implicit conversion of a list to a Boolean is made, with the convention that only the empty list converts to `False`.

At times, it is necessary to handle at the same time the values of a list along with their positions (indices) within the list. This can be implemented as follows:

```
for index in range(len(L)):
    value = L[index]
        # ... handling of index and value
```

The function `enumerate` allows a more compact expression of this loop:

```
for index, value in enumerate(L):
        # ... handling of index and value
```

For a dictionary, the following loop iterates simultaneously over the keys and values:

```
for key, value in dic.items():
        # ... handling of key and value
```

1.2.2   Specificities: List and Dictionary Comprehension, Iterators

List and Dictionary Comprehension
The language Python provides a syntax close to the notation used in mathematics for certain objects. To describe the list of squares from 0 to n^2, it is possible to use a *list comprehension*:

```
>>> n = 5
>>> squared_numbers = [x ** 2 for x in range(n + 1)]
>>> squared_numbers
[0, 1, 4, 9, 16, 25]
```

which corresponds to the set $\{x^2 | x = 0, \dots, n\}$ in mathematics.

This is particularly useful to initialise a list of length n:

```
>>> t = [0 for _ in range(n)]
>>> t
[0, 0, 0, 0, 0]
```

or to initialise counters for the letters in a string:

```
>>> my_string = "cowboy bebop"
>>> nb_occurrences = {letter: 0 for letter in my_string}
>>> nb_occurrences
{'c': 0, 'o': 0, 'w': 0, 'b': 0, 'y': 0, ' ': 0, 'e': 0, 'p': 0}
```

The second line, a *dictionary comprehension*, is equivalent to the following:

```
nb_occurrences = {}
for letter in my_string:
    nb_occurrences[letter] = 0
```

Ranges and Other Iterators

To loop over ranges of integers, the code for i in range(n): can be used to run over the integers from 0 to $n - 1$. Several variants exist:

$$
\begin{array}{ll}
\texttt{range(k, n)} & \text{from } k \text{ to } n - 1 \\
\texttt{range(k, n, 2)} & \text{from } k \text{ to } n - 1 \text{ two by two} \\
\texttt{range(n - 1, -1, -1)} & \text{from } n - 1 \text{ to } 0 \, (-1 \text{ excluded}) \text{ in decreasing order.}
\end{array}
$$

In early versions of Python, range returned a list. Nowadays, for efficiency, it returns an object known as an *iterator*, which produces integers one by one, if and when the for loop claims a value. Any function can serve as an iterator, as long as it can produce elements at different moments of its execution using the keyword yield. For example, the following function iterates over all pairs of elements of a given list:.

```
def all_pairs(L):
    n = len(L)
    for i in range(n):
        for j in range(i + 1, n):
            yield (L[i], L[j])
```

1.2.3 Useful Modules and Packages

Modules

Certain Python objects must be imported from a module or a package with the command import. A package is a collection of modules. Two methods can be used; the second avoids potential naming collisions between the methods in different modules:

```
>>> from math import sqrt
>>> sqrt(4)
2
>>> import math
>>> math.sqrt(4)
2
```

math   This module contains mathematical functions and constants such as `log`, `sqrt`, `pi`, etc. Python operates on integers with arbitrary precision, thus there is no limit on their size. As a consequence, there is no integer equivalent to represent $-\infty$ or $+\infty$. For floating point numbers on the other hand, `float('-inf')` and `float('inf')` can be used. Beginning with Python 3.5, `math.inf` (or `from math import inf`) is equivalent to `float('inf')`.

fractions   This module exports the class `Fraction`, which allows computations with fractions without the loss of precision of floating point calculations. For example, if `f` is an instance of the class Fraction, then `str(f)` returns a string similar to the form "3/2", expressing f as an irreducible fraction.

bisect   Provides binary (dichotomous) search functions on a sorted list.

heapq   Provides functions to manipulate a list as a heap, thus allowing an element to be added or the smallest element removed in time logarithmic in the size of the heap; see Section 1.5.4 on page 22.

string   This module provides, for example, the function `ascii_lowercase`, which returns its argument converted to lowercase characters. Note that the strings themselves already provide numerous useful methods, such as `strip`, which removes whitespace from the beginning and end of a string and returns the result, `lower`, which converts all the characters to lowercase, and especially `split`, which detects the substrings separated by spaces (or by another separator passed as an argument). For example, "12/OCT/2018".split("/") returns ["12", "OCT", "2018"].

Packages

One of the strengths of Python is the existence of a large variety of code packages. Some are part of the standard installation of the language, while others must be imported with the shell command `pip`. They are indexed and documented at the web site `pypi.org`. Here is a non-exhaustive list of very useful packages.

tryalgo   All the code of the present book is available in a package called `tryalgo` and can be imported in the following manner: `pip install tryalgo`.

```
>>> import tryalgo
>>> help(tryalgo)        # for the list of modules
>>> help(tryalgo.arithm) # for a particular module
```

collections   To simplify life, the class `from collections import Counter` can be used. For an object c of this class, the expression `c[x]` will return 0 if x is not a key in c. Only modification of the value associated with x will create an entry in c, such as, for example, when executing the instruction c[x] += 1. This is thus slightly more practical than a dictionary, as is illustrated below.

```
>>> c = {}                    # dictionary
>>> c['a'] += 1               # the key does not exist
Traceback (most recent call last):
  File "<stdin>", line 1, in <module>
KeyError: 'a'
>>> c['a'] = 1
>>> c['a'] += 1               # now it does
>>> c
{'a': 2}
>>> from collections import Counter
>>> c = Counter()
>>> c['a'] += 1               # the key does not exist, so it is created
Counter({'a': 1})
>>> c = Counter('cowboy bebop')
Counter({'o': 3, 'b': 3, 'c': 1, 'w': 1, 'y': 1, ' ': 1, 'e': 1, 'p': 1})
```

The collections package also provides the class deque, for *double-ended queue*, see Section 1.5.3 on page 21. With this structure, elements can be added or removed either from the left (head) or from the right (tail) of the queue. This helps implement Dijkstra's algorithm in the case where the edges have only weights 0 or 1, see Section 8.2 on page 126.

This package also provides the class defaultdict, which is a dictionary that assigns default values to keys that are yet in the dictionary, hence a generalisation of the class Counter.

```
>>> from collections import defaultdict
>>> g = defaultdict(list)
>>> g['paris'].append('marseille')  # 'paris' key is created on the fly
>>> g['paris'].append('lyon')
>>> g
defaultdict(<class 'list'>, {'paris': ['marseille', 'lyon']})
>>> g['paris']  # behaves like a dict
['marseille', 'lyon']
```

See also Section 1.3 on page 13 for an example of reading a graph given as input.

numpy   This package provides general tools for numerical calculations involving manipulations of large matrices. For example, numpy.linalg.solve solves a linear system, while numpy.fft.fft calculates a (fast) discrete Fourier transform.

While writing the code of this book, we have followed the norm PEP8, which provides precise recommendations on the usage of blanks, the choice of names for variables, etc. We advise the readers to also follow these indications, using, for example, the tool pycodestyle to validate the structure of their code.

1.2.4   Interpreters `Python`, `PyPy`, and `PyPy3`

We have chosen to implement our algorithms in Python 3, which is already over 12 years old,[2] while ensuring backwards compatibility with Python 2. The principal changes affecting the code appearing in this text concern `print` and division between integers. In Python 3, $5 / 2$ is equal to 2.5, whereas it gives 2 in Python 2. The integer division operator `//` gives the same result for both versions. As for `print`, in Python 2 it is a keyword, whereas in Python 3 it is a function, and hence requires the parameters to be enclosed by parentheses.

The interpreter of reference is CPython, and its executable is just called `python`. According to your installation, the interpreter of Python 3 could be called `python` or `python3`. Another much more efficient interpreter is PyPy, whose executable is called `pypy` in version 2 and `pypy3` in version 3. It implements a subset of the Python language, called RPython, with quite minimal restrictions, which essentially allow the inference of the type of a variable by an analysis of the source code. The inconvenience is that `pypy` is still under development and certain modules are not yet available. But it can save your life during a contest with time limits!

1.2.5   Frequent Errors

Copy
An error often made by beginners in Python concerns the copying of lists. In the following example, the list B is in fact just a reference to A. Thus a modification of $B[0]$ results also in a modification of $A[0]$.

```
A = [1, 2, 3]
B = A  # Beware! Both variables refer to the same object
```

For B to be a distinct copy of A, the following syntax should be used:

```
A = [1, 2, 3]
B = A[:]  # B becomes a distinct copy of A
```

The notation [:] can be used to make a copy of a list. It is also possible to make a copy of all but the first element, $A[1 :]$, or all but the last element, $A[: -1]$, or even in reverse order $A[:: -1]$. For example, the following code creates a matrix M, all of whose rows are the same, and the modification of $M[0][0]$ modifies the whole of the first column of M.

```
M = [[0] * 10] * 10  # Do not write this!
```

---

[2] Python 3.0 final was released on 3 December, 2008.

A square matrix can be correctly initialised using one of the following expressions:

```
M1 = [[0] * 10 for _ in range(10)]
M2 = [[0 for j in range(10)] for i in range(10)]
```

The module numpy permits easy manipulations of matrices; however, we have chosen not to profit from it in this text, in order to have generic code that is easy to translate to Java or C++.

Ranges
Another typical error concerns the use of the function range. For example, the following code processes the elements of a list *A* between the indices 0 and 9 inclusive, in order.

```
for i in range(0, 10):   # 0 included, 10 excluded
    process(A[i])
```

To process the elements in descending order, it is not sufficient to just swap the arguments. In fact, range(10, 0, -1)—the third argument indicates the step—is the list of elements with indices 10 (included) to 0 (excluded). Thus the loop must be written as:

```
for i in range(9, -1, -1):  # 9 included, -1 excluded
    process(A[i])
```

1.3 Input-Output

1.3.1 Read the Standard Input

For most problems posed by programming contests, the input data are read from *standard input*, and the responses displayed on *standard output*. For example, if the input file is called test.in, and your program is prog.py, the contents of the input file can be directed to your program with the following command, launched from a command window:

```
python prog.py < test.in
```

In general, under Mac OS X, a command window can be obtained by typing *Command-Space Terminal*, and under Windows, via *Start → Run → cmd*.
If you are running Linux, the keyboard shortcut is generally *Alt-F2*, but that you probably already knew...

If you wish to save the output of your program to a file called test.out, type:

```
python prog.py < test.in > test.out
```

A little hint: if you want to display the output at the same time as it is being written to a file test.out, use the following (the command tee is not present by default in Windows):

```
python prog.py < test.in | tee test.out
```

The inputs can be read line by line via the command input(), which returns the next input line in the form of a string, excluding the end-of-line characters.[3] The module sys contains a similar function stdin.readline(), which does not suppress the end-of-line characters, but according to our experience has the advantage of being four times as fast!

If the input line is meant to contain an integer, we can convert the string with the function int (if it is a floating point number, then we must use float instead). In the case of a line containing several integers separated by spaces, the string can first be cut into different substrings using split(); these can then be converted into integers with the method map. For example, in the case of two integers height and width to be read on the same line, separated by a space, the following command suffices:

```
import sys

height, width = map(int, sys.stdin.readline().split())
```

If your program exhibits performance problems while reading the inputs, our experience shows that a factor of two can be gained by reading the whole of the inputs with a single system call. The following code fragment assumes that the inputs are made up of only integers, eventually on multiple lines. The parameter 0 in the function os.read means that the read is from standard input, and the constant M must be an upper bound on the size of the file. For example, if the file contains 10^7 integers, each between 0 and 10^9, then as each integer is written with at most 10 characters and there are at most 2 characters separating the integers (\n and \r), we can choose $M = 12 \cdot 10^7$.

---

[3] According to the operating system, the end-of-line is indicated by the characters \r, \n, or both, but this is not important when reading with input(). Note that in Python 2 the behaviour of input() is different, so it is necessary to use the equivalent function raw_input().

```
import os

instance = list(map(int, os.read(0, M).split()))
```

Example – Read a Graph on Input
If the inputs are given in the form:

```
3
paris tokyo 9471
paris new-york 5545
new-york singapore 15344
```

where 3 is the number of edges of a graph and each edge is represented by <departure> <arrival> <distance>, then the following code, using defaultdict to initialise the new keys in an empty dictionary, allows the construction of the graph:

```
from collections import defaultdict

nb_edges = int(input())

g = defaultdict(dict)
for _ in range(nb_edges):
    u, v, weight = input().split()
    g[u][v] = int(weight)
    # g[v][u] = int(weight)   # For an undirected graph
```

Example—read three matrices A, B, C and test if $AB = C$
In this example, the inputs are in the following form: the first line contains a single integer n. It is followed by $3n$ lines each containing n integers separated by spaces, coding the values contained in three $n \times n$ matrices A, B, C, given row by row. The goal is to test if the product A times B is equal to the matrix C. A direct approach by matrix multiplication would have a complexity $O(n^3)$. However, a probabilistic solution exists in $O(n^2)$, which consists in randomly choosing a vector x and testing whether $A(Bx) = Cx$. This is the *Freivalds test* (1979). What is the probability that the algorithm outputs equality even if $AB \neq C$? Whenever the computations are made modulo d, the probability of error is at most $1/d$. This error probability can be made arbitrarily small by repeating the test several times. The following code has an error probability bounded above by 10^{-6}.

```
from random import randint
from sys import stdin


def readint():
    return int(stdin.readline())


def readarray(typ):
    return list(map(typ, stdin.readline().split()))
def readmatrix(n):
    M = []
    for _ in range(n):
        row = readarray(int)
        assert len(row) == n
        M.append(row)
    return M


def mult(M, v):
    n = len(M)
    return [sum(M[i][j] * v[j] for j in range(n)) for i in range(n)]


def freivalds(A, B, C):
    n = len(A)
    x = [randint(0, 1000000) for j in range(n)]
    return mult(A, mult(B, x)) == mult(C, x)


if __name__ == "__main__":
    n = readint()
    A = readmatrix(n)
    B = readmatrix(n)
    C = readmatrix(n)
    print(freivalds(A, B, C))
```

Note the test on the variable __name__. This test is evaluated as True if the file containing this code is called directly, and as False if the file is included with the import keyword.

Problem
Enormous Input Test [spoj:INTEST]

1.3.2   Output Format

The outputs of your program are displayed with the command print, which produces a new line with the values of its arguments. The generation of end-of-line characters can be suppressed by passing end='' as an argument.

To display numbers with fixed precision and length, there are at least two possibilities in Python. First of all, there is the operator % that works like the function printf in the language C. The syntax is s % a, where s is a format string, a character string including typed display indicators beginning with %, and where a consists of one or more arguments that will replace the display indicators in the format string.

```
>>> i_test = 1
>>> answer = 1.2142
>>> print("Case #%d: %.2f gigawatts!!!" % (i_test, answer))
Case #1: 1.21 gigawatts!!!
```

The letter d after the % indicates that the first argument should be interpreted as an integer and inserted in place of the %d in the format string. Similarly, the letter f is used for floats and s for strings. A percentage can be displayed by indicating %% in the format string. Between the character % and the letter indicating the type, further numerical indications can be given. For example, %.2f indicates that up to two digits should be displayed after the decimal point.

Another possibility is to use the method format of a string, which follows the syntax of the language C#. This method provides more formatting possibilities and is in general easier to manipulate.

```
>>> print("Case #{}: {:.2f} gigawatts!!!".format(i_test, answer))
Case #1: 1.21 gigawatts!!!
```

Finally, beginning with Python 3.6, *f-strings*, or formatted string literals, exist.

```
>>> print(f"Case #{testCase}: {answer:.2f} gigawatts!!!")
Case #1: 1.21 gigawatts!!!
```

In this case, the floating point precision itself can be a variable, and the formatting is embedded with each argument.

```
>>> precision = 2
>>> print(f"Case #{testCase}: {answer:.{precision}f} gigawatts!!!")
Case #1: 1.21 gigawatts!!!
```

1.4   Complexity

To write an efficient program, it is first necessary to find an algorithm of appropriate complexity. This complexity is expressed as a function of the size of the inputs. In order to easily compare complexities, the notation of Landau symbols is used.

Landau Symbols

The complexity of an algorithm is, for example, said to be $O(n^2)$ if the execution time can be bounded above by a quadratic function in n, where n represents the size or some parameter of the input. More precisely, for two functions f, g we denote $f \in O(g)$ if positive constants n_0, c exist, such that for every $n \geq n_0$, $f(n) \leq c \cdot g(n)$. By an abuse of notation, we also write $f = O(g)$. This notation allows us to ignore the multiplicative and additive constants in a function f and brings out the magnitude and form of the dependence on a parameter.

Similarly, if for constants $n_0, c > 0$ we have $f(n) \geq c \cdot g(n)$ for every $n \geq n_0$, then we write $f \in \Omega(g)$. If $f \in O(g)$ and $f \in \Omega(g)$, then we write $f \in \Theta(g)$, indicating that f and g have the same order of magnitude of complexity. Finally, if $f \in O(g)$ but not $g \in O(f)$, then we write $f \in o(g)$

Complexity Classes

If the complexity of an algorithm is $O(n^c)$ for some constant c, it is said to be *polynomial* in n. A problem for which a polynomial algorithm exists is said to be *polynomial*, and the class of such problems bears the name P. Unhappily, not all problems are polynomial, and numerous problems exist for which no polynomial algorithm has been found to this day.

One such problem is k-SAT: Given n Boolean variables and m clauses each containing k literals (a variable or its negation), is it possible to assign to each variable a Boolean value in such a manner that each clause contains at least one literal with the value True (SAT is the version of this problem without a restriction on the number of variables in a clause)? The particularity of each of these problems is that a potential solution (assignment to each of the variables) satisfying all the constraints can be verified in polynomial time by evaluating all the clauses: they are in the class NP (for Non-deterministic Polynomial). We can easily solve 1-SAT in polynomial time, hence 1-SAT is in P. 2-SAT is also in P; this is the subject of Section 6.9 on page 110. However, from 3-SAT onwards, the answer is not known. We only know that solving 3-SAT is at least as difficult as solving SAT.

It turns out that $P \subseteq NP$—intuitively, if we can construct a solution in polynomial time, then we can also verify a solution in polynomial time. It is believed that $P \neq NP$, but this conjecture remains unproven to this day. In the meantime, researchers have linked NP problems among themselves using *reductions*, which transform in polynomial time an algorithm for a problem A into an algorithm for a problem B. Hence, if A is in P, then B is also in P: A is 'at least as difficult' as B.

The problems that are at least as difficult as SAT constitute the class of problems NP-hard, and among these we distinguish the NP-complete problems, which are defined as those being at the same time NP-hard and in NP. Solve any one of these in polynomial time and you will have solved them all, and will be gratified by eternal recognition, accompanied by a million dollars.[4] At present, to solve these problems in an acceptable time, it is necessary to restrict them to instances with properties

---

[4] www.claymath.org/millennium-problems/p-vs-np-problem

that can aid the resolution (planarity of a graph, for example), permit the program to answer correctly with only a constant probability or produce a solution only close to an optimal solution.

Happily, most of the problems encountered in programming contests are polynomial.

If these questions of complexity classes interest you, we recommend Christos H. Papadimitriou's book on computational complexity (2003).

For programming contests in particular, the programs must give a response within a few seconds, which gives current processors the time to execute on the order of tens or hundreds of millions of operations. The following table gives a rough idea of the acceptable complexities for a response time of a second. These numbers are to be taken with caution and, of course, depend on the language used,[5] the machine that will execute the code and the type of operation (integer or floating point calculations, calls to mathematical functions, etc.).

size of input	acceptable complexity
1000000	$O(n)$
100000	$O(n \log n)$
1000	$O(n^2)$

The reader is invited to conduct experiments with simple programs to test the time necessary to execute n integer multiplications for different values of n. We insist here on the fact that the constants lurking behind the Landau symbols can be very large, and at times, in practice, an algorithm with greater asymptotic complexity may be preferred. An example is the multiplication of two $n \times n$ matrices. The naive method costs $O(n^3)$ operations, whereas a recursive procedure discovered by Strassen (1969) costs only $O(n^{2.81})$. However, the hidden multiplicative constant is so large that for the size of matrices that you might need to manipulate, the naive method without doubt will be more efficient.

In Python, adding an element to a list takes constant time, as does access to an element with a given index. The creation of a sublist with $L[i : j]$ requires time $O(\max\{1, j - i\})$. Dictionaries are represented by hash tables, and the insertion of a key-value pair can be done in constant time, see Section 1.5.2 on page 21. However, this time constant is non-negligible, hence if the keys of the dictionary are the integers from 0 to $n - 1$, it is preferable to use a list.

Amortised Complexity

For certain data structures, the notion of amortised time complexity is used. For example, a list in Python is represented internally by an array, equipped with a variable *length* storing the size. When a new element is added to the array with the method append, it is stored in the array at the index indicated by the variable length, and then

---

[5] Roughly consider Java twice as slow and Python four times as slow as C++.

the variable length is incremented. If the capacity of the array is no longer sufficient, a new array twice as large is allocated, and the contents of the original array are copied over. Hence, for n successive calls to append on a list initially empty, the time of each call is usually constant, and it is occasionally linear in the current size of the list. However, the sum of the time of these calls is $O(n)$, which, once spread out over each of the calls, gives an amortised time $O(1)$.

1.5   Abstract Types and Essential Data Structures

We will now tackle a theme that is at the heart of the notion of efficient programming: the data structures underlying our programs to solve problems.

An *abstract type* is a description of the possible values that a set of objects can take on, the operations that can be performed on these objects and the behaviour of these operations. An abstract type can thus be seen as a *specification*.

A *data structure* is a concrete way to organise the data in order to treat them efficiently, respecting the clauses in the specification. Thus, we can implement an abstract type by one or more different data structures and determine the complexity in time and memory of each operation. Thereby, based on the frequency of the operations that need to be executed, we will prefer one or another of the implementations of an abstract type to solve a given problem.

To program well, a mastery of the data structures offered by a language and its associated standard library is essential. In this section, we review the most useful data structures for programming competitions.

1.5.1   Stacks

A **stack** (see Figure 1.2) is an object that keeps track of a set of elements and provides the following operations: test if the stack is empty, add an element to the top of the stack *(push)*, access the element at the top of the stack and remove an element *(pop)*. Python lists can serve as stacks. An element is pushed with the method append(element) and popped with the method pop().

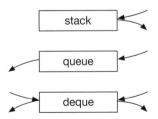

Figure 1.2 The three principal sequential access data structures provided by Python.

If a list is used as a Boolean, for example as the condition of an if or while instruction, it takes on the value True if and only if it is non-empty. In fact, this is the case for all objects implementing the method __len__; for these, if x: behaves exactly like if len(x) > 0:. All of these operations execute in constant time.

1.5.2 Dictionaries

A **dictionary** allows the association of keys to values, in the same manner that an array associates indices to values. The internal workings are based on a hash table, which uses a hash function to associate the elements with indices in an array, and implements a mechanism of collision management in the case where different elements are sent to the same index. In the best case, the read and write operations on a dictionary execute in constant time, but in the worst case they execute in linear time if it is necessary to run through a linear number of keys to handle the collisions. In practice, this degenerate case arrives only rarely, and in this book, we generally assume that accesses to dictionary entries take constant time. If the keys are of the form $0, 1, \ldots, n - 1$, it is, of course, always preferable for performance reasons to use a simple array.

Problems
Encryption [spoj:CENCRY]
Phone List [spoj:PHONELST]
A concrete simulation [spoj:ACS]

1.5.3 Queues

A **queue** is similar to a stack, with the difference that elements are added to the end of the queue (enqueued) and are removed from the front of the queue (dequeued). A queue is also known as a FIFO queue (*first in, first out*, like a waiting line), whereas a stack is called LIFO (*last in, first out*, like a pile of plates).

In the Python standard library, there are two classes implementing a queue. The first, Queue, is a synchronised implementation, meaning that several processes can access it simultaneously. As the programs of this book do not exploit parallelism, the use of this class is not recommended, as it entails a slowdown because of the use of semaphores for the synchronisation. The second class is deque (for *double-ended queue*). In addition to the methods append(element) and popleft(), which, respectively, add to the end of the queue and remove from the head of the queue, deque offers the methods appendleft(element) and pop(), which add to the head of the queue and remove from the end of the queue. We can thus speak of a **queue with two ends**. This more sophisticated structure will be found useful in Section 8.2 on page 126, where it is used to find the shortest path in a graph the edges of which have weights 0 or 1.

We recommend the use of deque—and in general, the use of the data structures provided by the standard library of the language—but as an example we illustrate here how to implement a queue using two stacks. One stack corresponds to the head of the queue for extraction and the other corresponds to the tail for insertion. Once the head stack is empty, it is swapped with the tail stack (reversed). The operator `__len__` uses `len(q)` to recover the number of elements in the queue q, and then `if q` can be used to test if q is non-empty, happily in constant time.

```python
class OurQueue:
    def __init__(self):
        self.in_stack = []          # tail
        self.out_stack = []         # head

    def __len__(self):
        return len(self.in_stack) + len(self.out_stack)

    def push(self, obj):
        self.in_stack.append(obj)
    def pop(self):
        if not self.out_stack:      # head is empty
            # Note that the in_stack is assigned to the out_stack
            #  in reverse order. This is because the in_stack stores
            #  elements from oldest to newest whereas the out_stack
            #  needs to pop elements from newest to oldest
            self.out_stack = self.in_stack[::-1]
            self.in_stack = []
        return self.out_stack.pop()
```

1.5.4   Priority Queues and Heaps

A **priority queue** is an abstract type allowing elements to be added and an element with minimal key to be removed. It turns out to be very useful, for example, in sorting an array (heapsort), in the construction of a Huffman code (see Section 10.1 on page 172) and in the search for the shortest path between two nodes in a graph (see Dijkstra's algorithm, Section 8.3 on page 127). It is typically implemented with a heap, which is a data structure in the form of a tree.

Perfect and Quasi-Perfect Binary Trees

We begin by examining a very specific type of data structure: the quasi-perfect binary tree. For more information on these trees, see Chapter 10 on page 171, dedicated to them.

A binary tree is either empty or is made up of a node with two children or subtrees, left and right. The node at the top of the tree is the root, while the nodes with two empty children, at the bottom of the tree, are the leaves. A binary tree is *perfect* if all its leaves are at the same distance from the root. It is *quasi-perfect* if all its leaves are on, at most, two levels, the second level from the bottom is completely full and all the leaves on the bottom level are grouped to the left. Such a tree can conveniently be represented by an array, see Figure 1.3. The element at index 0 of this array is ignored. The root is found at index 1, and the two children of a node i are at $2i$ and $2i + 1$. Simple index manipulations allow us to ascend or descend in the tree.

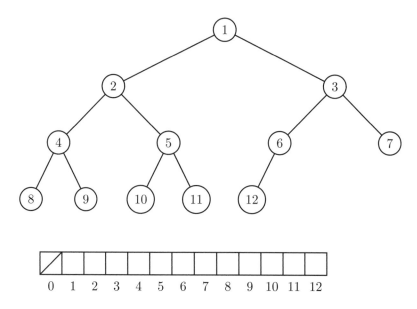

Figure 1.3 A quasi-perfect binary tree and its representation by an array.

Priority Queues and Heaps

A *heap*, also known as a tournament tree, is a tree verifying the heap property: each node has a key smaller than each of its children, for a certain order relation. The root of a heap is thus the element with the smallest key. A variant known as a *max-heap* exists, wherein each node has a key greater that each of its children.

In general, we are interested in binary heaps, which are quasi-perfect binary tournament trees. This data structure allows the extraction of the smallest element and the insertion of a new element with a logarithmic cost, which is advantageous. The objects in question can be from an arbitrary set of elements equipped with a total order relation. A heap also allows an update of the priority of an element, which is a useful operation for Dijkstra's algorithm (see Section 8.1 on page 125) when a shorter path has been discovered towards a summit.

In Python, heaps are implemented by the module heapq. This module provides a function to transform an array A into a heap (heapify(A)), which results in an array representing a quasi-perfect tree as described in the preceding section, except that the element with index 0 does not remain empty and instead contains the root. The module also allows the insertion of a new element (heappush(heap,element)) and the extraction of the minimal element (heappop(heap)).

However, this module does not permit the value of an element in the heap to be changed, an operation useful for Dijkstra's algorithm to improve the time complexity. We thus propose the following implementation, which is more complete.

Implementation details

The structure contains an array heap, storing the heap itself, as well as a dictionary rank, allowing the determination of the index of an element stored in the heap. The principal operations are push and pop. A new element is inserted with push: it is added as the last leaf in the heap, and then the heap is reorganised to respect the heap order. The minimal element is extracted with pop: the root is replaced by the last leaf in the heap, and then the heap is reorganised to respect the heap order, see Figure 1.4.

The operator __len__ returns the number of elements in the heap. The existence of this operator permits the inner workings of Python to implicitly convert a heap to a Boolean and to perform such conditional tests as, for example, while h, which loops while the heap h is non-empty.

The average complexity of the operations on our heap is $O(\log n)$; however, the worst-case complexity is $O(n)$, due to the use of the dictionary (rank).

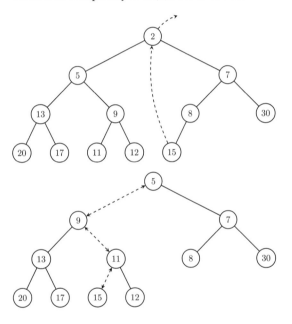

Figure 1.4 The operation pop removes and returns the value 2 of the heap and replaces it by the last leaf 15. Then the operation down performs a series of exchanges to place 15 in a position respecting the heap order.

```
class OurHeap:
    def __init__(self, items):
        self.heap = [None]  # index 0 will be ignored
        self.rank = {}
        for x in items:
            self.push(x)

    def __len__(self):
        return len(self.heap) - 1

    def push(self, x):
        assert x not in self.rank
        i = len(self.heap)
        self.heap.append(x)      # add a new leaf
        self.rank[x] = i
        self.up(i)               # maintain heap order

    def pop(self):
        root = self.heap[1]
        del self.rank[root]
        x = self.heap.pop()      # remove last leaf
        if self:                 # if heap is not empty
            self.heap[1] = x     # move the last leaf
            self.rank[x] = 1     # to the root
            self.down(1)         # maintain heap order
        return root
```

The reorganisation is done with the operations up(i) and down(i), which are called whenever an element with index *i* is too small with respect to its parent (for up) or too large for its children (for down). Hence, up effects a series of exchanges of a node with its parents, climbing up the tree until the heap order is respected. The action of down is similar, for an exchange between a node and its child with the smallest value.

Finally, the method update permits the value of a heap element to be changed. It then calls up or down to preserve the heap order. It is this method that requires the introduction of the dictionary rank.

```
def up(self, i):
    x = self.heap[i]
    while i > 1 and x < self.heap[i // 2]:
        self.heap[i] = self.heap[i // 2]
        self.rank[self.heap[i // 2]] = i
        i //= 2
    self.heap[i] = x          # insertion index found
    self.rank[x] = i


def down(self, i):
    x = self.heap[i]
    n = len(self.heap)
    while True:
        left = 2 * i         # climb down the tree
        right = left + 1
        if (right < n and self.heap[right] < x and
                self.heap[right] < self.heap[left]):
            self.heap[i] = self.heap[right]
            self.rank[self.heap[right]] = i   # move right child up
            i = right
        elif left < n and self.heap[left] < x:
            self.heap[i] = self.heap[left]
            self.rank[self.heap[left]] = i    # move left child up
            i = left
        else:
            self.heap[i] = x   # insertion index found
            self.rank[x] = i
            return


def update(self, old, new):
    i = self.rank[old]       # change value at index i
    del self.rank[old]
    self.heap[i] = new
    self.rank[new] = i
    if old < new:            # maintain heap order
        self.down(i)
    else:
        self.up(i)
```

1.5.5   Union-Find

Definition

Union-find is a data structure used to store a partition of a universe V and that allows the following operations, also known as *requests* in the context of dynamic data structures:

- `find(v)` returns a canonical element of the set containing v. To test if u and v are in the same set, it suffices to compare `find(u)` with `find(v)`.
- `union(u,v)` combines the set containing u with that containing v.

Application

Our principal application of this structure is to determine the connected components of a graph, see Section 6.5 on page 94. Every addition of an edge will correspond to a call to `union`, while `find` is used to test if two vertices are in the same component. Union-find is also used in Kruskal's algorithm to determine a minimal spanning tree of a weighted graph, see Section 10.4 on page 179.

Data Structures with Quasi-Constant Time per Request

We organise the elements of a set in an oriented tree towards a canonical element, see Figure 1.5. Each element v has a reference `parent[v]` towards an element higher in the tree. The root v—the canonical element of the set—is indicated by a special value in `parent[v]`: we can choose 0, -1, or v itself, as long as we are consistent. We also store the size of the set in an array `size[v]`, where v is the canonical element. There are two ideas in this data structure:

1. When traversing an element on the way to the root, we take advantage of the opportunity to compress the path, i.e. we link directly to the root that the elements encountered.
2. During a union, we hang the tree of smaller rank beneath the root of the tree of larger rank. The *rank* of a tree corresponds to the depth it would have if none of the paths were compressed.

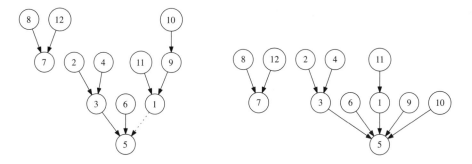

Figure 1.5 On the left: The structure union-find for a graph with two components $\{7, 8, 12\}$ and $\{2, 3, 4, 5, 6, 9, 10, 11\}$. On the right: after a call to `find(10)`, all the vertices on the path to~the root now point directly to the root 5. This accelerates future calls to `find` for these vertices.

This gives us:

```python
class UnionFind:
    def __init__(self, n):
        self.up_bound = list(range(n))
        self.rank = [0] * n

    def find(self, x_index):
        if self.up_bound[x_index] == x_index:
            return x_index
        self.up_bound[x_index] = self.find(self.up_bound[x_index])
        return self.up_bound[x_index]

    def union(self, x_index, y_index):
        repr_x = self.find(x_index)
        repr_y = self.find(y_index)
        if repr_x == repr_y:         # already in the same component
            return False
        if self.rank[repr_x] == self.rank[repr_y]:
            self.rank[repr_x] += 1
            self.up_bound[repr_y] = repr_x
        elif self.rank[repr_x] > self.rank[repr_y]:
            self.up_bound[repr_y] = repr_x
        else:
            self.up_bound[repr_x] = repr_y
        return True
```

It can be proved that any arbitrary sequence of m operations union or find on a universe of size n costs a time $O((m+n)\alpha(n))$, where α is the inverse of Ackermann's function, which in practice can be considered as the constant 4.

Problem
Havannah [gcj:2013round3B]

1.6   Techniques

1.6.1   Comparison

In Python, a comparison between n-tuples is based on lexicographical order. This allows us, for example, to find, at the same time, the largest value in an array along with the corresponding index, taking the largest index in the case of equality.

```python
max((tab[i], i) for i,tab_i in enumerate(tab))
```

The most common element of an array can be found by using a dictionary to count the number of occurrences of each element, and then using the above technique to select the element with the largest count, or the first element in lexicographical order if there are several candidates with the maximal count. Our implementation has a complexity of $O(nk)$ on average, but $O(n^2k)$ in the worst case because of the use of a dictionary, where n is the number of words given and k is the maximal length of a word.

```python
def majority(L):
    count = {}
    for word in L:
        if word in count:
            count[word] += 1
        else:
            count[word] = 1
    # Using min() like this gives the first word with
    #    maximal count "for free"
    val_1st_max, arg_1st_max = min((-count[word], word) for word in count)
    return arg_1st_max
```

1.6.2   Sorting

An array of n elements in Python can be sorted in time $O(n \log n)$. We distinguish two kinds of sorts:

- a sort with the method `sort()` modifies the list in question (it is said to sort 'in place') ;
- a sort with the function `sorted()` returns a sorted copy of the list in question.

Given a list L of n distinct integers, we would like to determine two integers in L with minimal difference. This problem can be solved by sorting L, and then running through L to select the pair with the smallest difference. Note the use of minimum over a collection of pairs of integers, compared in lexicographical order. Hence, `valmin` will contain the smallest distance between two successive elements of L and `argmin` will contain the corresponding index.

```python
def closest_values(L):
    assert len(L) >= 2
    L.sort()
    valmin, argmin = min((L[i] - L[i - 1], i) for i in range(1, len(L)))
    return L[argmin - 1], L[argmin]
```

Sorting n elements requires $\Omega(n \log n)$ comparisons between the elements in the worst case. To be convinced, consider an input of n distinct integers. An algorithm must select one among $n!$ possible orders. Each comparison returns one of two values (greater or smaller) and thus divides the search space in two. Finally, it requires at most $\lceil \log_2(n!) \rceil$ comparisons to identify a particular order, giving the lower bound $\Omega(\log(n!)) = \Omega(n \log n)$.

Variants
In certain cases, an array of n integers can be sorted in time $O(n)$, for example when they are all found between 0 and cn for some constant c. In this case, we can simply

scan the input and store the number of occurrences of each element in an array count of size cn. We then scan count by increasing index, and write the values from 0 to cn to the output array, repeating them as often as necessary. This technique is known as *counting sort*; a similar variant is *pigeonhole sort*.

Problems
Spelling Lists [spoj:MIB]
Yodaness Level [spoj:YODANESS]

1.6.3   Sweep Line

Numerous problems in geometry can be solved with the *sweep line* technique, including many problems concerning intervals, i.e. one-dimensional geometric objects. The idea is to sweep over the different input elements from left to right and perform a specific processing for each element encountered.

Example—Intersection of Intervals
Given n intervals $[\ell_i, r_i)$ for $i = 0, \ldots, n - 1$, we wish to find a value x included in a maximum number of intervals. Here is a solution in time $O(n \log n)$. We sort the endpoints, and then sweep them from left to right with an imaginary pointer x. A counter c keeps track of the number of intervals whose beginning has been seen, but not yet the end, hence it counts the number of intervals containing x.

Note that the order of processing of the elements of B guarantees that the right endpoints of the intervals are handled before the left endpoints of the intervals, which is necessary when dealing with intervals that are half-open to the right.

```python
def max_interval_intersec(S):
    B = ([(left,  +1) for left, right in S] +
         [(right, -1) for left, right in S])
    B.sort()
    c = 0
    best = (c, None)
    for x, d in B:
        c += d
        if best[0] < c:
            best = (c, x)
    return best
```

Problem
Back to the future [prologin:demi2012]

1.6.4   Greedy Algorithms

We illustrate here an important algorithmic technique: informally, a greedy algorithm produces a solution step by step, at each step making a choice to maximise a local criterion. A formal notion exists that is related to combinatorial structures known as *matroids*, and it can be used to prove the optimality or the non-optimality of greedy algorithms. We do not tackle this here, but refer to Kozen (1992) for a very good introduction.

For some problems, an optimal solution can be produced step by step, making a decision that is in a certain sense *locally optimal*. Such a proof is, in general, based on an *exchange argument*, showing that any optimal solution can be transformed into the solution produced by the algorithm without modifying the cost. The reader is invited to systematically at least sketch such a proof, as intuition can often be misleading and the problems that can be solved by a greedy algorithm are in fact quite rare.

An example is making change with coins, see Section 11.2 on page 184. Suppose you work in a store, and dispose of an infinity of coins with a finite number of distinct values. You must make change for a client for a specific sum and you wish to do it with as few coins as possible. In most countries, the values of the coins are of the form $x \cdot 10^i$ with $x \in \{1, 2, 5\}$ and $i \in \mathbb{N}$, and in this case we can in a greedy manner make change by repeatedly selecting the most valuable coin that is not larger than the remaining sum to return. However, in general, this approach does not work, for example with coins with values 1, 4 and 5, and with a total of 8 to return. The greedy approach generates a solution with 4 coins, i.e. $5 + 1 + 1 + 1$, whereas the optimal is composed of only 2 coins: $4 + 4$.

Example – Minimal Scalar Product

We introduce the technique with the aid of a simple example. Given two vectors x and y of n non-negative integers, find a permutation π of $\{1, \ldots, n\}$ such that the sum $\sum_i x_i y_{\pi(i)}$ is minimal.

Application

Suppose there are n tasks to be assigned to n workers in a *bijective* manner, i.e. where each task must be assigned to a different worker. Each task has a duration in hours and each worker has a price per hour. The goal is to find the assignment that minimises the total amount to be paid.

Algorithm in $O(n \log n)$

Since applying the same permutation to both x and y preserves the optimal solution, without loss of generality we can suppose that x is sorted in increasing order. We claim that a solution exists that multiplies x_0 by a maximal element y_j. Fix a permutation π with $\pi(0) = i$ and $\pi(k) = j$ for an index k and $y_i < y_j$. We observe that $x_0 y_i + x_k y_j$ is greater or equal to $x_0 y_j + x_k y_i$, which implies that without increasing the cost, π can be transformed such that x_0 is multiplied by y_j. The observation is justified by the following computation, which requires x_0, x_k to be non-negative:

$$x_0 \leq x_k$$
$$x_0(y_j - y_i) \leq x_k(y_j - y_i)$$

$$x_0 y_j - x_0 y_i \le x_k y_j - x_k y_i$$
$$x_0 y_j + x_k y_i \le x_0 y_i + x_k y_j.$$

By repeating the argument on the vector x with x_0 removed and on y with y_j removed, we find that the product is minimal when $i \mapsto y_{\pi(i)}$ is decreasing.

```python
def min_scalar_prod(x, y):
    x1 = sorted(x)   # make copies to preserve the input arguments
    y1 = sorted(y)
    return sum(x1[i] * y1[-i - 1] for i in range(len(x1)))
```

Problems
Minimum Scalar Product [gcj:2008round1A]
Minimal Coverage [timus:1303]

1.6.5 Dynamic Programming

Dynamic programming is one of the methods that must be part of your 'Swiss army knife' as a programmer. The idea is to store a few precious bits of information so as to not have to recompute them while solving a problem (a sort of a cache), and then to reflect on how to astutely combine these bits. More formally, we decompose a problem into subproblems, and we construct the optimal solution of the principal problem out of the solutions to the subproblems.

Typically, these problems are defined over recursive structures. For example, in a rooted tree, the descendants of the root are themselves roots of subtrees. Similarly, an interval of indices in an array is the union of two shorter intervals. The reader is invited to master the dynamic programming techniques presented in this text, as numerous problems in programming competitions are variants of these classic problems.

A classic example is the computation of the nth Fibonacci number, defined by the following recurrence:

$$F(0) = 0$$
$$F(1) = 1$$
$$F(i) = F(i-1) + F(i-2).$$

This number gives, for example, the number of possibilities to climb an n-step stairway by taking one or two steps at a time. A naive implementation of F by a recursive function is extremely inefficient, since for the same parameter i, $F(i)$ is computed several times, see Figure 1.6.

```python
def fibo_naive(n):
    if n <= 1:
        return n
    return fibo_naive(n - 1) + fibo_naive(n - 2)
```

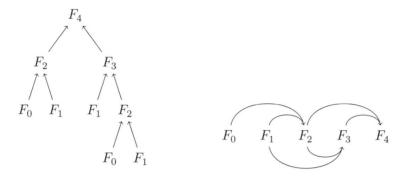

Figure 1.6 On the left, the exhaustive exploration tree of the recursive computation of the Fibonacci number F_4. On the right, the acyclic oriented graph of the value dependencies of dynamic programming, with many fewer nodes.

Try this function on a not-very-large value, $n = 32$, and you will see that the code can already take more than a second, even on a powerful machine; the computation time increases exponentially with n.

A solution by dynamic programming simply consists of storing in an array of size $n+1$ the values of $F(0)$ to $F(n)$, and filling it in increasing order of the indices. Hence, at the moment we compute $F(i)$, the values $F(i-1)$ and $F(i-2)$ will already have been computed; they are the last two values entered into the array.

```
def fibo_dp(n):
    mem = [0, 1]
    for i in range(2, n + 1):
        mem.append(mem[-2] + mem[-1])
    return mem[-1]
```

However, the above code uses $n + 1$ memory locations, whereas 2 are sufficient, those corresponding to the last two Fibonacci numbers computed.

```
def fibo_dp_mem(n):
    mem = [0, 1]
    for i in range(2, n + 1):
        mem[i % 2] = mem[0] + mem[1]
    return mem[n % 2]
```

In this way, the memory complexity is reduced from linear in n (hence, it is exponential in the input size $\log n$) to $O(\log n)$; hence, it is linear in the size of the data. Indeed, the Fibonacci number n can be expressed using $O(n)$ bits.

Now that you have a complete example of the principle of dynamic programming in mind, we can reveal to you a trick using the *decorator* @lru_cache(maxsize= None) present in the standard library functools. This decorator performs a *memoisation*,[6] i.e. it stores the successive calls of a function with their arguments in a

---

[6] To be more precise, LRU stands for 'Least Recently Used cache', but indicating 'maxsize=None' deactivates the cache mechanism, since the cache is then non-bounded, unless for physical considerations.

dictionary, to avoid the combinatorial explosion of the calls. In other words, adding
@lru_cache(maxsize=None) transforms any old naive recursive implementation into
a clever example of dynamic programming. Isn't life beautiful?

```
from functools import lru_cache


@lru_cache(maxsize=None)
def fibo_naive(n):
    if n <= 1:
        return n
    return fibo_naive(n - 1) + fibo_naive(n - 2)
```

This code is as fast as the implementation using dynamic programming, thanks to
the memoisation provided by the decorator @lru_cache.

Problem
Fibonacci Sum [spoj:FIBOSUM]

1.6.6   Encoding of Sets by Integers

A technique to efficiently handle sets of integers between 0 and k for an integer k
on the order of 63 consists of encoding them as integers.[7] More precisely, we use
the binary decomposition of an integer as the characteristic vector of the subset to be
represented. The encodings and operations are summarised in the following table:

value	encoding	explanation
{}	0	empty set
$\{i\}$	$1 << i$	this notation represents 2^i
$\{0, 1, \ldots, n-1\}$	$(1 << n) - 1$	$2^n - 1 = 2^0 + 2^1 + \cdots + 2^{n-1}$
$A \cup B$	$A \mid B$	the operator | is the binary *or*
$A \cap B$	$A \& B$	the operator & is the binary *and*
$(A \backslash B) \cup (B \backslash A)$	$A \char`^ B$	the operator ^ is the *exclusive or*
$A \subseteq B$	$A \& B == A$	test of inclusion
$i \in A$	$(1 << i) \& A$	test of membership
$\{\min A\}$	$-A \& A$	this expression equals 0 if A is empty

The justification of this last expression is shown in Figure 1.7. It is useful, for
example, to count in a loop the cardinality of a set. There is no equivalent expression
to obtain the maximum of a set.

To illustrate this encoding technique, we apply it to a classic problem.

---

[7] The limit comes from the fact that integers in Python are, in general, coded in a machine word, which
today is usually 63 bits plus a sign bit, for a total of 64 bits.

We wish to obtain the minimum of the set $\{3, 5, 6\}$ encoded by an integer. This integer is
$2^3 + 2^5 + 2^6 = 104$.

64+32+8=104	01101000
complement of 104	10010111
-104	10011000
-104&104 = 8	00001000

The result is 2^3 encoding the singleton $\{3\}$.

Figure 1.7 Example of the extraction of the minimum of a set.

Example – Fair Partition into Three Portions
Definition
Given n integers $x_0, \dots, x_{n-1}$, we wish to partition them into three sets with the same sum.

Naive Algorithm in Time $O(2^{2n})$
This algorithm uses exhaustive search. This consists of enumerating all the disjoint subsets $A, B \subseteq \{0, \dots, n-1\}$ and comparing the three values $f(A), f(B), f(C)$ with $C = \{0, \dots, n-1\} \setminus A \setminus B$ and $f(S) = \sum_{i \in S} x_i$. The implementation skips explicit computation of the set C by verifying that $f(A) = f(B)$ and $3f(A) = f(\{0, \dots, n-1\})$.

```
def three_partition(x):
    f = [0] * (1 << len(x))
    for i, _ in enumerate(x):
        for S in range(1 << i):
            f[S | (1 << i)] = f[S] + x[i]
    for A in range(1 << len(x)):
        for B in range(1 << len(x)):
            if A & B == 0 and f[A] == f[B] and 3 * f[A] == f[-1]:
                return (A, B, ((1 << len(x)) - 1) ^ A ^ B)
    return None
```

For another utilisation of this technique, see the resolution for numbers in the TV contest 'Des Chiffres et des Lettres' (1965), presented as 'Countdown' (1982) in the UK, Section 15.6 on page 243.

1.6.7 Binary (Dichotomic) Search

Definition
Let f be a Boolean function—in $\{0, 1\}$—with

$$f(0) \leq \dots \leq f(n-1) = 1.$$

We wish to find the smallest integer k such that $f(k) = 1$.

Algorithm in Time $O(\log n)$
The solution is sought in an interval $[\ell, h]$, initially $\ell = 0, h = n - 1$. Then f is tested in the middle of the interval at $m = \lfloor (\ell + h)/2 \rfloor$. As a function of the result, the search

space is reduced either to $[\ell,m]$ or to $[m+1,h]$. Note that because of the rounding below in the computation of m, the second interval is never empty, nor the first for that matter. The search terminates after $\lceil\log_2(n)\rceil$ iterations, when the search interval is reduced to a singleton.

```python
def discrete_binary_search(tab, lo, hi):
    while lo < hi:
        mid = lo + (hi - lo) // 2
        if tab[mid]:
            hi = mid
        else:
            lo = mid + 1
    return lo
```

Libraries
Binary search is provided in the standard module `bisect`, so that in many cases you will not have to write it yourself. Consider the case of a sorted array `tab` of n elements, where we want to find the insertion point of a new element x. The function `bisect_left(tab, x, 0, n)` returns the first index i such that `tab[i]` $\geq x$.

Continuous Domain
This technique can equally be applied when the domain of f is continuous and we seek the smallest value x_0 with $f(x) = 1$ for every $x \geq x_0$. The complexity will then depend on the precision required for x_0.

```python
def continuous_binary_search(f, lo, hi, gap=1e-4):
    while hi - lo > gap:
        mid = (lo + hi) / 2.0
        if f(mid):
            hi = mid
        else:
            lo = mid
    return lo
```

Search without a Known Upper Bound
Let f be a monotonic Boolean function with $f(0) = 0$ and the guarantee that an integer n exists such that $f(n) = 1$. The smallest integer n_0 with $f(n_0) = 1$ can be found in time $O(\log n_0)$, even in the absence of an upper bound for n_0. Initially, we set $n = 1$, and then repeatedly double it while $f(n) = 0$. Once a value n is found with $f(n) = 1$, we proceed with the standard binary search.

Ternary (Trichotomic) Search
Let f be a function on $\{0,\dots,n-1\}$, increasing and then decreasing, for which we seek to find the maximal value. In this case, it makes sense to divide the search interval $[l,h]$ not in two but in three portions $[l,a],[a+1,b],[b+1,h]$. By comparing the values of $f(a)$ with $f(b)$, we can decide which of the intervals $[l,b],[a+1,h]$ contains a

maximal value. The number of iterations necessary is again logarithmic, on the order of $\log_{3/2} n$.

Search in an Interval $[0, 2^k)$

In the case of a search space where the size n is a power of 2, it is possible to slightly improve the usual binary search, by using only bit manipulation operators, such as binary shifts or *exclusive or*. We begin with the index of the last element of the array, which in binary is written as a sequence of ones of length k. For each of the bits, we test whether its replacement by 0 results in an index i such that tab[i] remains true. In this case, we update the upper endpoint of the search interval.

```python
def optimized_binary_search(tab, logsize):
    hi = (1 << logsize) - 1
    intervalsize = (1 << logsize) >> 1
    while intervalsize > 0:
        if tab[hi ^ intervalsize]:
            hi ^= intervalsize
        intervalsize >>= 1
    return hi
```

Invert a Function

Let f be a continuous and strictly monotonic function. Thus there exists an inverse function f^{-1}, again monotonic. Imagine that f^{-1} is much easier to compute than f, in this case we can use it to compute $f(x)$ for a given value of x. Indeed, it suffices to find the smallest value y such that $f^{-1}(y) \geq x$.

Example—Filling Tasks

Suppose there are n tanks in the form of rectangular blocks at different heights, interconnected by a network of pipes. We pour into this system a volume V of liquid, and wish to know the resulting height of the liquid in the tanks.

```python
level = continuous_binary_search(lambda level: volume(level) >= V, 0, hi)
```

Problems
Fill the cisterns [spoj:CISTFILL]
Egg Drop [gcj:eggdrop]

1.7   Advice

Here is a bit of common sense advice to help you rapidly solve algorithmic problems and produce a working program. Be organised and systematic. For this, it is important to not be carried away with the desire to start hacking before all the details are clear. It is easy to leap into the implementation of a method that can never work for a reason that would not have escaped you if you had taken a bit more time to ponder before starting to pound on the keyboard.

When possible, in your program, separate the input of the instance from the computation of the solution. Be nice to yourself and systematically add to the comments the name of the problem, if possible with its URL, and specify the complexity of your algorithm. You will appreciate this effort when you revisit your code at a later date. Above all, stay coherent in your code and reuse the terms given in the problem statement to highlight the correspondence. There is little worse than having to debug a program whose variable names are not meaningful.

Carefully Read the Problem Statement

What complexity is acceptable?   Pay attention to the limits stated for the instances. Analyse your algorithm before implementing it.

Understand the example given.   Carefully read the typical example furnished with the problem statement. If the input describes a graph, draw its picture. Once you have an idea of a solution, of course verify it on the example or examples provided.

What guarantees on the inputs?   Do not deduce guarantees from the examples. Do not suppose anything. If it is not stated that the graph is not empty, there will probably be an instance with an empty graph. If it is not said that a character string does not contain a space, there will probably be an instance with such a string. Etc, etc.

What type of number should you choose?   Integer or floating point? Can the numbers be negative? If you are coding in C++ or Java, determine a bound on the largest intermediate value in your calculations, to decide between the use of 16-, 32- or 64-bit integers.

Which problem is easy?   For a competition involving several problems, start with a rapid overview to determine the type of each problem (greedy algorithm, implicit graph, dynamic programming, etc.) and estimate its level of difficulty. Concentrate then on the easiest problems in priority. During a team competition, distribute the problems according to the domains of expertise of each participant. Monitor the progress of the other teams to identify the problems that are easy to solve.

Plan Your Work

Understand the example.   Draw pictures. Discover the links with known problems. How can you exploit the particularities of the instances?

When possible, use existing modules.   Master the classics: binary search, sorting, dictionaries.

Use the same variable names as in the problem statement.   Preferably,   use names that are short but meaningful. Avoid variables such as O or l, which are too easily confused with numbers.

Initialise your variables.   Make sure that the variables are reinitialised before the processing of each new instance. Treading on the remnants of the preceding iteration is a classic error. Take, for example, a program solving a graph problem whose input consists of the number of instances, followed by each instance, beginning with two integers: the number of vertices n and the number of edges m. These are followed by two arrays of integers A, B of size m, encoding the endpoints of the edges for each instance. Imagine that the program encodes the graph in the form of an adjacency list G and for every $i = 0, \ldots, m - 1$, adds $B[i]$ to $G[A[i]]$ and $A[i]$ to $G[B[i]]$. If the lists are not emptied before the beginning of each input of an instance, the edges accumulate to form a superposition of all the graphs.

Debug

Make all your mistakes *now*   to have the proper reflexes later.

Generate test sets   for the limit cases (*Wrong Answer*) and for large instances (*Time Limit Exceeded* or *Runtime Error*).

Explain the algorithm   to a team-mate and add appropriate comments to the program. You must be capable of explaining each and every line.

Simplify your implementation.   Regroup all similar bits of code. Never go wild with copy-and-paste (note from the translators—one of the most observed sources of buggy programs from novice programmers!).

Take a step back   by passing to another problem, and come back later for a fresh look.

Compare   the environment of your local machine with that of the server where your code will be tested.

1.8   A Problem: 'Frosting on the Cake'

See [icpcarchive:8154].

Iskander the Baker is decorating a huge cake by covering the rectangular surface of the cake with frosting. For this purpose, he mixes frosting sugar with lemon juice and beetle juice, in order to produce three kinds of frosting: yellow, pink and white. These colours are identified by the numbers 0 for yellow, 1 for pink and 2 for white.

To obtain a nice pattern, he partitions the cake surface into vertical stripes of width $A_1, A_2, \ldots, A_n$ centimeters, and horizontal stripes of height $B_1, B_2, \ldots, B_n$ centimeters, for some positive integer n. These stripes split the cake surface into $n \times n$ rectangles. The intersection of vertical stripe i and horizontal stripe j has colour number $(i + j)$ mod 3 for all $1 \le i, j \le n$, see Figure 1.8. To prepare the frosting, Iskander wants to know the total surface in square centimeters to be coloured for each of the three colours, and asks for your help.

Input

The input consists of the following integers:

- on the first line: the integer n,
- on the second line: the values of $A_1, \ldots, A_n$, n integers separated by single spaces,
- on the third line: the values of $B_1, \ldots, B_n$, n integers separated by single spaces.

Limits

The input satisfies $3 \leq n \leq 100\,000$ and $1 \leq A_1, \ldots, A_n, B_1, \ldots, B_n \leq 10\,000$.

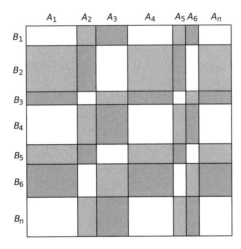

Figure 1.8 An instance of the problem 'Frosting on the Cake'

Output

The output should consist of three integers separated by single spaces, representing the total area for each colour 0, 1 and 2.

Solution

When you see the upper bound on n, you want to find a solution that runs in time $O(n)$ or possibly $O(n \log n)$. This rules out the naive solution which loops over all n^2 grid cells and accumulates their areas in variables corresponding to each colour. But with a little thought about the problem, we can make the following observation. Permuting columns or rows preserves the total area of each colour. Hence, we can reduce to the $n = 3$ case, by simply summing the values of each colour class A_{3k}, A_{3k+1} and A_{3k+2}. Then the answer per colour class is just the sum of the areas of three rectangles.

Hence, a solution could be as short as the following one. The tricky part relies in not mixing up the colours.

```python
def read_ints(): return [int(x) for x in input().split()]


def cat(l): return tuple(sum(l[n::3]) for n in [1, 2, 0])


input()   # n
A = cat(read_ints())
B = cat(read_ints())
print("{} {} {}".format(B[2] * A[0] + B[0] * A[2] + B[1] * A[1],
                        B[2] * A[1] + B[0] * A[0] + B[1] * A[2],
                        B[2] * A[2] + B[0] * A[1] + B[1] * A[0]))
```

2 Character Strings

The resolution of problems involving *character strings* (or simply *strings*) rapidly became an important domain in the study of algorithms. These problems occur, of course, in text processing, such as spell checking and the search for *factors (substrings)* or for more general *patterns*. With the development of bioinformatics, new problems arose in the alignment of DNA chains. This chapter presents a selection of string-processing algorithms that we consider important.

A character string could be represented internally by a list of symbols, but, in general, we use the Python native type `str`, which behaves essentially like a list. The characters can be encoded with two bytes for a *Unicode* encoding, but are usually encoded with only one byte, using the *ASCII* encoding: each integer between 0 and 127 corresponds to a distinct character, and the codes are organised in such a way that the successive symbols '0' to '9', 'a' to 'z' and 'A' to 'Z' are consecutive. Thereby, if a string s contains only capitals, we can recover the rank of the ith letter by computing `ord(s[i])-ord('A')`. Conversely, the jth capital letter of the alphabet numbered from~0—is obtained with `chr(j+ord('A'))`.

When we speak of a *factor* (or *substring*) of a string, we require the characters to be consecutive, in contrast with the more general notion of a *subsequence*.

2.1 Anagrams

Definition
A word w is an *anagram* of a word v if a permutation of the letters transforming w into v exists. Given a set of n words of length at most k, we would like to detect all possible anagrams.

> **input:** below the car is a rat drinking cider and bending its elbow while this thing is an arc that can act like a cat which cried during the night caused by pain in its bowel[1]
>
> **output:** {bowel below elbow}, {arc car}, {night thing}, {cried cider}, {act cat}

---

[1] Believe it or not: the authors did not consume cider in order to produce this sample input.

Complexity

The proposed algorithm solves this problem in time $O(nk \log k)$ on average, and in $O(n^2 k \log k)$ in the worst case, due to the use of a dictionary.

Algorithm

The idea is to compute a signature for each word, so that two words are anagrams of each other if and only if they have the same signature. This signature is simply a new string made up of the same letters sorted in lexicographical order.

The data structure used is a dictionary associating with each signature the list of words with this signature.

```
def anagrams(S):                    # S is a set of strings
    d = {}                          # maps s to list of words with signature s
    for word in S:                  # group words according to the signature
        s = ''.join(sorted(word))   # calculate the signature
        if s in d:
            d[s].append(word)       # append a word to an existing signature
        else:
            d[s] = [word]           # add a new signature and its first word
    # -- extract anagrams, ingoring anagram groups of size 1
    return [d[s] for s in d if len(d[s]) > 1]
```

Problem

Anagram verifier [spoj:ANGRAM]

2.2 T9—Text on 9 Keys

```
input:  2665687
output: bonjour
```

Application

Mobile telephones with keys offer an interesting input mode, sometimes called T9. The 26 letters of the alphabet are distributed over the keys 2 to 9, as in Figure 2.1. To input a word, it suffices to input the corresponding sequence of digits. However, as several words could begin with the same digits, a dictionary must be used to propose the most probable word. At any moment, the telephone displays the prefix of the most probable word corresponding to the sequence of digits entered.

Definition

The first part of the problem instance is a dictionary, composed of pairs (m, w) where m is a word over the alphabet of 26 lower-case letters, and w is a weight of the importance of the word. The second part is a series of sequences of digits from 2 to 9. For each sequence s, the word in the dictionary of maximal weight is to be displayed. A word m corresponds to s if s is a prefix of the sequence t obtained from m by replacing each letter by the corresponding digit, according to the correspondence table given in Figure 2.1. For example, 'bonjour' corresponds to 26, but also to 266 or 2665687.

Figure 2.1 The keys of a mobile phone.

Algorithm

The complexity is $O(nk)$ for the initialisation of the dictionary, and $O(k)$ for each request, where n is the number of words in the dictionary and k an upper bound on the length of the words.

In a first phase, we compute for each prefix p of a word in the dictionary the total weight of all the words with prefix p. This weight is stored in a dictionary total_weight. In a second phase, we store in a dictionary prop[seq] the prefix to be proposed for a given sequence seq. A scan over the keys in total_weight allows the determination of the prefix with greatest weight.

A principal ingredient is the function code_word, which for a given word returns the corresponding sequence of digits.

To improve readability, the implementation below is in $O(nk^2)$.

```
t9 = "2223334445556667777888999"
#      abcdefghijklmnopqrstuvwxyz     mapping on the phone


def letter_to_digit(x):
    assert 'a' <= x <= 'z'
    return t9[ord(x) - ord('a')]


def code_word(word):
    return ''.join(map(letter_to_digit, word))
def predictive_text(dic):
    # total_weight[p] = total weight of words having prefix p
    total_weight = {}
    for word, weight in dic:
        prefix = ""
        for x in word:
            prefix += x
            if prefix in total_weight:
                total_weight[prefix] += weight
            else:
                total_weight[prefix] = weight
    #   prop[s] = prefix to display for s
    prop = {}
    for prefix in total_weight:
        code = code_word(prefix)
        if (code not in prop
                or total_weight[prop[code]] < total_weight[prefix]):
            prop[code] = prefix
    return prop


def propose(prop, seq):
    if seq in prop:
        return prop[seq]
    return None
```

Problem
T9 [poj:1451]

2.3   Spell Checking with a Lexicographic Tree

Application
How should the words of a dictionary be stored in order to implement a spell checker? For a given word, we would like to quickly find a dictionary word close to it in the sense of the *Levenshtein edit distance*, see Section 3.2 on page 63. If we store the dictionary words in a hash table, then we lose all proximity information between words. It is better to store them in a *lexicographic tree*, also known as a *prefix tree* or a *trie* (pronounced like 'try').

Definition
A *trie* is a tree that stores a set of words. The edges of a node towards its children are labelled by distinct letters. Each word in the dictionary then corresponds to a path from the root to a node in the tree. The nodes are marked to distinguish those corresponding to words in the dictionary from those that are only strict prefixes of such words, see Figure 2.2.

Spell Checking
With such a structure, it is easy to find a dictionary word that is at a distance `dist` from a given word, for the *Levenshtein edit distance* defined in Section 3.2 on page 63. It suffices to simulate the edit operations at each node, and invoke recursive calls to the search with the parameter `dist` - 1.

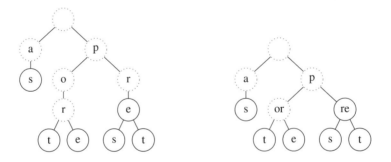

Figure 2.2 A lexicographic tree for the words as, port, pore, pré, près, prêt (but without the accents). In this figure, the label of each edge is indicated in the node of the child. The circles with solid boundaries mark the nodes that correspond to words in the dictionary. On the right, we show a *Patricia trie* for the same dictionary.

```python
from string import ascii_letters    # in Python 2 one would import letters


class TrieNode:
    def __init__(self):                          # each node will have
        self.is_word = False                     # 52 children -
        self.s = {c: None for c in ascii_letters}  # most will remain empty


def add(T, w, i=0):  # Add a word to the trie
    if T is None:
        T = TrieNode()
    if i == len(w):
        T.is_word = True
    else:
        T.s[w[i]] = add(T.s[w[i]], w, i + 1)
    return T
def Trie(S):  # Build the trie for the words in the dictionary S
    T = None
    for w in S:
        T = add(T, w)
    return T


def spell_check(T, w):  # Spell check a word against the trie
    assert T is not None
    dist = 0
    while True:
        u = search(T, dist, w)
        if u is not None:  # Match at distance dist
            return u
        dist += 1          # No match - try increasing the distance
def search(T, dist, w, i=0):
    if i == len(w):
        if T is not None and T.is_word and dist == 0:
            return ""
        else:
            return None
    if T is None:
        return None
    f = search(T.s[w[i]], dist, w, i + 1)        # matching
    if f is not None:
        return w[i] + f
    if dist == 0:
        return None
    for c in ascii_letters:
        f = search(T.s[c], dist - 1, w, i)       # insertion
        if f is not None:
            return c + f
        f = search(T.s[c], dist - 1, w, i + 1)   # substitution
        if f is not None:
            return c + f
    return search(T, dist - 1, w, i + 1)         # deletion
```

Variant

A more complex structure exists that merges nodes as long as they have a single child. A node is thus labelled with a word, rather than by a simple letter, see Figure 2.2. This structure, optimal in memory and in traversal time, is known as a *Patricia trie* (see Morrison, 1968).

Problem

Spell checker [icpcarchive:3872]

2.4   Searching for Patterns

```
input: lalopalalali lala
output         ^
```

Definition

Given a string s of length n and a pattern t of length m, we want to find the first index i such that t is a factor of s at the position i. The response should be -1 if t is not a factor of s.

Complexity

$O(n + m)$ (see Knuth et al., 1977).

Naive Algorithm

This consists of testing all possible alignments of t under s and for each alignment i verifying character by character if t corresponds to $s[i..i + m - 1]$. The complexity is $O(nm)$ in the worst case. The following example illustrates the comparisons performed by the algorithm for an example. Each line corresponds to a choice of i, and indicates the characters of the 'pattern motif' that match, or an $\times$ for a difference.

	l	a	l	o	p	a	l	a	l	a	l	i
0	l	a	l	×								
1		×										
2			l	×								
3				×								
4					×							
5						×						
6							l	a	l	a		

Observe that after handling a few i, we already know about a good portion of the string s. We could use this information to skip the comparison of $t[0]$ with $s[i]$ in the above example. This observation is extended to a study of the *boundaries* of the strings, leading to the optimal Knuth–Morris–Pratt algorithm, described in the next section.

2.5   Maximal Boundaries—Knuth–Morris–Pratt

entrée: abracadabra
sortie: abra abra

An important classic problem on character strings is the detection of occurrences of a pattern t in a string s. The Knuth–Morris–Pratt algorithm solves this problem in optimal linear time $O(|t| + |s|)$ (see Knuth et al., 1977). The essential ingredient of this algorithm is the search for the boundaries of a string, which is the subject of this section. At first sight this problem seems to be totally artificial and without any applications. However, do not be fooled—this problem is at the heart of several classic problems concerning character strings, and we will present a few of these. We begin by introducing a few formal notions. Note that in what follows, the terms 'word' and 'character string' are used interchangeably.

Definition
The *boundary* of a word w is a word that is at the same time a strict prefix and a strict suffix of w, where by *strict* we mean that the length of the boundary must be strictly less than the length of w. The *maximal boundary* of w is its longest boundary, and is denoted $\beta(w)$. For example, *abaababaa* has for boundaries *abaa*, *a* and the empty word ε, hence $\beta(abaababaa) = abaa$. See Figure 2.3 for an illustration.

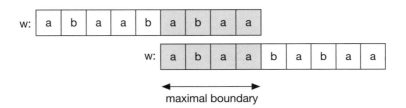

maximal boundary

Figure 2.3 Intuitively, the maximal boundary represents the longest *overlap* of a word with itself: take two copies of the word w one over the other, and slide the second to the right until the letters of the two words coincide. The portion of w corresponding to this overlap is then its maximal boundary.

Given a string $w = w_0 \cdots w_{n-1}$, we would like to compute its maximal boundary. As we will see further on, this problem is recursive in nature, and hence the solution is based on the computation of the maximal boundaries of each of its prefixes. As a boundary is completely described by its length, we will in fact compute the lengths of the maximal boundaries. We thus seek to efficiently construct the sequence of lengths $f_i = |\beta(w_0 \cdots w_i)|$ for $i = 0, \ldots, n - 1$, see Figure 2.4.

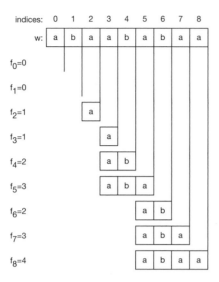

Figure 2.4 The array f of boundary lengths illustrated with an example. For a given string w, f_i is the largest value k such that the suffix $w_{i-k+1} \ldots w_i$ is equal to the prefix $w_0 \ldots w_{k-1}$.

Key Observation

The relation of being a boundary is transitive: if v is a boundary of a boundary b of u, then v is also a boundary of u. Moreover, if v is a boundary of u shorter than $\beta(u)$, then v is a boundary of $\beta(u)$, see Figure 2.5. Hence, the iterated application of β to a word w generates all the boundaries of w. For example, with $w = abaababa$, we have $\beta(w) = aba$, then $\beta(\beta(w)) = a$ and finally $\beta(\beta(\beta(w))) = \varepsilon$. This will prove very useful for our algorithm.

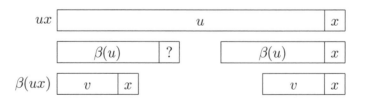

Figure 2.5 Visual explanation of the proof: every boundary of uw_i can be written vw_i where v is a boundary of u, hence knowing the lengths of the boundaries of u allows the identification of the longest boundary of uw_i.

Algorithm and Proof

Suppose that we know the maximal boundaries for the first i prefixes of w, i.e. up to the prefix $u = w_0 \cdots w_{i-1}$, for $1 \le i < n$. Consider the next prefix uw_i: if its maximal boundary is not the empty word, then it is of the form vw_i where v is a boundary of u. Thus, to find the longest boundary of uw_i it suffices to verify whether for each boundary v of u in order of decreasing length, the word vw_i is a boundary of uw_i, see Figure 2.5. We already know that vw_i is a suffix of uw_i and that v is a prefix of u, hence it suffices to compare the two letters $w_k =^? w_i$ where $k = |v|$: indeed, w_k is the letter following the prefix v in uw_i. How can we iterate over the boundaries v of u in order of decreasing size? We simply successively apply the function β to the word u, until we hit the empty word. Note that to perform this test, we only need to know the lengths of the boundaries v of u, which have been stored in the array f.

Illustration

We use a window that exposes a letter w_i of the first copy of w and a letter w_k of the second copy. Three cases must be considered:

1. If the two characters are equal, then we know that $w_0 \cdots w_k$ is the longest boundary of $w_0 \cdots w_i$, and set $f_i = k + 1$, since $|w_0 \cdots w_k| = k + 1$. The window is then shifted one step to the right in order to process the next prefix, see Figure 2.6; this corresponds to an increment of both i and k.
2. If not, in the case $w_k \neq w_i$ and $k > 0$, we move on to the next smaller boundary $\beta(w_0 \ldots w_{k-1})$, of size f_{k-1}. This boils down to shifting to the right the second copy of w, until its contents coincide with the first along the whole of the left part of the window, see Figure 2.6.
3. The final case corresponds to $k = 0$ and $w_0 \neq w_i$. At this point, we know that the maximal boundary of $w_0 \ldots w_i$ is the empty word. We thus set $f_i = 0$.

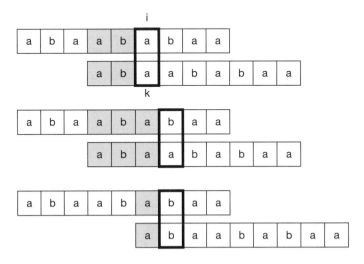

Figure 2.6 An example of the execution of the Knuth–Morris–Pratt algorithm. When the window reveals two identical characters, we set $f_i = k + 1$ and shift to the right, which comes down to incrementing i and k. However, when the window exposes two different characters, the bottom word must be shifted to the right, so that its prefix determined by the window is of length f_{k-1}.

Code

All these cases can be captured in just a few lines of code. An outer while loop looks for the boundary of a suitable prefix (case 2 above). We exit this loop for one of two reasons. First, if $k = 0$ (no non-empty boundary was found), then only a single character remains to test: $w_k =^? w_i$. If yes, then $f_i = 1$ (case 1); if not, $f_k = 0$ (case 3). Second, we exit because a non-empty boundary is found where $w_k = w_i$ and $f_i = k + 1$: we increment k and then assign k to f_i. We thus ensure that at each start of the loop for, the value of k corresponds to the length of the longest boundary of the preceding prefix.

```
def maximum_border_length(w):
    n = len(w)
    f = [0] * n                    # init f[0] = 0
    k = 0                          # current longest border length
    for i in range(1, n):          # compute f[i]
        while w[k] != w[i] and k > 0:
            k = f[k - 1]           # mismatch: try the next border
        if w[k] == w[i]:           # last characters match
            k += 1                 # we can increment the border length
        f[i] = k                   # we found the maximal border of w[:i + 1]
    return f
```

Complexity

This algorithm consists of a while loop nested in a for loop, which suggests a quadratic complexity. However, the behaviour of the algorithm should be considered using the example illustrated above. For each comparison $w_k =^? w_i$ in the algorithm, either the word on the bottom is shifted to the right or the window is shifted to the right. Each of these movements can only be executed at most $|w|$ times, which shows the linear complexity in $|w|$: we speak of amortised complexity, as the long iterations are on average compensated by other shorter iterations.

Application: Find the Longest Boundary Palindrome

input: lilipolilil
output: lil   lil

A word $x = x_0 x_1 \cdots x_{n-1}$ is a palindrome if $x = \overleftarrow{x}$, where $\overleftarrow{x} = x_{n-1} \cdots x_1 x_0$. Given a word x, we look for the longest palindrome u such that x can be written in the form $x = uvu$ for a word v. This problem comes down to seeking the longest boundary of $x\overleftarrow{x}$.

Application: Find a Pattern t in the String s

input: fragil supercalifragilisticexpialidocious
output: ^

The most important application of the maximal boundary algorithm is the search for the first occurrence of a pattern t within a string s whose length is greater than $|t|$. The naive approach consists of testing all the possible positions of t with respect to s. More precisely, for each position $i = 0 \ldots n - m$ in s we test if the substring $s[i : i + m]$ is equal to t. This equality test involves comparing for every $j = 0 \ldots m - 1$ the character $s[i + j]$ with $t[j]$. These two nested loops have complexity $O(nm)$.

The Knuth–Morris–Pratt algorithm selects a letter # occurring neither in t nor in s and we consider the lengths f_i of the maximal boundaries of the prefixes of $w = t\#s$. Note that these boundaries can never be longer than t, due to the character #, hence $f_i \leq |t|$. However, if ever $f_i = |t|$, then we have found an occurrence of t in s. In the positive case, the answer to the problem is the index $i - 2|t|$: the length of t is subtracted twice from i, once to arrive at the start of the boundary and another time to obtain the index in s rather than in w, see Figure 2.7. Note that this algorithm is a bit different from the classic presentation of the Knuth–Morris–Pratt algorithm, composed of a pre-computation of the array f of boundaries of t followed by a very similar portion seeking the maximal alignments of t with the prefixes of s.

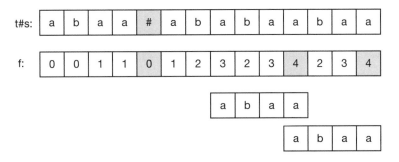

Figure 2.7 An execution of the maximal boundary search algorithm. Each occurrence of t in s corresponds to a boundary of length $|t|$ in the array f of lengths of maximal boundaries.

```
def knuth_morris_pratt(s, t):
    sep = '\x00'                        # special unused character
    assert sep not in t and sep not in s
    f = maximum_border_length(t + sep + s)
    n = len(t)
    for i, fi in enumerate(f):
        if fi == n:                     # found a border of the length of t
            return i - 2 * n            # beginning of the border in s
    return -1
```

Method Provided by the Language Python

Note that the language Python provides an integrated method find, allowing the search of a pattern t in a string s, simply with the expression s.find(t). A second optional parameter permits the search to be started at a certain index in s. This functionality will be useful in the problem of the determination of the period of a word, presented below.

Note

All standard libraries of common programming languages propose a function that looks for a pattern needle in a string haystack. However, the function provided by Java 10 has worst-case complexity $\Theta(nm)$, which is astonishingly expensive. We invite the reader to measure, for their favourite language, the execution time as a function of n of the search for the pattern $a^n b$ in the string a^{2n}, and protest if it is not linear.

Application: Determine the Largest Integer Power of a Word

```
input:   blablabla
output:  (bla)^{3}
```

Given a word x, we would like to identify the largest integer k such that x can be written as z^k for a word z. If $k > 1$, then we say that x is not *primitive*.

We can use our Swiss army knife of the computation of boundaries to solve this problem: if x can be written as y^ℓ, then all the y^p for $p = 0, \ldots, \ell - 1$ are boundaries of x. It remains to prove that $y^{\ell-1}$ is the maximal boundary of x. So, if n is the length of u and if $n - f_n$ divides n, the word is not primitive and the largest value of k we seek is $n/(n - f_n)$, see Figure 2.8.

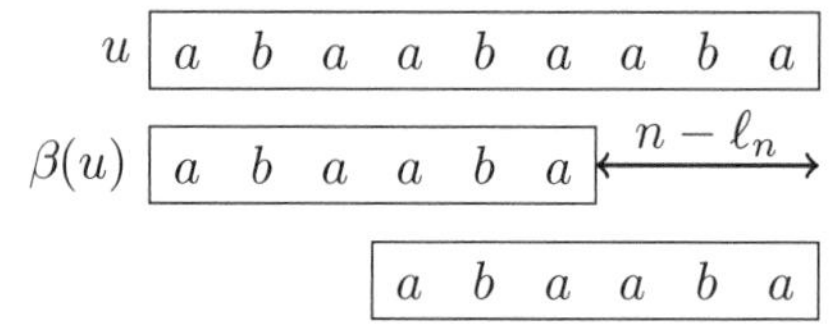

Figure 2.8 Knowing the maximal boundary of a periodic word allows the determination of its smallest period, here aba.

Proof

Suppose that $w = z^k$ for k maximal and $\beta(w)$ can be written as $z^{k-1}q$ where $qb = z$ for a certain non-empty b. First, note that $z = qb = bq$ (see Figure 2.9), hence $|b| \leq |q|$, otherwise $z^{k-1}b$ would be a larger boundary of w. Hence, b is a boundary of z and $bz = zb = bqb$. Thus, $bw = wb$, meaning that at the same time b is a boundary of w and w is a boundary of bw. We now prove the key observation: as long as b^ℓ is smaller that w, then b^ℓ is a boundary of w. We already know this is true for $\ell = 1$, and if it is true for b^ℓ, then bb^ℓ is a boundary of $bw = wb$; hence $b^{\ell+1}$ and w are boundaries of bw. This means that either $b^{\ell+1}$ is a boundary of w, or w is a boundary of $b^{\ell+1}$. Let L be the largest integer for which b^L is a boundary of w: then $w = b^L r = r b^L$ for a word r strictly smaller than b. If r is non-empty, then we have found a boundary larger than the maximal boundary $z^{k-1}q$, a contradiction. Hence, r is empty and since $|b| < |z|$, the factorisation b^L is suitable for $L > k$, again a contradiction. See Figure 2.9

```
def powerstring_by_border(u):
    f = maximum_border_length(u)
    n = len(u)
    if n % (n - f[-1]) == 0:         # does the alignment shift divide n ?
        return n // (n - f[-1])      # we found a power decomposition
    return 1
```

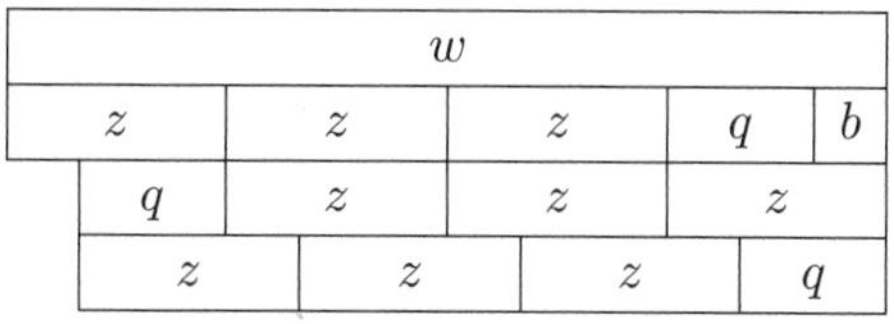

w				
z	z	z	q	b
q	z	z	z	
z	z	z	q	

Figure 2.9 If $w = z^4 = z^3qb$ and we suppose that the maximal boundary of w is z^3q, then the boundary property allows us to see that $z = bq = qb$.

Note that a shorter implementation exists using the substring search function integrated with Python, see Figure 2.10.

```
def powerstring_by_find(u):
    return len(x) // (x + x).find(x, 1)
```

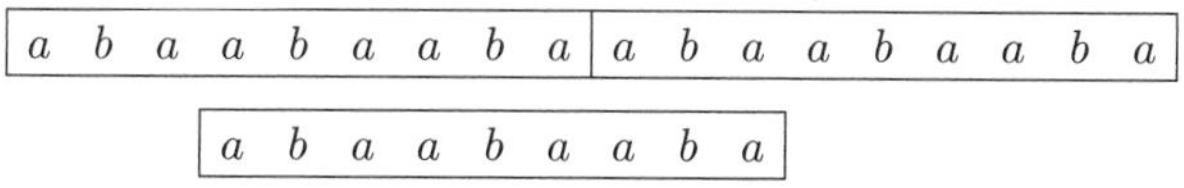

a	b	a	a	b	a	a	b	a	a	b	a	a	b	a	a	b	a

a	b	a	a	b	a	a	b	a

Figure 2.10 Detection of the first non-trivial position of x in xx allows the identification of its smallest period, here 3.

Application: Conjugate of a Word

```
input:  sweetsour   soursweet
output: sweet|sour sour|sweet
```

Another classic problem consists in detecting whether two words x and y are conjugate, i.e. if they can be written as $x = uv$ and $y = vu$ for words u and v. In the affirmative case, we would like to find the decomposition of x and y minimising the length of u. This boils down to simply looking for the first occurrence of y in the word xx.

Problems

Find the maximal product of string prefixes [codility:carbo2013]
A Needle in the Haystack [spoj:NHAY]
Power strings [kattis:powerstrings]
Period [spoj:PERIOD]

2.6   Pattern Matching—Rabin–Karp

Complexity
The expected time is $O(n + m)$, but the worst case complexity is $O(nm)$.

Algorithm
The Rabin–Karp algorithm 1987 is based on a completely different idea from Knuth–Morris–Pratt. To find a pattern t in a large string s, we slide a window of length len(t) over s and verify if the content of this window is equal to t. Since a character-by-character test is very costly, we instead maintain a hash value for the contents of the current window and compare it to the hash value of the search string t. If ever the hash values coincide, we proceed to the expensive character-by-character test, see Figure 2.11. To obtain an interesting complexity, it is necessary to efficiently update the hash value as the window shifts. We thus use what is known as a *rolling hash function*.

If the hash function, with values in $\{0, 1, \ldots, p - 1\}$, is well-chosen, we would expect a collision—i.e. when two distinct strings u, v with the same size, selected uniformly, give the same hash value—to occur with probability on the order of $1/p$. In this case, the mean complexity of the algorithm is $O(n + m + m/p)$. Our implementation uses p on the order of 2^{56}, hence in practice the complexity is $O(n + m)$, but in the worst case, it is $O(nm)$.

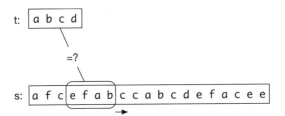

Figure 2.11 The idea of the Rabin–Karp algorithm is to first compare the hash values between t and a window on s before performing a costly character-by-character comparison.

Rolling Hash Function
Our hash function first transforms an m-character string into m integers $x_0, \ldots, x_{m-1}$, corresponding to their ASCII codes, lying between 0 and 127. The value of the hash function is then the multilinear expression

$$h(x_0, \ldots, x_{m-1}) = (x_0 \cdot 128^{m-1} + x_1 \cdot 128^{m-2} + \cdots + x_{m-2} \cdot 128 + x_{m-1}) \bmod p$$

where all of the operations are performed modulo a large prime number p. In practice, care should be taken so that all of the values calculated can be manipulated on a 64-bit machine, where a machine word (CPU register) contains signed integer values between -2^{63} and $2^{63} - 1$. The largest intermediate value calculated by the algorithm is $128 \cdot (p - 1) = 2^7 \cdot (p - 1)$, hence for our implementation we have chosen $p < 2^{56}$.

The polynomial form of this hash function allows us to calculate in constant time the value of $h(x_1, \ldots, x_m)$ in terms of x_0, x_m and $h(x_0, \ldots, x_{m-1})$: removing the first character amounts to subtracting the first term, shifting the characters to the left corresponds to a multiplication by 128 and modifying the last character is done by adding a term. Consequently, shifting the window on s, updating the hash value and comparing it with that of t takes constant time.

Note in the code below the addition of the value DOMAIN * PRIME (which is of course 0 mod p) to ensure that the calculations remain in the non-negative integers. This is not strictly necessary in Python but is required in languages such as C++, where the calculation of modulo can return a negative number.

```
PRIME = 72057594037927931      # < 2^{56}
DOMAIN = 128


def roll_hash(old_val, out_digit, in_digit, last_pos):
    val = (old_val - out_digit * last_pos + DOMAIN * PRIME) % PRIME
    val = (val * DOMAIN) % PRIME
    return (val + in_digit) % PRIME
```

The implementation of the algorithm begins with a function to compare character-by-character factors of length k in s at the position i and in t at the position j.

```
def matches(s, t, i, j, k):
    # tests if s[i:i + k] equals t[j:j + k]
    for d in range(k):
        if s[i + d] != t[j + d]:
            return False
    return True
```

Next, the implementation of the Rabin–Karp algorithm itself begins with the computation of the hash values of t and of the first window on s, followed by a loop over all the factors of s, until a match is found.

```
def rabin_karp_matching(s, t):
    hash_s = 0
    hash_t = 0
    len_s = len(s)
    len_t = len(t)
    last_pos = pow(DOMAIN, len_t - 1) % PRIME
    if len_s < len_t:                    # substring too long
        return -1
    for i in range(len_t):               # preprocessing
        hash_s = (DOMAIN * hash_s + ord(s[i])) % PRIME
        hash_t = (DOMAIN * hash_t + ord(t[i])) % PRIME
    for i in range(len_s - len_t + 1):
        if hash_s == hash_t:             # hashes match
            # check character by character
            if matches(s, t, i, 0, len_t):
                return i
        if i < len_s - len_t:
            # shift window and calculate new hash on s
            hash_s = roll_hash(hash_s, ord(s[i]), ord(s[i + len_t]),
                               last_pos)
    return -1                            # no match
```

This algorithm is less efficient than that of Knuth–Morris–Pratt: our experiments measured roughly a factor of 3 increase in the computation time. Nevertheless, its interest lies in the fact that its technique can be applied to solve several interesting variants of this problem.

Variant: The Search for Multiple Patterns

The Rabin–Karp algorithm which verifies if a string t is a factor of a given string s can naturally be generalised to a set $\mathcal{T}$ of strings to be found in s, in the case where all of the strings of $\mathcal{T}$ have the same length. It suffices to store the hash values of the strings in $\mathcal{T}$ in a dictionary to_search and for each window on s to verify whether the associated hash value is contained in to_search.

Variant: Common Factor

Given two strings s, t and a length k, we look for a string f of length k that is at the same time a factor of s and of t. To solve this problem, we first consider all of the factors of length k of the string t. These substrings are obtained in an analogous method to the Rabin–Karp algorithm, by sliding a window of size k across t and storing the resulting hash values in a dictionary pos. With each hash value, we associate the start positions of the corresponding windows.

Next, for each factor x of s of length k, we verify whether the hash value v is in pos, in which case we compare character-by-character x with the factors in t at the positions of pos[v].

For this algorithm, we must pay attention to the choice of the hash function. If s and t are of length n, it is necessary to choose $p \in \Omega(n^2)$, so that the number of collisions between the hash values of one of the $O(n)$ windows of t with one of the $O(n)$ windows of s is roughly constant. For a precise analysis, see Karp and Rabin (1987).

Variant: Common Factor with Maximal Length

Given two strings s, t, finding the longest common factor can be done with a binary search on the length k by using the previous algorithm. The complexity is $O(n \log m)$ where n is the total length of s and t, and m is the length of the optimal factor.

```
def rabin_karp_factor(s, t, k):
    last_pos = pow(DOMAIN, k - 1) % PRIME
    pos = {}
    assert k > 0
    if len(s) < k or len(t) < k:
        return None
    hash_t = 0


    # First calculate hash values of factors of t
    for j in range(k):
        hash_t = (DOMAIN * hash_t + ord(t[j])) % PRIME
    for j in range(len(t) - k + 1):
        # store the start position with the hash value
        if hash_t in pos:
            pos[hash_t].append(j)
        else:
            pos[hash_t] = [j]
        if j < len(t) - k:
            hash_t = roll_hash(hash_t, ord(t[j]), ord(t[j + k]), last_pos)


    hash_s = 0
    # Now check for matching factors in s
    for i in range(k):            # preprocessing
        hash_s = (DOMAIN * hash_s + ord(s[i])) % PRIME
    for i in range(len(s) - k + 1):
        if hash_s in pos:         # is this signature in s?
            for j in pos[hash_s]:
                if matches(s, t, i, j, k):
                    return (i, j)
        if i < len(s) - k:
            hash_s = roll_hash(hash_s, ord(s[i]), ord(s[i + k]), last_pos)
    return None
```

Problem
Longest Common Substring [spoj:LCS]

2.7   Longest Palindrome of a String—Manacher

```
input: babcbabcbaccba
output:  abcbabcba
```

Definition
A word s is a palindrome if the first character of s is equal to the last, the second is equal to the next-to-last and so on.

The problem of the longest palindrome consists in determining the longest factor that is a palindrome.

Complexity

This problem can be solved in quadratic time with the naive algorithm, in time $O(n \log n)$ with suffix arrays, but in time $O(n)$ with Manacher's algorithm (1975), described here.

Algorithm

First, we transform the input s by inserting a separator # around each character and by adding sentinels ^ and $ around the string. For example, abc is transformed into ^#a#b#c#$. Let t be the resulting string. This allows us to process in an equivalent manner palindromes of both even and odd length. Note that with this transformation, every palindrome begins and ends with the separator #. Thus, the two ends of a palindrome have indices with the same parity, which simplifies the transformation of a solution on the string t into one on the string s. The sentinels avoid special care for the border cases.

> The word nonne contains a palindrome of length 2 (nn) and one of length 3 (non). Their equivalents in
>
> ```
>      |-----|
> ^#n#o#n#n#e#$
>      |---|
> ```
>
> all begin and end with the separator #.

The output of the algorithm is an array p indicating for each position i, the largest radius r such that the factor from $i - r$ to $i + r$ is a palindrome. The naive algorithm is the following: for each i, we initialise $p[i] = 0$ and increment $p[i]$ until we find the longest palindrome $t[i - p[i], \dots, i + p[i]]$ centred on i.

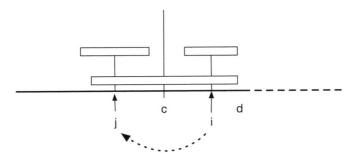

Figure 2.12 Manacher's algorithm. Having already computed p for the indices $< i$, we wish to compute $p[i]$. Suppose there is a palindrome centred on c of radius $d - c$ with d maximal, and let j be the mirror image of i with respect to c. By symmetry, the palindrome centred on j of radius $p[j]$ must be equal to the word centred on i, at least up to the radius $d - i$. Consequently, $p[j]$ is a lower bound for the value $p[i]$.

Manacher's improvement concerns the initialisation of $p[i]$. Suppose we already know a palindrome centred on c with radius r, hence terminating on the right at

$d = c + r$. Let j be the mirror image of i with respect to c, see Figure 2.12. There is a strong relation between $p[i]$ and $p[j]$. In the case where $i + p[j]$ is not greater than d, we can initialise $p[i]$ by $p[j]$. This is a valid operation, as the palindrome centred on j of radius $p[j]$ is included in the first half of the palindrome centred on c and of radius $d - c$; hence it is also found in the second half.

After having computed $p[i]$, we must update c and d, to preserve the invariant that they code a palindrome with $d - c$ maximal. The complexity is linear, since each comparison of a character is responsible for an incrementation of d.

```python
def manacher(s):
    assert set.isdisjoint({'$', '^', '#'}, s)  # Forbidden letters
    if s == "":
        return (0, 1)
    t = "^#" + "#".join(s) + "#$"
    c = 1
    d = 1
    p = [0] * len(t)
    for i in range(2, len(t) - 1):
        #                          -- reflect index i with respect to c
        mirror = 2 * c - i         # = c - (i-c)
        p[i] = max(0, min(d - i, p[mirror]))
        #                          -- grow palindrome centered in i
        while t[i + 1 + p[i]] == t[i - 1 - p[i]]:
            p[i] += 1
        #                          -- adjust center if necessary
        if i + p[i] > d:
            c = i
            d = i + p[i]
    (k, i) = max((p[i], i) for i in range(1, len(t) - 1))
    return ((i - k) // 2, (i + k) // 2)  # extract solution
```

Application
A man is walking around town, and his smartphone registers all of his movements. We recover this trace and seek to identify a certain type of trajectory during the day, notably round trips between two locations that use the same route. For this, we extract from the trace a list of street intersections and check it for palindromes.

Problems
Longest Palindromic Substring [spoj:LPS]
Casting Spells [kattis:castingspells]

3   Sequences

What is dynamic programming? It is a method to break down the resolution of a problem into a combination of solutions of some of its sub-problems. We first compute the solution of the subproblems and store them to be used later on (principle of *memoisation*), in an order fixed according to a *sweep*. This technique is particularly well-adapted to problems on sequences, where the sub-problems are, for example, defined on the prefixes of a sequence.

3.1   Shortest Path in a Grid

Definition
Consider a grid of $(n + 1) \times (m + 1)$ cells, labelled (i, j) with $0 \le i \le n$ and $0 \le j \le m$. The cells are linked by weighted arcs: the predecessors of a cell (i, j) are $(i - 1, j), (i - 1, j - 1)$ and $(i, j - 1)$, with the exception of the cells in the first column and first row (see Figure 3.1). The goal is to find the shortest path from $(0, 0)$ to (n, m).

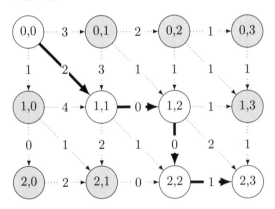

Figure 3.1 Shortest path in a directed grid, illustrated by the heavy arcs.

Algorithm in $O(nm)$
As this graph is directed and acyclic (abbreviated DAG, for *directed acyclic graph*), we can solve this problem by dynamic programming, by computing the distances from

(0,0) to all of the cells (i, j) in a certain order. First of all, the distances to the cells of the first row and first column are easy to compute, since a unique path towards these cells exists. Next, we compute the distances to the cells (i, j) with $1 \leq i \leq n, 1 \leq j \leq m$ in lexicographical order. Each distance from $(0,0)$ to an (i, j) is the minimum of three alternatives, which can be determined in constant time, as the distances to the predecessors of (i, j) have already been computed.

Variants
Several classic problems can be reduced to this simple problem, as described in the following sections.

Problem
Philosophers Stone [spoj:BYTESM2]

3.2 The Levenshtein Edit Distance

```
input: AUDI, LADA
output: LA-DA
       -AUDI
3 operations: deletion L, insertion U, substitution A by I
```

Definition
Given two strings x, y, we wish to know how many operations (insertion, deletion, or substitution) are required to transform x into y. This distance is used, for example, in the Unix command diff, which displays line-by-line a minimal number of operations to transform one file into another.

Algorithm in $O(nm)$
For $n = |x|, m = |y|$, we present an algorithm in $O(nm)$ using dynamic programming, see Figure 3.2. We construct an array $A[i, j]$ giving the distance between the prefix of x of length i and the prefix of y of length j. To begin, we initialise $A[0, j] = j$ and $A[i, 0] = i$ (the distances from the empty string to the various prefixes of x and y). Then, in general, when $i, j \geq 1$, there are three possibilities for the last letters of the prefixes. Either x_i is deleted, or y_j is inserted (at the end), or x_i is replaced by y_j (if they are not already equal). This gives the following recurrence formula, where match is a Boolean function which returns 1 if its arguments are identical:

$$A[i, j] = \min \begin{cases} A[i - 1, j - 1] + \text{match}(x_i, y_j) \\ A[i, j - 1] + 1 \\ A[i - 1, j] + 1. \end{cases}$$

This function encodes the cost of a letter substitution, which can be adjusted if desired. For example, the cost could depend on the distance between letters on the keyboard.

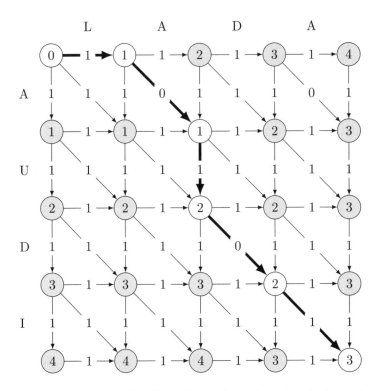

Figure 3.2 Shortest path in a directed graph, determining the edit distance between two words.

Sequence of Operations

As well as computing the edit distance between the strings, it would be nice to know the operations necessary to transform x into y. This can be done as in the search for the shortest path in a graph. By examining the distances of its predecessors, we can determine a choice that realises a minimal distance to a node. Thus we can trace the path from the node (n, m) back to $(0, 0)$, and along this path produce the list of operations corresponding to the optimal edits. At the end, it suffices to reverse this list.

Implementation Details

Note that in the description of the dynamic program, the dimension of the array A is $(n + 1) \times (m + 1)$, whereas the strings are of length n and m. This is because A takes into account *all* prefixes of x and y, *including the empty string ϵ*. So x has $n + 1$ prefixes, and y has $m + 1$.

```
def levenshtein(x, y):
    n = len(x)
    m = len(y)
    # Create the table A
    #   Row 0 and column 0 are initialized as required
    #   The remaining entries will be overwritten during the computation
    A = [[i + j for j in range(m + 1)] for i in range(n + 1)]
    for i in range(n):
        for j in range(m):
            A[i + 1][j + 1] = min(A[i][j + 1] + 1,              # insert
                                  A[i + 1][j] + 1,              # delete
                                  A[i][j] + int(x[i] != y[j]))  # subst.
    return A[n][m]
```

To Go Further
Algorithms with better performance in practice have been proposed. For example, if
an upper bound s is known for the edit distance, then the above dynamic program can
be restricted to entries in A at a distance of at most s from the diagonal, to obtain a
complexity of $O(s \min\{n, m\})$ (Ukkonen, 1985).

Problems
Edit distance [spoj:EDIST]
Advanced Edit Distance [spoj:ADVEDIST]

3.3   Longest Common Subsequence

```
input: GAC, AGCAT
output: A G C A T
           |   |
           G   A C
```

Definition
Let Σ be a set of symbols. For two sequences $s, x \in \Sigma^\star$, s is said to be a subsequence
of x if indices $i_1 < \ldots < i_{|s|}$ exist such that $x_{i_k} = s_k$ for every $k = 1, \ldots, |s|$. Given
two sequences $x, y \in \Sigma^\star$, we wish to find a maximal length sequence $s \in \Sigma^\star$, which
is a subsequence of both x and y.

Another way to see the problem involves *matchings*, see Section 9.1 on page 139. We seek a maximum matching between equal letters of x and y such that the links between the matches do not cross each other, see Figure 3.3.

Application
The program 'diff' reports differences between two files, expressed as a minimal list of line changes to bring either file into agreement with the other (Hunt and McIlroy, 1976). To do this, it is necessary to identify the largest common subsequence of lines between both files

This problem also arises in bioinformatics, for example when aligning two chains of nitrogenous bases.

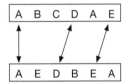

Figure 3.3 The problem of the longest common subsequence can be seen as a maximal alignment without crossings between equal elements of the two given sequences. For example, an additional alignment of the letters B would cross the alignment of the letters D.

Algorithm in $O(nm)$
We present an algorithm in $O(nm)$, where $n = |x|, m = |y|$. The idea is to compute for every $0 \le i \le n$ and $0 \le j \le m$ the longest common subsequence of the prefixes $x_1 \ldots x_i$ and $y_1 \ldots y_j$. This gives $n \cdot m$ subproblems. The optimal solution for (i, j) can be computed from the solutions for $(i - 1, j), (i, j - 1)$, and $(i - 1, j - 1)$, in constant time. We can thus solve the problem for (n, m) in time $O(nm)$. The algorithm is based on the following observation.

Key Observation
Let $A[i, j]$ be a longest common subsequence of $x_1 \ldots x_i$ and $y_1 \ldots y_j$. If $i = 0$ or $j = 0$, then $A[i, j]$ is empty. If $x_i \ne y_j$, then necessarily one of the letters x_i, y_j is not matched in an optimal solution and $A[i, j]$ is the longest sequence between $A[i - 1, j]$ and $A[i, j - 1]$. If $x_i = y_j$, then an optimal solution exists that makes a match between these letters and $A[i, j]$ is $A[i - 1, j - 1] \cdot x_i$. Here, the symbol '·' represents concatenation, and by *maximum* we mean the sequence of maximal length.

Implementation
In the simplified implementation given below, the variable `A[i][j]` does not represent the sequence $A[i, j]$, but instead represents its length.

```
def longest_common_subsequence(x, y):
    n = len(x)
    m = len(y)

    #                        -- compute optimal length
    A = [[0 for j in range(m + 1)] for i in range(n + 1)]
    for i in range(n):
        for j in range(m):
            if x[i] == y[j]:
                A[i + 1][j + 1] = A[i][j] + 1
            else:
                A[i + 1][j + 1] = max(A[i][j + 1],  A[i + 1][j])

    #                        -- extract solution in reverse order
    sol = []
    i, j = n, m
    while A[i][j] > 0:
        if A[i][j] == A[i - 1][j]:
            i -= 1
        elif A[i][j] == A[i][j - 1]:
            j -= 1
        else:
            i -= 1
            j -= 1
            sol.append(x[i])
    return ''.join(sol[::-1])  # reverse the list to obtain the solution
```

Variant for Several Given Sequences

Suppose that we seek a longest common subsequence, not for 2, but for k given sequences, of length $n_1, \ldots, n_k$, respectively. Then the above approach can be generalised. We generate a matrix A of dimension k, computing the longest common sequence for every combination of prefixes of the given sequences. The complexity of this algorithm is $O(2^k \prod_{i=1}^k n_i)$.

Variant with Two Sorted Sequences

The problem can be solved in time $O(n + m)$ if both sequences are sorted; in this case, we can proceed as in the merge of two sorted lists (see Section 4.1 on page 73).

In Practice

The algorithm BLAST (for *Basic Local Alignment Search Tool*) is widely used, but it does not always guarantee to produce an optimal solution.

Problems

Longest Common Substring [spoj:LCS]
Longest Common Subsequence [spoj:LCS0]

3.4   Longest Increasing Subsequence

Definition
Given a sequence of n integers x, find a strictly increasing subsequence of s of maximal length.

Application
Consider a straight road leading to the sea, with houses built along the road. Each house has several floors and enjoys a sea view if all the houses between it and the sea have fewer floors. We wish to give each house a sea view. What is the minimal number of houses that must be demolished to reach this goal (see Figure 3.4)?

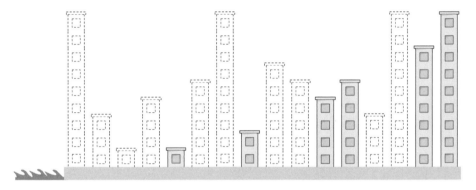

Figure 3.4 Demolish the least number of houses so that the rest have a sea view.

Algorithm in $O(n \log n)$
More precisely, the complexity is $O(n \log m)$ where m is the size of the solution produced by the algorithm. Using a greedy approach, for each index i, we want to append x_i to an increasing subsequence[1] of the prefix $x_1, \ldots, x_{i-1}$. But which of these subsequences will lead to an optimal solution? Consider the set of subsequences of the prefix. In a subsequence y two attributes are important: its length and the last element. Intuitively: we like the subsequences to be long—as this is the attribute to optimise—and we like them to end with a small element, since this allows more opportunities to easily complete it.

To formalise this intuition, denote by $|y|$ the length of a subsequence y and by y_{-1} the last element of y. The sequence y is said to *dominate* z if $|y| \geq |z|$ and $y_{-1} \leq z_{-1}$ and at least one of these inequalities is strict. It suffices to consider the non-dominated subsequences that can possibly be extended to an optimal subsequence.

The non-dominated subsequences of the prefix $x_1, \ldots, x_{i-1}$ differ by their length. Thus, for each length k we keep a subsequence of length k ending with a minimal integer. More specifically, we maintain an array b such that $b[k]$ is the last element of the longest subsequence of length k. By convention, $b[0] = -\infty$.

The key observation is that the array b is strictly increasing. Hence, when x_i is considered, at most one of the subsequences needs to be updated. In particular, if k is

---

[1] We omit the adjective *increasing* from now on for readability.

such that $b[k-1] < x_i < b[k]$, then we can improve the sequence of length $k-1$ by appending x_i, and obtain a better subsequence of length k, since it ends with a smaller element. If x_i is greater than all the elements of b, we can extend b with the element x_i. This is the only possible improvement, and the search for the index k can be done by dichotomy in time $O(\log |b|)$, where $|b|$ is the size of b.

Implementation Details

The subsequences are represented by linked lists with the aid of arrays h and p. The heads of the lists are held in h, such that $b[k] = x[h[k]]$, while the predecessor of an element j is $p[j]$. The lists are terminated by the constant None, see Figure 3.5.

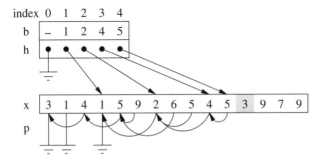

Figure 3.5 Computation of the longest increasing subsequence. In grey the input x being processed. For the prefix considered, the sequences so far are $(), (1), (1,2), (1,2,4), (1,2,4,5)$. After processing the element 3, the sequence $(1,2,4)$ is dethroned by $(1,2,3)$.

```
from bisect import bisect_left


def longest_increasing_subsequence(x):
    n = len(x)
    p = [None] * n
    h = [None]
    b = [float('-inf')]   # - infinity
    for i in range(n):
        if x[i] > b[-1]:
            p[i] = h[-1]
            h.append(i)
            b.append(x[i])
        else:
            #    -- binary search: b[k - 1] < x[i] <= b[k]
            k = bisect_left(b, x[i])
            h[k] = i
            b[k] = x[i]
            p[i] = h[k - 1]
    # extract solution in reverse order
    q = h[-1]
    s = []
    while q is not None:
        s.append(x[q])
        q = p[q]
    return s[::-1]   # reverse the list to obtain the solution
```

Variant: Non-Decreasing Subsequence
If the subsequence does not need to be strictly increasing, but merely non-decreasing, then instead of searching for k such that $b[k-1] < x[i] \leq b[k]$, we look for k such that $b[k-1] \leq x[i] < b[k]$. This can be done using the Python function `bisect_right`.

Variant: Longest Common Increasing Subsequence
Given two sequences x and y, we wish to find the longest common increasing subsequence. This problem can easily be solved in cubic time, by first sorting y to produce a sequence z, and then looking for a common subsequence to x, y, z. A better algorithm in time $O(|x| \cdot |y|)$ was published in 2005 by Yang et al.; however, this complexity was already required to solve a problem posed during the ACM/ICPC/NEERC competition a couple years earlier, in 2003.

Problem
Easy Longest Increasing Subsequence [spoj:ELIS]

3.5   Winning Strategy in a Two-Player Game

Definition
Consider a game over a stack of positive integers played by two players (in this instance, both players are female, in order to avoid convoluted grammar), see Figure 3.6. Player 0 starts. If the stack is empty, she loses. If not, then if the top of the stack contains an integer x, she has the choice between popping one element or popping x times. The latter option is authorised only if the stack contains at least x elements. Then it is the turn of Player 1 to play, and so on. Suppose you are given a stack P with n integers; the question is whether Player 0 has a winning strategy, i.e. if she can play in a way that wins no matter what Player 1 chooses to do.

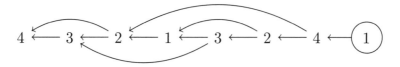

Figure 3.6 A configuration of the game.

Complexity
The complexity is linear using dynamic programming.

Algorithm by Dynamic Programming
Simulating the game would be too expensive, as the binary choices would lead to a combinatorial explosion. This is where dynamic programming can come in handy. Let G be a Boolean array of size n, where $G[i]$ indicates whether it is possible for a player to win if she begins the match with a stack reduced to the first i elements. The idea is

that Player 0 has a winning strategy if she manages in one shot to place Player 1 in a position where she can never win.

The base case is $G[0] = $ False, and the inductive case for $i > 0$ is

$$G[i] = \begin{cases} \overline{G[i-1] \vee \overline{G[i - P[i]]}} & \text{if } P[i] \leq i \\ \overline{G[i-1]} & \text{otherwise.} \end{cases}$$

By a simple scan in a linear number of steps, the array G can be populated, and the problem is solved by returning $G[n-1]$.

4   Arrays

Arrays figure as one of the most important of the elementary data types. For many simple problems, no other data structure is required. In Python, arrays are stored in the data type called *list*. The choice of this name might be confusing, because Python lists have nothing to do with *linked lists*, which are standard objects in C++ (*std::list*) and Java (*LinkedList*). Typically, a linked list allows the deletion or insertion of a given element at a given position in constant time. However, inserting into a Python list requires building in linear time a new list consisting of a prefix, the new element and a suffix. The elements of a Python list are indexed from 0. This must be taken into consideration when reading or displaying data, if ever the numbering of the elements begins at 1 in the format of the inputs or outputs.

In what follows, we use 'array' as the generic language-independent term, and 'list' when referring to the specific Python data structure.

An array can be used to represent a binary tree in a very simple manner. The parent of a node at index i is found at $\lfloor i/2 \rfloor$, its left child at index $2i$ and its right child at index $2i + 1$. The root is at index 1 and the element at index 0 is simply ignored.

This section deals with classic problems on arrays, and presents data structures to perform operations on intervals of indices known as *ranges*, for example, the computation of a minimal value within a range. Two of the sections describe dynamic data structures used to provide efficient operations of element modification and queries over such ranges.

> Recall: In Python, the last element of a list t can be accessed with the index -1. A reversed copy of t is obtained with $t[::-1]$. A new element is added with the method append. In this sense, Python lists are similar to the class `ArrayList` of Java or the class `vector` of C++.

Section 1.2.1 on page 6 contains a more complete introduction to Python lists.

4.1   Merge of Sorted Lists

Definition
Given two sorted lists x and y, produce a sorted list z, containing the elements of x and y.

Application
This operation is useful for the merge sort algorithm. To sort a list, we divide it into two portions of equal size (up to a difference of one element if the length is odd). The two portions are then sorted recursively, and the sorted results are merged using the procedure described below. This algorithm has an optimal complexity of $O(n \log n)$ comparisons.

Algorithm in Linear Time
The solution consists of conjointly running over the two lists and constructing z as we go. The key is to advance at each step within the list having the smallest current element. This ensures that the result itself will be sorted.

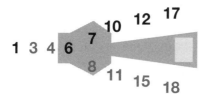

Figure 4.1 Merging two lists works a bit like a zipper with minimum selection instead of alternation.

```
def merge(x, y):
    z = []
    i = 0
    j = 0
    while i < len(x) or j < len(y):
        if j == len(y) or i < len(x) and x[i] <= y[j]:   # priority on x
            z.append(x[i])
            i += 1
        else:
            z.append(y[j])                               # now switch to y
            j += 1
    return z
```

Variant with k Lists
To rapidly identify the list in which we need to advance, we can store the k current elements of each list in a priority queue. The complexity is then $O(n \log k)$ where n is the length of the resulting list.

Problem
Mergesort [spoj:MERGSORT]

4.2   Sum Over a Range

Definition
Each request is of the form of an interval of indices $[i, j)$ and must return the sum of the elements of t between the indices i (included) and j (excluded).

Data Structure in $O(1)$ per Request and Initialisation in $O(n)$
It suffices to compute an array s of size $n + 1$, containing all the sums of prefixes of t. More specifically, $s[j] = \sum_{i<j} t[i]$. In particular, $s[0] = 0, s[1] = t[0], s[n] = \sum_{i=0}^{n-1} t[i]$. Then the response to the request $[i, j)$ is $s[j] - s[i]$.

4.3   Duplicates in a Range

Definition
Each request is in the form of an interval of indices $[i, j)$ and we must either find an element x of t appearing at least twice within this interval or announce that all the elements are distinct.

Data Structure in $O(1)$ per Request and Initialisation in $O(n)$
With a sweep from left to right, we construct an array p indicating for each j the largest index $i < j$ such that $t[i] = t[j]$. When $t[j]$ is seen for the first time, we set $p[j] = -1$.

The computation of p requires storing, for each element x, the index of the last occurrence of x observed in t during the sweep. This can be done with an array if there is a guarantee on the domain of the elements of t, or otherwise with a dictionary based on a hash table.

In parallel, we store in an array q, for each j, the largest value of $p[i]$ for all $i \leq j$. In response to a request $[i, j)$, if ever $q[j - 1] < i$ then all the elements in $[i, j)$ are distinct, otherwise $t[q[j - 1]]$ is a duplicate.

To determine the indices of two occurrences, it suffices to compute in parallel with $q[j]$ the index i that realises the maximum.

index	0	1	2	3	4	5	6	7	8	9
t		a	b	a	a	c	d	b	a	b	c
p		-1	-1	0	2	-1	-1| 1	3	6	4
q		-1	-1	0	2	2	2	2	3	6	6

Figure 4.2 The algorithm for finding duplicates on an example. In the interval $[3, 6)$ all elements of t are distinct because $q[5] < 3$. However, the interval $[4, 10)$ contains duplicates, for example, b at the positions $q[9]$ and $p[q[9]]$.

Problem

Unique Encryption Keys [icpcarchive:5881]

4.4   Maximum Subarray Sum

Definition

This statistical problem seeks to find, for an array of values t, the maximum of $t[i] + t[i + 1] + \cdots + t[j]$ over every pair of indices i, j with $i \leq j$.

Algorithm in $O(n)$

This solution by dynamic programming was found by Jay Kadane in 1984. For each index j we look for the maximal sum $t[i] + \cdots + t[j]$ over all indices $0 \leq i \leq j$. Denote $A[j]$ as this value. This value must be either $t[j]$ itself, or made up of $t[j]$ plus a sum of the form $t[i] + \cdots + t[j - 1]$, which is itself maximal. Hence, $A[0] = t[0]$, as this is the only option, and for $j \geq 1$, we have the recurrence relation $A[j] = t[j] + \max\{A[j - 1], 0\}$.

Variants

This problem can be generalised to matrices. Given a matrix M of dimension $n \times m$, a range of row indices $[a, b]$ and a range of column indices $[i, j]$ define a rectangle $[a, b] \otimes [i, j]$ within the matrix. We wish to find the rectangle with the largest sum. For this, it suffices to loop over all pairs of row indices $[a, b], a \leq b$, and for each pair generate an array t of length m, such that $t[i] = M[a, i] + \cdots + M[b, i]$. This array can be obtained in time $O(m)$ from the array of the previous iteration corresponding to the pair $[a, b - 1]$, by simply adding the bth row of M. With the aid of the above algorithm, we can find in time $O(m)$ a range of columns $[i, j]$ which describes a rectangle $[a, b] \otimes [i, j]$ of maximal sum bounded by the rows a and b. The largest sum seen when looping over a and b gives the maximal sum for M. This approach produces a solution with complexity $O(n^2 m)$.

Problems

Maximum Sum Sequences [spoj:MAXSUMSQ]

Largest Rectangle [codechef:LARGEST]

4.5   Query for the Minimum of a Range—Segment Tree

Definition

We wish to maintain a data structure storing an array t of n values and allowing the following operations:

- change $t[i]$ for a given index i.
- calculate $\min_{i \leq j < k} t[j]$ for a given range of indices i, k.

Variant
With only minor changes we can also determine the index of the minimum element along with its value.

Data Structure with $O(\log n)$ per Request
The idea is to complement the array t with a binary tree, known as a *segment tree*. This data structure is also known as a *BIT-tree* (*Binary Index Tree*). Each node is responsible for a range of indices in t, see Figure 4.3. The size of a range is a power of 2, and the two children of a node are responsible for the two halves of the range. The leaf nodes at the bottom level of the tree contain the values of t. For each node, we simply store the minimum of the values of the array in the associated range.

An update of an array entry requires a logarithmic number of updates in the structure, on each node on the path down from the element in question. The search for the minimum over a given range $[i, k)$ is done with a recursive exploration of the tree. The function _range_min(j, start, span, i, k) returns the minimum of the array t among the indices of [start, start+span) $\cap$ $[i, k)$, where j is the index of the node corresponding to this range. The search terminates when either the range of the current node is contained in $[i, k)$—in which case, we return the value of the node—or when the range of the current node is disjoint from $[i, k)$—in which case, we return $+\infty$.

1											
1						5					
1		2		5				∞			
1	8	3	2	5		∞		∞		∞	
3	1	9	8	3	4	2	7	5	∞	∞	∞	∞	∞	∞

Figure 4.3 The tree used in the structure to determine the minimum in a range.

Analysis of the Complexity
To convince ourselves that the time taken per request is $O(\log n)$, we distinguish four types of nodes encountered in the traversal. Let $[s, t)$ be the range corresponding to a node.

- The node is said to be *empty* if $[s, t)$ is disjoint from $[i, k)$.
- The node is said to be *full* if $[s, t) \subseteq [i, k)$.
- The node is said to be *strict* if $[s, t) \supset [i, k)$.
- Otherwise, the node is said to be *overlapping*.

Note that for an overlapping node, the ranges $[s, t)$ and $[i, k)$ intersect, but without one being included in the other. The analysis follows from a bound on the number of nodes of each type.

The search range_min traverses a logarithmic number of full nodes, which correspond to the decomposition of $[i, k)$ into disjoint ranges. This is the same for the empty nodes, which correspond to a decomposition of the complement of $[i, k)$ into ranges.

The analysis terminates with the observation that the children of an overlapping node are always either full or empty, and that only the root can be a strict node.

```
class RangeMinQuery:
    def __init__(self, t, INF=float('inf')):
        self.INF = INF
        self.N = 1
        while self.N < len(t):                    # find size N
            self.N *= 2
        self.s = [self.INF] * (2 * self.N)
        for i in range(len(t)):                    # store values of t
            self.s[self.N + i] = t[i]              # in the leaf nodes
        for p in range(self.N - 1, 0, -1):        # fill inner nodes
            self.s[p] = min(self.s[2 * p], self.s[2 * p + 1])

    def __getitem__(self, i):
        return self.s[self.N + i]

    def __setitem__(self, i, v):
        p = self.N + i
        self.s[p] = v
        p //= 2                                    # climb up the tree
        while p > 0:                               # update node
            self.s[p] = min(self.s[2 * p], self.s[2 * p + 1])
            p //= 2

    def range_min(self, i, k):
        return self._range_min(1, 0, self.N, i, k)

    def _range_min(self, p, start, span, i, k):
        if start + span <= i or k <= start:        # disjoint intervals
            return self.INF
        if i <= start and start + span <= k:       # contained intervals
            return self.s[p]
        left = self._range_min(2 * p, start, span // 2,
                               i, k)
        right = self._range_min(2 * p + 1, start + span // 2, span // 2,
                                i, k)
        return min(left, right)
```

A weighted variant of this structure is put to use in order to efficiently calculate the area of a union of rectangles, see Section 13.5 on page 205.

Problem
Negative Score [spoj:RPLN]

4.6   Query the Sum over a Range—Fenwick Tree

Definition
We wish to maintain a data structure t storing n values and allowing the following operations for a given index $a \in \{0, \dots, n-1\}$:

- update $t[a]$.
- calculate $t[0] + \cdots + t[a]$.

For technical reasons, internally we work with an array T whose indices vary from 1 to n, with $t[a] = T[a + 1]$. Hence, in Python, $T[0]$ is ignored, and the length of T will actually be $n + 1$!. The first statement in the access methods to our structure is a shift of the index, in order to hide this technical detail from the users.

This problem can be solved using a segment tree, as described in the previous section. By replacing the constant ∞ by 0 and the operation min by an addition, we obtain a structure that solves the problem with a complexity $O(\log n)$ per request. The structure described in this section has a similar performance, but is quicker to implement.

Variant
With a slight modification, this structure can also be used to perform the following operations in time $O(\log n)$.

- add a value across the whole of an interval $t[a], t[a + 1], \ldots, t[b]$ for given indices a, b.
- request the value of $t[a]$ for a given index a.

For this, it suffices to use a Fenwick tree storing an array t', with $t[a] = t'[0] + \cdots + t'[a]$. Hence, reading $t[a]$ reduces to calculating the sum of a prefix in t', and adding a value to a suffix in t involves modifying a value in t'. Hence, adding a value to an interval of indices in t comes down to modifying two values in t' at the endpoints of the interval.

Data Structure with $O(\log n)$ per Request
(see Fenwick, 1994). The idea of the structure is to store, not the array T itself, but instead the sums over intervals of T. To this end, we create a new array s such that for $i \in \{1, \ldots, n\}$, $s[i]$ is the sum of $T[j]$ over $j \in I(i)$, where $I(i)$ is an interval defined below. The element $s[0]$ is ignored. These intervals are organised in the form of a tree by inclusion in the following manner, with two relations: parent and left neighbour (see Figure 4.4).

- The element $s[i]$ where the binary representation[1] of i is of the form $x10^k$ for $x \in \{0, 1\}^*$ contains the sum of elements of T over the interval $I(i) = \{x0^k 1, \ldots, i\}$.
- The parent of the index $i = x10^k$ is $i + 10^k$.

---

[1] We usually use subscript 2 to denote the binary representation, but it is omitted if no confusion is possible.

- The left neighbour of the index $i = x10^k$ is $j = x00^k$. The interval $I(j)$ is the one touching $I(i)$ on the left.

Hence, the sum of the prefix $T[1] + \cdots + T[i]$ with $i = x10^k$ is $s[i]$ plus the sum of the prefix $T[1] + \cdots + T[x00^k]$, in a recursive manner.

For example, in Figure 4.4, updating $T[11]$ must change $s[11 = 01011_2]$, $s[12 = 01100_2]$ and $s[16 = 10000_2]$, and the sum of the prefix $T[1] \ldots T[11]$ is the sum of $s[11 = 01011_2]$, $s[10 = 01010_2]$ and $s[8 = 01000_2]$.

An important operation to implement this structure consists of isolating the least significant non-zero digit in the binary representation i, i.e. to transform a number in binary notation $x10^k$ into 10^k. This operation is simply i&-i. As follows:

$$i = x10^k$$
$$\bar{i} = \bar{x}01^k$$
$$-i = \bar{i} + 1 = \bar{x}10^k$$
$$i \& -i = 10^k$$

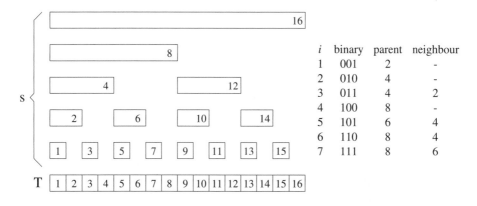

Figure 4.4 Example of a Fenwick tree. The relation 'is parent of' can be read vertically from top to bottom. For example, 8 is the parent of 4, 6 and 7. An index i is left neighbour of j if the interval $I(i)$ touches $I(j)$ on the left. For example, 4 is the left neighbour of 5 and 6.

```
class Fenwick:
    def __init__(self, t):
        self.s = [0] * (len(t) + 1)   # create internal storage
        for a, v in enumerate(t):
            self.add(a, v)                # initialize

    def prefixSum(self, a):
        i = a + 1                         # internal index starts at 1
        total = 0
        while i > 0:                      # loops over neighbors
            total += self.s[i]            # cumulative sum
            i -= (i & -i)                 # left neighbor
        return total

    def intervalSum(self, a, b):
        return self.prefixSum(b) - self.prefixSum(a-1)

    def add(self, a, val):
        i = a + 1                         # internal index starts at 1
        while i < len(self.s):            # loops over parents
            self.s[i] += val              # update node
            i += (i & -i)                 # parent

    # variante:
    def intervalAdd(self, a, b, val):
        self.add(a,     +val)
        self.add(b + 1, -val)

    def get(self, a):
        return self.prefixSum(a)
```

4.7   Windows with k Distinct Elements

Definition
Given a sequence x of n elements and an integer k, we wish to determine all the intervals $[i, j)$, maximal by inclusion, such that $x_i, \dots, x_{j-1}$ include exactly k distinct elements, see Figure 4.5.

Figure 4.5 A window containing exactly 2 distinct elements.

Application
A cache is a rapid-access memory which is placed in front of a slower memory. The address space of the slow memory is partitioned into equal-sized blocks, known as

pages. The cache has limited capacity and can only hold k pages. The memory access of a processor over time forms a sequence x whose elements are the pages requested. When a requested page is in the cache, access to it is very fast, otherwise we speak of a *cache miss* and the page must be loaded into the cache from slow memory in place of another page (one that is used infrequently or has not been used in a long time). Looking for intervals in x containing exactly k distinct elements reduces to finding the intervals of time during which no cache misses have occurred, under the hypothesis of a favourable initial cache configuration.

Algorithm in $O(n)$

The idea is to run over the sequence x with two cursors i and j that define a window. We maintain the number of distinct elements of the set $x_i, \ldots, x_{j-1}$ in a variable dist, with the aid of a counter of occurrences occ for each element. When dist exceeds the parameter k, we advance i, otherwise we advance j. The following implementation returns an iterator, and can be used by another function to individually process each interval. As each of the two cursors i and j only advance, we perform at most $2n$ operations, hence the linear time complexity.

```
def windows_k_distinct(x, k):
    dist, i, j = 0, 0, 0           # dist = |{x[i], ..., x[j-1]}|
    occ = {xi: 0 for xi in x}      # number of occurrences in x[i:j]
    while j < len(x):
        while dist == k:           # move start of interval
            occ[x[i]] -= 1         # update counters
            if occ[x[i]] == 0:
                dist -= 1
            i += 1
        while j < len(x) and (dist < k or occ[x[j]]):
            if occ[x[j]] == 0:     # update counters
                dist += 1
            occ[x[j]] += 1
            j += 1                 # move end of interval
        if dist == k:
            yield (i, j)           # one interval found
```

Variant

Given a ring of symbols (a list of characters looping back on itself), what is the length of the smallest interval containing at least one instance of each symbol? This is indeed a variant, as it suffices to run through the list concatenated with itself and determine the smallest interval containing k distinct elements, where k is the total number of symbols. A solution with two cursors again has linear complexity.

Problem

Épiphanie [prologin:2011:epiphanie]

5 Intervals

Several problems concerning intervals can be solved by dynamic programming. The set of intervals that are before or after a threshold can form two independent sub-instances.

If the problem permits, it is convenient to use half-open intervals of the form $[s,t)$, as the number of integers that they contain is then easy to compute (here simply $t - s$, as long as s, t are integers).

5.1 Interval Trees

Definition

The problem consists of storing n given intervals in a structure in order to rapidly answer queries of the following form: *for a given value p, what is the list of all the intervals containing p?* We suppose that all the intervals are of the half-open form $[l, h)$, but the structure can be adapted to other forms.

Data Structure with $O(\log n + m)$ per Query

Here, m is the number of intervals returned. The structure is a binary tree constructed as follows. Let S be a set of intervals to store. We choose a value center as described below. This value divides the intervals into three groups: the set L of intervals to the left of center, the set C of intervals containing center and the set R of intervals to the right of center. Then the root of the tree stores center and C, and in a recursive manner, the left and right subtrees store L and R, see Figure 5.1.

In order to quickly answer queries, the set C is stored in the form of sorted lists. The list by_low stores the intervals of C ordered by their left endpoints, whereas the list by_high stores the intervals of C ordered by their right endpoints.

To reply to a query for a point p, it suffices to compare p with center. If $p <$ center, then we recursively look for intervals containing p in the left subtree and add the intervals $[l, h)$ of C with $l \leq p$. This is correct, since by construction these intervals satisfy $h >$ center and hence $p \in [l, h)$. If not, and $p \geq$ center, then we recursively look for intervals containing p in the right subtree and add the intervals $[l, h)$ of C with $p < h$.

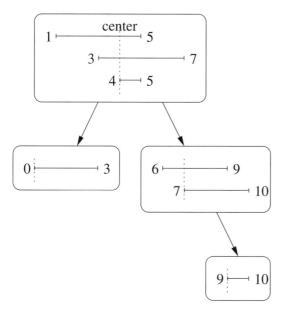

Figure 5.1 A tree storing 7 intervals.

Choice of center

For the binary tree to be balanced, we can choose center as the median value of the left endpoints of the intervals to be stored. Then half the intervals will be stored in the right subtree, guaranteeing a logarithmic depth. In a manner similar to the behaviour of the sort algorithm quicksort, if the centre is chosen randomly among the left endpoints, the performance will be similar in expectation.

Complexity

The construction of the tree takes time $O(n \log n)$, and the processing of a query costs $O(\log n + m)$, where the logarithmic term is due to the binary search in the sorted lists.

Implementation Details

In our implementation, the intervals are represented by n-tuples whose first two elements contain the endpoints of an interval. Other elements can be added to transport supplementary information.

The binary search is done via the function bisect_right(t,x), which returns i such that $t[j] > x$ if and only if $j > i$. Note that you should not loop in the array by_high with the aid of the sublist selection by_high[i:], as the creation of the sublist is linear in len(by_high), thus increasing the complexity to $O(\log n + n)$ instead of $O(\log n + m)$, where m is the size of the list returned.

The arrays contain pairs (value, interval), thus we search with bisect_right the insertion point of an element x of the form $(p, (\infty, \infty))$.

```
class _Node:
    def __init__(self, center, by_low, by_high, left, right):
        self.center = center
        self.by_low = by_low
        self.by_high = by_high
        self.left = left
        self.right = right


def interval_tree(intervals):
    if intervals == []:
        return None
    center = intervals[len(intervals) // 2][0]
    L = []
    R = []
    C = []
    for I in intervals:
        if I[1] <= center:
            L.append(I)
        elif center < I[0]:
            R.append(I)
        else:
            C.append(I)
    by_low = sorted((I[0], I) for I in C)
    by_high = sorted((I[1], I) for I in C)
    IL = interval_tree(L)
    IR = interval_tree(R)
    return _Node(center, by_low, by_high, IL, IR)


def intervals_containing(t, p):
    INF = float('inf')
    if t is None:
        return []
    if p < t.center:
        retval = intervals_containing(t.left, p)
        j = bisect_right(t.by_low, (p, (INF, INF)))
        for i in range(j):
            retval.append(t.by_low[i][1])
    else:
        retval = intervals_containing(t.right, p)
        i = bisect_right(t.by_high, (p, (INF, INF)))
        for j in range(i, len(t.by_high)):
            retval.append(t.by_high[j][1])
    return retval
```

Variant

If the goal is only to determine the *number* of intervals containing a given value, and not the list, then a much simpler solution exists with a sweep line algorithm. We sweep the intervals contained in a node from left to right, advancing from one end to the other. At any given moment, we maintain the number of intervals *open* (i.e. the right endpoint has not yet been seen), and thus produce an array containing pairs of the form (x, k), such that for two successive pairs $(x, k), (x', k')$, the number of intervals containing p is k for $x \leq p < x'$.

5.2   Union of Intervals

Definition
Given a set S of n intervals, we wish to determine their union, in the form of an ordered list L of disjoint intervals, with the property $\bigcup_{I \in S} = \bigcup_{I \in L}$.

Algorithm
The complexity is $O(n \log n)$ using a sweep line algorithm. We sweep the endpoints of the intervals from left to right. At any given moment, we maintain in nb_open the number of intervals *open* (i.e. the right endpoint has not yet been seen). When this number becomes zero, we add to the solution a new interval [last,x], where x is the current position of the sweep line and last is the last sweep position where nb_open became positive.

Implementation Details
Note the order in which the endpoints of the intervals are processed. This order is correct when the intervals are closed or half-open. For open intervals, the end of the interval (x, y) must be handled before the beginning of the interval (y, z).

```python
def intervals_union(S):
    E = [(low, -1) for (low, high) in S]
    E += [(high, +1) for (low, high) in S]
    nb_open = 0
    last = None
    retval = []
    for x, _dir in sorted(E):
        if _dir == -1:
            if nb_open == 0:
                last = x
            nb_open += 1
        else:
            nb_open -= 1
            if nb_open == 0:
                retval.append((last, x))
    return retval
```

5.3   The Interval Point Cover Problem

Application
We need to install a minimal number of antennas along a straight beach in order to provide coverage to a number of small offshore islands (as small as individual points!).

An antenna can cover all of the islands within a given radius r (too bad for islands further out than r), which is the same for all the antennas.

Observation
The intersection of the beach with a circle of radius r drawn around an island defines an interval on the beach that must contain an antenna. The problem thus reduces to the following, see Figure 5.2.

Definition
For n given intervals, find a minimal set of points S such that each interval intersects S.

Algorithm
The complexity is $O(n \log n)$ using the sweep line technique. We process the intervals in increasing order of their right endpoint. At every step, we maintain a solution S for the intervals already seen, which minimises $|S|$ and in case of equality maximises max S.

The algorithm is simple. If for an interval $[l, r]$ we have $l \leq$ max S, then we do nothing, otherwise we add r to S. The idea is that in any case we must cover $[l, r]$, and by choosing the largest value that covers it, we increase the chance to additionally cover subsequent intervals.

To be convinced of the optimality, let S_n be the solution constructed for the set of intervals $I_1, \ldots, I_n$ already processed. Obviously, S_1 is optimal for I_1. Suppose S_n is optimal, and consider $I_{n+1} = [l, r]$. Either $l \leq$ max S_n, in which case S_n is already an optimal solution for I_{n+1}, or $l >$ max S_n, and $|S_{n+1}| = |S_n| + 1$. In the latter case,

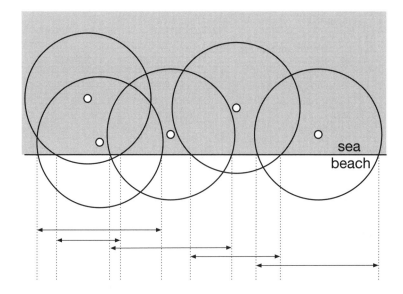

Figure 5.2 How many antennas are needed to cover all the islands? This problem reduces to the interval point cover problem.

suppose S'_{n+1} is an optimal solution for $I_1, \ldots, I_{n+1}$. Then $S'_{n+1} \setminus \{\max S'_{n+1}\}$ must cover $I_1, \ldots, I_n$, and hence, by the optimality of S_n, $|S'_{n+1}| = |S_n| + 1 = |S_{n+1}|$.

```python
def interval_cover(I):
    S = []
    # sort by right endpoints
    for start, end in sorted(I, key=lambda v: v[1]):
        if not S or S[-1] < start:
            S.append(end)
    return S
```

Problem
Radar Installation [onlinejudge:1193]

6 Graphs

A graph is a combinatorial object composed of a set of vertices V (also known as nodes) and a set of edges E. The edges correspond to pairs of vertices, which are generally distinct, and without a notion of order in the sense where (u, v) and (v, u) denote the same edge.

At times, we consider a variant, the *directed graph*, where the edges have an orientation. In this case, the edges are usually known as *arcs*. The arc (u, v) has origin u and destination v. Most of the algorithms described in this book operate on directed graphs but can be applied to non-directed graphs by replacing each edge (u, v) by two arcs (u, v) and (v, u).

Graphs can contain additional information, such as weights or letters, in the form of labels on the vertices or the edges.

6.1   Encoding in Python

A simple manner to encode a graph is to identify the n vertices by the integers from 0 to $n - 1$. However, it is common to number the vertices starting from 1 when displaying a graph, or when reading from an input file. Thus, remember to add or subtract 1 from the indices when displaying or reading a graph.

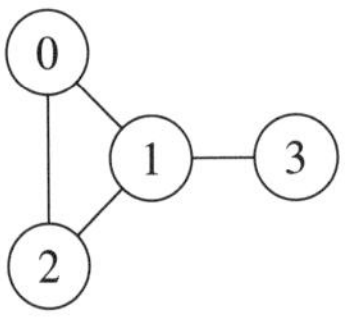

```
# adjacency list
G = [[1,2],[0,2,3],[0,1],[1]]

# adjacency matrix
G = [[0,1,1,0],
     [1,0,1,1],
     [1,1,0,0],
     [0,1,0,0]]
```

Figure 6.1 A graph and its possible encodings.

The edges can essentially be represented in two manners, by adjacency list or by adjacency matrix. The latter is sometimes simpler to implement but is more demanding in memory: the graph is represented by a binary matrix E such that $E[u, v]$ indicates the existence of an arc (u, v), see Figure 6.1.

The representation by adjacency list consists of symbolising the graph by a list of lists G. For a vertex u, $G[u]$ is the list of neighbours of u. The vertices can also be designated by a textual identifier, in which case G could be a dictionary whose keys are strings and whose values are the lists of neighbours. For example, the triangle composed of three vertices 'axel', 'bill' and 'carl' would be encoded by the following dictionary:

```
{'axel': ['bill','carl'], 'bill': ['axel','carl'], 'carl': ['axel','bill']}
```

The algorithms presented in this book generally work with adjacency lists.

In a directed graph, at times we require two structures G_out, G_in, containing the arcs originating from and terminating on each vertex. However, rather than storing the arc, we store the endpoints of the arcs. Hence, for each vertex u, G_out[u] contains the list of vertices v for each outgoing arc (u, v) and G_in[u] the list of vertices v for each incoming arc (v, u).

A simple way to store labels on the vertices and the edges is to use complementary arrays indexed by the vertices or matrices indexed by pairs of vertices. In this way the structure of the encoding of the graph G itself is not affected, and G can be used without modification in the portions of the code that are not concerned with the labels.

Certain implementations of graph algorithms require the vertices to be simply the integers between 0 and $n - 1$, whereas at times the vertices need to be identified by a name or by a more complex but immutable object, such as a string or an n-tuple of integers. To provide an interface between these code fragments, a small class can be written, translating between the index of a vertex and the complex object that it represents. Such a class would contain a dictionary name2node relating the name of a vertex to its index, and an array node2name providing the inverse function. If G is an instance of the class Graph, then the expression len(G) should return the number of its vertices and G[u] the adjacency list of the vertex with index u. Then the class behaves exactly like an adjacency list, and in addition allows vertices and edges to be added using the names of the vertices.

```
class Graph:
    def __init__(self):
        self.neighbors = []
        self.name2node = {}
        self.node2name = []
        self.weight = []

    def __len__(self):
        return len(self.node2name)

    def __getitem__(self, v):
        return self.neighbors[v]
    def add_node(self, name):
        assert name not in self.name2node
        self.name2node[name] = len(self.name2node)
        self.node2name.append(name)
        self.neighbors.append([])
        self.weight.append({})
        return self.name2node[name]

    def add_edge(self, name_u, name_v, weight_uv=None):
        self.add_arc(name_u, name_v, weight_uv)
        self.add_arc(name_v, name_u, weight_uv)

    def add_arc(self, name_u, name_v, weight_uv=None):
        u = self.name2node[name_u]
        v = self.name2node[name_v]
        self.neighbors[u].append(v)
        self.weight[u][v] = weight_uv
```

6.2   Implicit Graphs

At times, the graph is given implicitly, for example, in the form of a grid, where the vertices are the cells of the grid and the edges correspond to the adjacent cells, as in a labyrinth. Another example of a graph given implicitly is with combinatorial objects, where an arc corresponds to a local modification.

Example: Rush Hour

RUSH HOUR is a commercially available puzzle. The playing board is a 6×6 grid, see Figure 6.2. Cars (of length 2) and trucks (of length 3) are placed on the grid, without overlapping and without going outside the boundary of the grid. A specific car is marked in darker shade, and the goal is for it to exit the grid via the unique opening on the boundary. For this, it is possible to move the vehicles forwards or backwards.

The modelisation with a graph is straightforward. The data for each of the k vehicles includes a fixed part and a variable part. The fixed part includes the size, the orientation and the fixed coordinate (for example, the column for a vehicle oriented vertically). The variable part consists of the free coordinate. The vector of all these coordinates completely encodes a configuration of the grid. The key of an exploration of this graph is a function, which from a given configuration vector enumerates all the configuration

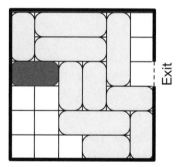

Figure 6.2 A configuration of the game RUSH HOUR.

vectors reachable in one move. The encoding of the configuration given in Figure 6.2
is the following.

```
orient = [1, 0, 1, 0, 0, 1, 1, 0, 0, 1, 0]   # 0 = horizontal, 1 = vertical
length = [2, 3, 3, 3, 2, 2, 2, 2, 3, 2, 2]   # 2 = car, 3 = truck
coofix = [0, 0, 4, 1, 2, 2, 3, 3, 4, 5, 5]
coovar = [0, 1, 0, 1, 0, 2, 2, 4, 2, 4, 3]
red = 4                                        # index of red car
```

For example, if orient[i] = 0, then the vehicle i occupies all the cells (x, y) for
coovar[i] $\leq x <$ coovar[i] + length[i] and $y =$ coofix[i]. If orient[i] = 1, then
the vehicle i occupies all the cells (x, y) for $x =$ coofix[i] and coovar[i] $\leq y <$
coovar[i] + length[i].

Problem
Ricochet Robots [kattis:ricochetrobots]

6.3   Depth-First Search—DFS

Definition
Depth-first search is an exploration of a graph that begins at a given vertex and
recursively explores its neighbours.

Complexity
The complexity in time is $O(|V| + |E|)$.

Application
The principal application is to discover all the nodes accessible starting from a given
vertex of a graph. This technique is the basis for several algorithms that we will tackle
further on, such as the detection of biconnected components or topological sort, see
Sections 6.6 on page 97 and 6.7 on page 102.

Implementation Details
In order to avoid repeatedly exploring the neighbours of a vertex, we mark the vertices
already visited, using a Boolean array.

```
def dfs_recursive(graph, node, seen):
    seen[node] = True
    for neighbor in graph[node]:
        if not seen[neighbor]:
            dfs_recursive(graph, neighbor, seen)
```

Improved Implementation

The above recursive implementation cannot handle very large graphs, as the call stack is limited. In Python, the function setrecursionlimit allows this limit to be somewhat exceeded, but, in general, to not more than a depth of some thousands of recursive calls. To overcome this problem and for better efficiency, we propose an iterative implementation. The stack to_visit contains the vertices discovered but not yet processed.

```
def dfs_iterative(graph, start, seen):
    seen[start] = True
    to_visit = [start]
    while to_visit:
        node = to_visit.pop()
        for neighbor in graph[node]:
            if not seen[neighbor]:
                seen[neighbor] = True
                to_visit.append(neighbor)
```

The Case of a Grid

Consider a grid where certain cells can be visited (marked by the character '.') and certain cannot be (marked by '#'), as in a labyrinth. From any given cell, we can attempt to visit the four neighbouring cells, except for those on the boundary, which have fewer neighbours. In the following implementation, we use the grid itself to mark the visited cells with the letter X. To simplify readability, the recursive traversal is presented.

```
def dfs_grid(grid, i, j, mark='X', free='.'):
    height = len(grid)
    width = len(grid[0])
    to_visit = [(i, j)]
    grid[i][j] = mark
    while to_visit:
        i1, j1 = to_visit.pop()
        for i2, j2 in [(i1 + 1, j1), (i1, j1 + 1),
                       (i1 - 1, j1), (i1, j1 - 1)]:
            if (0 <= i2 < height and 0 <= j2 < width and
                    grid[i2][j2] == free):
                grid[i2][j2] = mark   # mark path
                to_visit.append((i2, j2))
```

Problems
ABC Path [spoj:ABCPATH]
A Bug's Life [spoj:BUGLIFE]

6.4   Breadth-First Search—BFS

Definition
Rather than exploring as far as possible starting from the current node (*depth-first search*), we can enumerate the nodes of a graph by their increasing distance from an initial node (*breadth-first search*, abbreviated *BFS*).

Key Observation
We must process the nodes by increasing distance from an initial node, hence we need a data structure to efficiently maintain this order. A queue is a good choice: if for every vertex extracted from the head of the queue we add its neighbours to the end of the queue, it is easy to see that at a given moment, it only contains nodes at a distance d at the head and $d + 1$ at the tail, since as long as vertices at distance d remain at the head, there can only be vertices at distance $d + 1$ added to the queue.

Algorithm in Linear Time $O(|V| + |E|)$
Breadth-first traversal has the same structure as the iterative depth-first traversal, except that we use a queue instead of a stack. Another difference is that the vertices are marked at the moment when they are added to the queue and not when they are removed, otherwise the time would be quadratic.

Implementation Details
The principal interest of breadth-first traversal is to determine the distances away from a given starting node in a non-weighted graph. Our implementation computes these distances as well as the predecessors in the shortest path tree. The array of distances is also used to mark the vertices visited.

```
from collections import deque


def bfs(graph, start=0):
    to_visit = deque()
    dist = [float('inf')] * len(graph)
    prec = [None] * len(graph)
    dist[start] = 0
    to_visit.appendleft(start)
    while to_visit:                    # an empty queue is considered False
        node = to_visit.pop()
        for neighbor in graph[node]:
            if dist[neighbor] == float('inf'):
                dist[neighbor] = dist[node] + 1
                prec[neighbor] = node
                to_visit.appendleft(neighbor)
    return dist, prec
```

Problem
Hike on a Graph [spoj:HIKE] Prime Path [spoj:PPATH]

Example: Prime Path
Consider the set S of prime numbers that can be written with exactly four digits, where
the leading digit is different from zero. Two numbers in S are said to be neighbours
if they differ by exactly one digit. Given two numbers x, y in S, we wish to find the
shortest sequence $z_0, z_1, \dots, z_k$ in S with $z_0 = x$, $z_k = y$ and for every $1 \leq i \leq k$, z_{i-1}
and z_i are neighbours. For this problem, it suffices to generate the set S with the Sieve
of Eratosthenes (see Section 14.5 on page 217), and to construct for each number in
S the set of its neighbours, by testing the presence in S of its at most 4×9 potential
neighbours. Then, a breadth-first traversal of the graph reveals a shortest path between
two given numbers.

6.5   Connected Components

Definition
A subset $A \subset V$ of a graph is called a *connected component* if for every pair of
vertices u, v in A, there exists a path from u to v. We could, for example, wish to know
the number of connected components of a graph. A graph is said to be *connected* if it
has exactly one connected component.

Algorithm by Depth-First Search
A depth-first traversal starting at a vertex u explores all vertices reachable from u, and
only these, thus exactly the connected component containing u. We use the index of
the current component as the visit marker.

```
def dfs_grid(grid, i, j, mark, free):
    grid[i][j] = mark
    height = len(grid)
    width = len(grid[0])
    for ni, nj in [(i + 1, j), (i, j + 1),      # 4-neighborhood
                   (i - 1, j), (i, j - 1)]:
        if 0 <= ni < height and 0 <= nj < width:
            if grid[ni][nj] == free:
                dfs_grid(grid, ni, nj, mark, free)
```

Application
Consider a photo taken from above of a die on a table. We would like to easily
determine the number of pips on the exposed face. For this, we posterise[1] the image
with a greyscale threshold to obtain an image in black and white, so that each pip
corresponds to a connected component in the image, see Figure 6.3.

Figure 6.4 shows the logo of the British electronic music group Clean Bandit in
ASCII art. It can be seen as a graph on a grid whose vertices are the sharps and two

---

[1] I.e. we reduce the number of colours.

 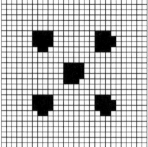

Figure 6.3 A photo of a die and its posterised image.

vertices are linked by an edge if and only if they touch, horizontally or vertically. This graph is made up of four connected components.

```
.....................................          ..................................
.................#.......####......            ..................1.......22222......
...............###.....######......            .................111.......2222222.....
..............####....########.....            ...............11111....222222222.....
.............######....######......            .............1111111....2222222......
............########....####.......            ...........111111111...22222.......
...........#########............               ...........11111111111..........
..........############..........               ..........11111111111..........
.........##############.........               .........111111111111111.........
..........############..........               .........11111111111111.........
...........#########............               ..........11111111111..........
......#.....#########..........                .........3....11111111...........
.....###...######...########.....              ........333.....1111111...444444444.....
...####.....####...########.....               .......33333.....11111....444444444.....
...######.....###....########.....             .......3333333.....111....444444444.....
..########....#.....########.....              .....333333333.....1......444444444.....
.##########..........########.....             ....33333333333..........444444444.....
.....................................          ..................................
```

Figure 6.4 The state of the grid before and after the execution of the algorithm on the graph of Clean Bandit.

We execute as many depth-first searches as there are connected components. We sweep the grid from top to bottom and from left to right. As soon as a cell containing a sharp is found, we know that we are dealing with a new connected component and a depth-first search is launched from this cell to determine it completely.

```
def nb_connected_components_grid(grid, free='#'):
    nb_components = 0
    height = len(grid)
    width = len(grid[0])
    for i in range(height):
        for j in range(width):
            if grid[i][j] == free:
                nb_components += 1
                dfs_grid(grid, i, j, str(nb_components), free)
    return nb_components
```

Each cell containing a sharp is visited only once, so the algorithm is $O(|V|)$, i.e. it is linear in the number of vertices.

Algorithm with the Structure Union-Find

As the graph is undirected, the relation 'there exists a path between u and v' is an equivalence relation. Thus, the connected components are exactly the equivalence classes for this relation, and union-find is a suitable structure to represent our problem, see Section 1.5.5 on page 26.

Complexity

The complexity of this method is slightly worse than that of our first approach; nevertheless, it becomes necessary when we have a graph whose number of edges evolves in time and we wish to know at each moment the number of connected components.

```python
def nb_connected_components(graph):
    n = len(graph)
    uf = UnionFind(n)
    nb_components = n
    for node in range(n):
        for neighbor in graph[node]:
            if uf.union(node, neighbor):
                nb_components -= 1
    return nb_components
```

Application to the Disconnection of a Graph

Given a graph whose edges disappear progressively with time, i.e. there is a sequence $e_1, \ldots, e_{|E|}$ of edges such that e_i disappears at time i, we wish to determine the first instant at which the graph becomes disconnected.

We begin with the graph without edges at time $t = |E|$ (which thus contains $|V|$ connected components). Working backwards from $e_{|E|}$, at each step we add an edge from the sequence and check to see if the number of components has evolved. As soon as the number of components reaches 1, we know the graph is connected, by definition, and $t + 1$ is the value we seek.

Problems

The Ant [spoj:ANTTT]

Lego [spoj:LEGO]

6.6   Biconnected Components

Input

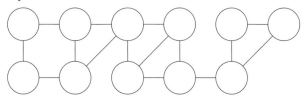

Output

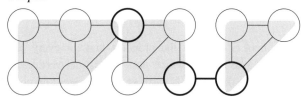

Application

Given a graph with costs of sabotage for each vertex and each edge, we wish to determine a unique vertex or a unique edge of minimal cost which disconnects the graph. Note the difference with the problem of finding a minimal *set* of edges which disconnect the graph, the *minimum cut* problem, described in Section 9.8 on page 162.

Definition

Let G be an undirected connected graph.

- A *cut vertex*—also called an *articulation point*—is a vertex whose suppression disconnects the graph.
- A *cut edge*—also called a *bridge*—is an edge whose deletion disconnects the graph, see Figure 6.5.
- A *biconnected component* is a maximal set of edges, such that within the induced graph (restrained to this set of edges and the incident vertices) neither cut vertices nor cut edges exists.
- The edges that are not bridges can be partitioned into biconnected components.

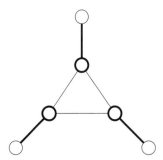

Figure 6.5 An edge between two cut vertices (vertices shown in bold) is not always a cut edge and the endpoints of a cut edge (edges shown in bold) are not always cut vertices.

A biconnected component S also has the property that for every pair of vertices $s, t \in S$ two paths from s to t exist, which pass by distinct vertices. Note that the biconnected components are defined by a partition of the edges and not by a partition of the vertices. Indeed, a vertex can belong to several biconnected components, see vertex 5 in Figure 6.8.

Given an undirected graph, the goal is to decompose it into biconnected components.

Complexity
Linear by a depth-first traversal (see Hopcroft and Tarjan, 1973).

Details of the Depth-First Search
In a previous section, we described a depth-first traversal (DFS) of a graph. We will now add supplementary information to the vertices and the edges. First of all, the vertices are numbered in the order of their processing. The array dfs_num contains this information.

A non-directed graph can be represented as a directed graph by the generation of two arcs for each edge. The DFS traversal explores the arcs of the graph, classified as follows (see Figures 6.6 and 6.7). An arc (u, v) is:

- a *tree arc* if v is seen for the first time during the processing of u. These arcs form a spanning tree constructed by the traversal, also known as the DFS tree;
- an *inverse tree arc* if (v, u) is a tree arc;
- a *back arc* if v has already been seen and is an ancestor of u in the DFS tree;
- a *forward arc* if v has already been seen and is a descendant of u in the DFS tree.

For a depth-first traversal of a directed graph, an additional type of arc exists, a *cross arc*, which goes to a vertex already seen, but is neither ancestor nor descendant. As in this section we only consider non-directed graphs, we can ignore this type of arc.

Determination of the Type of an Arc

The type of an arc is easy to determine by comparing the values dfs_num of its endpoints. More precisely, in addition to dfs_num[v] for each vertex v, we compute a value dfs_low[v], crucial for the algorithm. It is defined as the minimum of dfs_num[u] over all the back arcs (w, u) where w is a descendant of v. The minimum is thus taken over the vertices u that can be reached from v by a sequence of tree arcs (that can be empty) followed by a back arc. If there is no such vertex, we set dfs_low[u] $= \infty$.

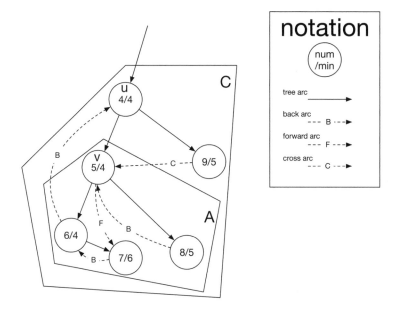

Figure 6.6 The classification of the arcs during a DFS traversal.

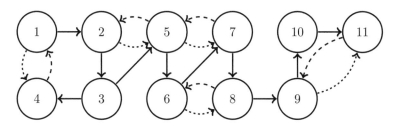

Figure 6.7 The vertices are labelled by the number in their order of processing, stored in dfs_num. The line style is solid for tree arcs, in dashes for back arcs and in dots for forward arcs. For every tree arc (u, v) an inverse tree arc exists (v, u), not shown for readability.

Key Observation

The values of dfs_low allow us to determine the cut vertices and edges.

1. A vertex u at the root of the DFS tree is a cut vertex if and only if it has at least two children in the tree.
    Note that each child v satisfies dfs_low[v] $\geq$ dfs_num[u].
2. A vertex u which is not the root is a cut vertex if and only if it has at least one child v with dfs_low[v] $\geq$ dfs_num[u].
3. An edge (u, v)—up to a swap of u and v—is a cut edge if and only if (u, v) is a tree arc and dfs_low[u] $\geq$ dfs_num[v].

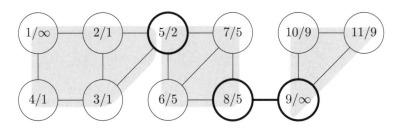

Figure 6.8 The vertices are labelled with dfs_num followed by dfs_low. The cut vertices and edge are highlighted in bold.

To determine the biconnected components, it thus suffices to apply the above definitions in order to detect when a new biconnected component starts.

Implementation Details

The array parent contains the predecessor in the DFS tree of each vertex and also allows the identification of the roots of the DFS trees. For each vertex u, we count in critical_children[u] the number of children v in the tree such that dfs_low[v] $\geq$ dfs_num[u]. This information allows us at the end of the traversal to determine the cut vertices and edges. The value dfs_low[v] is updated for every back arc detected emanating from v. At the end of the process, this value is propagated up to the parent vertex in the DFS tree.

```
# to ease readiness, variables do not have dfs_ prefix
def cut_nodes_edges(graph):
    n = len(graph)
    time = 0
    num = [None] * n
    low = [n] * n
    parent = [None] * n          # parent[v] = None if root else parent of v
    critical_children = [0] * n  # cc[u] = #{children v | low[v] >= num[u]}
    times_seen = [-1] * n
    for start in range(n):
        if times_seen[start] == -1:                    # init DFS path
            times_seen[start] = 0
            to_visit = [start]
            while to_visit:
                node = to_visit[-1]
                if times_seen[node] == 0:         # start processing
                    num[node] = time
                    time += 1
                    low[node] = float('inf')
                children = graph[node]
                if times_seen[node] == len(children):  # end processing
                    to_visit.pop()
                    up = parent[node]                  # propagate low to parent
                    if up is not None:
                        low[up] = min(low[up], low[node])
                        if low[node] >= num[up]:
                            critical_children[up] += 1
                else:
                    child = children[times_seen[node]]    # next arrow
                    times_seen[node] += 1
                    if times_seen[child] == -1:    # not visited yet
                        parent[child] = node       # link arrow
                        times_seen[child] = 0
                        to_visit.append(child)     # (below) back arrow
                    elif num[child] < num[node] and parent[node] != child:
                        low[node] = min(low[node], num[child])
    cut_edges = []
    cut_nodes = []                                  # extract solution
    for node in range(n):
        if parent[node] is None:                    # characteristics
            if critical_children[node] >= 2:
                cut_nodes.append(node)
        else:                                       # internal nodes
            if critical_children[node] >= 1:
                cut_nodes.append(node)
            if low[node] >= num[node]:
                cut_edges.append((parent[node], node))
    return cut_nodes, cut_edges
```

Problem
Police Query [spoj:POLQUERY]

6.7   Topological Sort

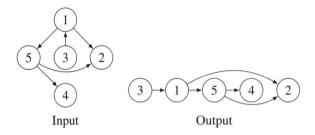

Input   Output

Definition
Given a directed graph $G(V, A)$, we want to order the vertices according to a rank function r in such a way that for every arc (u, v), we have $r(u) < r(v)$.

Application
The graph could represent a set of tasks where the arcs encode the dependencies $u \rightarrow v \Leftrightarrow$ 'u must be executed before v'. We are interested in an execution order compatible with the dependencies.

First of all, a few remarks:

- Several topological sorts for a given graph can exist. For example, if the sequence s is a topological sort of G_1 and the sequence t a topological sort of G_2, then, for example, the sequences st and ts are topological sorts of the graph formed by the union of G_1 and G_2.
- A graph containing a cycle never admits a topological sort: each vertex of a cycle would require the prior processing of all the others before it (including itself!).
- A graph without cycles admits a topological sort. See below.

Complexity
The execution time is linear in the size of the input.

Algorithm with a DFS Traversal
If we process each node only after all its neighbouring descendants, then we obtain an inverse topological order. Indeed, if $u \rightarrow v$ is a dependency, then:

- either v was seen before u, in which case v was already handled (if not, this would mean that u is accessible from v, hence the graph contains a cycle) and the inverse topological order is respected;
- or v is reached from u, in which case u will be handled after v, hence the inverse topological order is again respected.

The DFS traversal described previously must be adapted, as it does not allow determination of when the processing of a vertex is complete.

The following implementation uses an array seen, which is set to -1 for all vertices that have not yet been seen, and then to the number of direct descendants that have already been seen. When this counter is equal to the number of children of the node, then the processing of the node is finished, and the node is added to the sequence order. This sequence contains an inverse topological order, which must be reversed at the end of the algorithm.

```python
def topological_order_dfs(graph):
    n = len(graph)
    order = []
    times_seen = [-1] * n
    for start in range(n):
        if times_seen[start] == -1:
            times_seen[start] = 0
            to_visit = [start]
            while to_visit:
                node = to_visit[-1]
                children = graph[node]
                if times_seen[node] == len(children):
                    to_visit.pop()
                    order.append(node)
                else:
                    child = children[times_seen[node]]
                    times_seen[node] += 1
                    if times_seen[child] == -1:
                        times_seen[child] = 0
                        to_visit.append(child)
    return order[::-1]
```

Greedy Algorithm

An alternative solution is based on the input degree of the vertices. Consider an acyclic graph. Intuitively, we can begin by adding to the solution sequence the nodes without predecessors in an arbitrary order, trimming them from the graph, then adding to the sequence the new nodes without predecessors in an arbitrary order, and so on. This process terminates because an acyclic graph always contains a vertex without predecessors, and the deletion of nodes preserves the absence of cycles.

```python
def topological_order(graph):
    V = range(len(graph))
    indeg = [0 for _ in V]
    for node in V:                  # compute indegree
        for neighbor in graph[node]:
            indeg[neighbor] += 1
    Q = [node for node in V if indeg[node] == 0]
    order = []
    while Q:
        node = Q.pop()              # node without incoming arrows
        order.append(node)
        for neighbor in graph[node]:
            indeg[neighbor] -= 1
            if indeg[neighbor] == 0:
                Q.append(neighbor)
    return order
```

Applications

Given an acyclic graph and two vertices s, t, we might like to count the number of paths from s to t, or discover the longest path when there are weights on the arcs. A solution in linear time consists of performing a topological sort and executing a dynamic program on the nodes in that order.

For example, the dynamic program $P[s] = 0, P[v] = 1 + \max_u P[u]$ computes the longest path from s to t where the maximisation is made over all the arcs (u, v) terminating on v.

Problems

Topological Sorting [spoj:TOPOSORT]

Project File Dependencies [spoj:PFDEP]

Example: All Disks Considered [spoj:ALL]

The packages of a GNU/Linux distribution are stored on two DVDs. There is a dependency order between packages: each given package can be installed only after the installation of a certain set of prerequisite packages. We want to find an order for the installation of the packages that respects the dependencies while minimising the number of reloads of DVDs in the single DVD reader of the machine being installed.

Formally, we are given a directed graph without cycles whose vertices are coloured white or black (white corresponds to packages on one of the DVDs, and black to those on the other). This graph defines a partial order. The graph does not necessarily contain transitive arcs: we can have (u, v) and (v, w) without (u, w). The goal is to produce a total order minimizing the number of colour changes along this ordering. This can be done in linear time. Essentially, we proceed as for a topological sort, but seeking at each step to avoid colour changes. We can show with an exchange argument that the solution thus produced is optimal.

A package p is said to be *accessible* if all the packages on which p depends are already installed. The algorithm maintains two sets, the first containing all the white accessible packages and the second containing all the black accessible packages. To quickly determine when a package becomes accessible, the algorithm keeps a counter for each package p. This counter keeps track of the number of packages not yet installed on which p depends. Initially, the sets contain all the packages with no dependencies, whose counters are thus 0. Then, the algorithm selects an initial colour c. Two executions are thus necessary to determine the best choice. The solution will be in the form of a sequence of vertices.

The algorithm starts with an empty sequence. As long as at least one of the sets is non-empty, the algorithm performs the following steps. If the current colour set c is empty, the algorithm switches c over to the other colour. It then extracts a package p from the colour c set and appends it to the solution. Then, it decrements the counters of all the packages q depending on p. The packages q which become accessible (whose counters become 0) are added to the set of their colour. The algorithm is in linear time, as the work carried out on each arc is in constant time.

6.8　Strongly Connected Components

Definition
A subset $A \subset V$ of a directed graph is called a *strongly connected component* if for every pair (u, v) of vertices of A a path in A exists that links u to v. Note that in this case, a path in A exists that links v to u, see Figure 6.9.

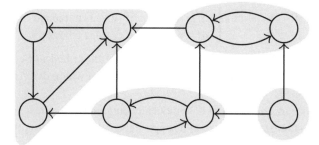

Figure 6.9　An example of the partition of a graph into strongly connected components.

Observation
The component (or reduced) graph is defined as the result of the contraction of the strongly connected components into 'super vertices'. This graph is acyclic, as each cycle of a directed graph is included in exactly one strongly connected component.

Complexity
The following algorithms execute in linear time in the size of the graph ($|V| + |E|$).

Tarjan's Algorithm
Tarjan's algorithm (1972) consists of a single depth-first search, numbering the vertices in the order of the beginning of their processing. It also places the vertices encountered into a stack waiting of nodes waiting to be grouped in a strongly connected component. Once a component is detected, it is trimmed from the graph and removed from the stack waiting. This means that all the arcs entering into an already discovered component are ignored.

A depth-first search enters into a component C by a first vertex v_0, and then explores all the vertices and eventually also the components reachable from C. Vertex v_0 is processed after all its descendants in the DFS tree. By construction, at the moment of the final processing of v_0, clearly the stack waiting contains above v_0 all the vertices of C. The vertex v_0 is known as the *representative* of C. The vertices are numbered by their order of processing, hence the representative of C has the smallest such number. All the difficulty lies in determining the representative of a component.

For this, the algorithm computes two values for each vertex v, the order number `dfs_num[v]`, attributed at the beginning of the processing of the vertex, and `dfs_min[v]`. The latter value is defined as the minimum of `dfs_num[u]` over all the vertices u that are not already in a strongly connected component—and hence still waiting—and reachable from v by a sequence of tree arcs, eventually followed by a single back arc. This value is defined as follows, where the minimum is taken over all outgoing arcs (v, u):

$$\text{dfs\_min[v]} := \min_u \begin{cases} \text{dfs\_num[v]} \\ \text{dfs\_min[u]} & \text{if } (v, u) \text{ is a tree arc} \\ \text{dfs\_num[u]} & \text{if } (v, u) \text{ is a back arc} \end{cases}$$

Note that this value differs from the value `dfs_low[v]` described in Section 6.6 on page 97, where there was no notion of *waiting vertices* and where `dfs_low[v]` could take on the value ∞.

Consider the case of a component C without any outgoing arcs, and a vertex $v \in C$. Let A be the DFS subtree with root v, and suppose that a back arc exists that leaves A towards a vertex u, predecessor of v. As C does not have any outgoing arcs, u must belong to C and v is not the representative of C. In this case, we have `dfs_min[v]` < `dfs_num[v]`. If a back arc leaving A does not exist, then it contains a strongly connected component, and since it is included in C, this tree covers C, and v is its representative. This situation is detected by `dfs_min[v]` == `dfs_num[v]`.

Implementation Details

In parallel with the stack `waiting`, the algorithm maintains a Boolean array `waits`, which allows the presence in the stack to be tested in constant time. This way, it is easy to trim a component by setting the corresponding elements to `False`.

The algorithm returns a list of lists, each containing the vertices of one of the components. Note that the components are determined in reverse topological order. This will be useful when we come to the resolution of a 2-SAT formula later on.

```
def tarjan_recursif(graph):
    global sccp, waiting, dfs_time, dfs_num
    sccp = []
    waiting = []
    waits = [False] * len(graph)
    dfs_time = 0
    dfs_num = [None] * len(graph)


    def dfs(node):
        global sccp, waiting, dfs_time, dfs_num
        waiting.append(node)            # new node is waiting
        waits[node] = True
        dfs_num[node] = dfs_time        # mark visit
        dfs_time += 1
        dfs_min = dfs_num[node]         # compute dfs_min
        for neighbor in graph[node]:
            if dfs_num[neighbor] is None:
                dfs_min = min(dfs_min, dfs(neighbor))
            elif waits[neighbor] and dfs_min > dfs_num[neighbor]:
                dfs_min = dfs_num[neighbor]
        if dfs_min == dfs_num[node]:    # representative of a component
            sccp.append([])            # make a component
            while True:                # add waiting nodes
                u = waiting.pop()
                waits[u] = False
                sccp[-1].append(u)
                if u == node:          # until representative
                    break
        return dfs_min


    for node in range(len(graph)):
        if dfs_num[node] is None:
            dfs(node)
    return sccp
```

Iterative Version

The iterative version of the algorithm is required for very large graphs, larger than, say, 100,000 vertices. Here, a counter `times_seen` allows us at the same time to mark the vertices encountered and to memorise the number of neighbours already considered.

```python
def tarjan(graph):
    n = len(graph)
    dfs_num = [None] * n
    dfs_min = [n] * n
    waiting = []
    waits = [False] * n   # invariant: waits[v] iff v in waiting
    sccp = []             # list of detected components
    dfs_time = 0
    times_seen = [-1] * n
    for start in range(n):
        if times_seen[start] == -1:              # initiate path
            times_seen[start] = 0
            to_visit = [start]
            while to_visit:
                node = to_visit[-1]              # top of stack
                if times_seen[node] == 0:        # start process
                    dfs_num[node] = dfs_time
                    dfs_min[node] = dfs_time
                    dfs_time += 1
                    waiting.append(node)
                    waits[node] = True
                children = graph[node]
                if times_seen[node] == len(children):  # end of process
                    to_visit.pop()                      # remove from stack
                    dfs_min[node] = dfs_num[node]       # compute dfs_min
                    for child in children:
                        if waits[child] and dfs_min[child] < dfs_min[node]:
                            dfs_min[node] = dfs_min[child]
                    if dfs_min[node] == dfs_num[node]:  # representative
                        component = []                   # make component
                        while True:                      # add nodes
                            u = waiting.pop()
                            waits[u] = False
                            component.append(u)
                            if u == node:                # until repr.
                                break
                        sccp.append(component)
                else:
                    child = children[times_seen[node]]
                    times_seen[node] += 1
                    if times_seen[child] == -1:          # not visited yet
                        times_seen[child] = 0
                        to_visit.append(child)
    return sccp
```

Kosaraju's Algorithm

A different algorithm was proposed by Kosaraju (1979). Its complexity is also linear, and in practice quite comparable to Tarjan's algorithm; however, it is perhaps easier to understand.

The principle consists in performing a first depth-first search, and then a second on the graph with the orientation of the arcs reversed. Formally, denote $A^T :=$ $\{(v,u)|(u,v) \in A\}$ the result of the reversal of the arcs. The algorithm is then composed of the following steps:

1. Perform a depth-first search of $G(V, A)$ and store as $f[v]$ the time of the completion of processing of the vertex v.
2. Perform a depth-first search of $G(V, A^T)$, selecting roots v in order of decreasing $f[v]$.

Each tree encountered in the second traversal is a strongly connected component.

The validity of the algorithm is based on the idea that if we associate with each strongly connected component C the integer $F(C) := \max_{u \in C} f_u$, then F gives a topological order on the graph induced by the strongly connected components in $G(V, A^T)$. Hence, each tree generated by the second traversal remains in the interior of a component, since the only outgoing arcs lead to components already traversed.

Implementation Details

The list sccp (for strongly connected component) contains the list of strongly connected components.

```
def kosaraju_dfs(graph, nodes, order, sccp):
    times_seen = [-1] * len(graph)
    for start in nodes:
        if times_seen[start] == -1:                    # initiate DFS
            to_visit = [start]
            times_seen[start] = 0
            sccp.append([start])
            while to_visit:
                node = to_visit[-1]
                children = graph[node]
                if times_seen[node] == len(children):   # end of process
                    to_visit.pop()
                    order.append(node)
                else:
                    child = children[times_seen[node]]
                    times_seen[node] += 1
                    if times_seen[child] == -1:          # new node
                        times_seen[child] = 0
                        to_visit.append(child)
                        sccp[-1].append(child)


def reverse(graph):
    rev_graph = [[] for node in graph]
    for node, _ in enumerate(graph):
        for neighbor in graph[node]:
            rev_graph[neighbor].append(node)
    return rev_graph


def kosaraju(graph):
    n = len(graph)
    order = []
    sccp = []
    kosaraju_dfs(graph, range(n), order, [])
    kosaraju_dfs(reverse(graph), order[::-1], [], sccp)
    return sccp[::-1]  # follow inverse topological order
```

Problem
Capital City [spoj:CAPCITY]

6.9   2-Satisfiability

Many decision problems can be modelled as a problem of satisfiability of a Boolean formula. The satisfiability problem is the following.

Definition
We are given n Boolean variables. A *literal* is a variable or the negation of a variable. A *clause* is a *disjunction (OR)* of several literals, so that a clause is satisfied (i.e., made true) if at least one of its literals is true. A *formula* is a *conjunction (AND)* of several clauses, so that a formula is satisfied if *all* its clauses are satisfied. The goal is to see whether there exists an assignment to the variables that satisfies the formula.

A formula is said to be of class *2-SAT* if each clause contains at most two literals. One of the fundamental results in complexity theory is that we can verify in linear time if a 2-SAT formula is satisfiable, whereas in general (for a 3-SAT formula, for example), in the worst case, a polynomial time algorithm is not known (it is *NP-hard*).

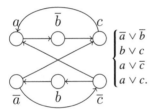

$$\begin{cases} \bar{a} \vee \bar{b} \\ b \vee c \\ a \vee \bar{c} \\ a \vee c. \end{cases}$$

Figure 6.10 Graph obtained from an instance of 2-SAT. There are two strongly connected components. The bottom one points to the top one, hence assigning 'False' to all the literals on the bottom and 'True' to all on top will satisfy this formula.

Complexity
The complexity is linear, i.e. time $O(n + m)$ for n and m the number of variables and clauses (see Aspvall et al., 1979).

Modelisation by a Directed Graph
The disjunction of two literals $x \vee y$ is equivalent to the implication $\bar{x} \Rightarrow y$ or $\bar{y} \Rightarrow x$. We associate with a 2-SAT formula an implication graph, where the vertices correspond to the literals, and the arcs correspond to the implications, equivalent to the clauses, see Figure 6.10. This graph presents a high degree of symmetry.

Key Observation

We can easily show that a 2-SAT formula is not satisfiable if for some x there is a path from x to $\overline{x}$ and a path from $\overline{x}$ to x in the implication graph. What is surprising is that the converse is also true!

As the implications are transitive, clearly if $x \Rightarrow \overline{x} \Rightarrow x$ is implied by the formula, then it cannot be satisfied, since each of the assignments $x = $ False or $x = $ True leads to a contradiction False $\Rightarrow$ True. Conversely, suppose that each variable is in a different strongly connected component from its negation.

As the directed graph is symmetric, we can consider pairs of strongly connected components, where each contains all the negations of literals of the other. Moreover, all the literals of a strongly connected component must have the same Boolean value. From this graph, it is thus possible to determine an assignment satisfying the formula: it suffices to assign True to all the literals of a component without any outgoing arcs. There is forcibly one, as the component graph is acyclic. Then we assign False to the opposing component, trim the two components from the graph and recurse.

To perform this efficiently, note that the algorithm presented previously to determine the strongly connected components finds them in reverse topological order. It thus suffices to traverse the components in this order, assign True to each component that does not yet have a value and assign False to the opposite component.

Implementation Details

We encode the literals by integers, such that $+1, \ldots, +n$ encode the n variables and $-1, \ldots, -n$ encode their negations. A clause is encoded by a pair of integers and a formula as a list of clauses. Each literal corresponds to one of the $2n$ nodes of the associated directed graph. These nodes are numbered from 0 to $2n - 1$, where $2i$ encodes the variable x_{i+1} and $2i + 1$ encodes $\overline{x_{i+1}}$. Here is the corresponding code.

```
def _vertex(lit):  # integer encoding of a litteral
    if lit > 0:
        return 2 * (lit - 1)
    return 2 * (-lit - 1) + 1


def two_sat(formula):
    # num_variables is the number of variables
    num_variables = max(abs(clause[p])
                        for p in (0, 1) for clause in formula)
    graph = [[] for node in range(2 * num_variables)]
    for x_idx, y_idx in formula:
        graph[_vertex(-x_idx)].append(_vertex(y_idx))     # x_idx or y_idx
        graph[_vertex(-y_idx)].append(_vertex(x_idx))     # -x_idx => y_idx
    sccp = tarjan(graph)                                  # -y_idx => x_idx
    comp_id = [None] * (2 * num_variables)  # each node's component ID
    assignment = [None] * (2 * num_variables)
    for component in sccp:
        rep = min(component)                  # representative of the component
        for vtx in component:
            comp_id[vtx] = rep
            if assignment[vtx] is None:
                assignment[vtx] = True
                assignment[vtx ^ 1] = False    # complementary literal
    for i in range(num_variables):
        if comp_id[2 * i] == comp_id[2 * i + 1]:
            return None                        # insatisfiable formula
    return assignment[::2]
```

Problems

Manhattan [kattis:manhattan]

Soldiers on Parade [spoj:SOPARADE]

7 Cycles in Graphs

Several classic problems concern cycles in graphs, whether they refer to geographical displacements or to anomalies in a dependency graph. The simplest problems consist of detecting the existence of cycles, the existence of cycles with negative weight or the identification of a minimal total weight or minimal mean weight cycle.

Other problems are concerned with exploring the whole of a graph to find paths traversing each edge exactly once (Eulerian path) or, when this is not possible, at least once (Chinese postman problem). These problems are polynomial, whereas determining a cycle that visits each vertex exactly once (Hamiltonian cycle) is NP-hard.

Search Algorithms for Cycles		
detection of a cycle	$O(|V| + |E|)$	depth-first search
cycle of minimal total weight	$O(|V| \cdot |E|)$	Bellman-Ford
cycle of minimal mean weight	$O(|V| \cdot |E|)$	Karp
cycle of minimal cost-to-time ratio	$O(|V| \cdot |E| \cdot \log \sum t)$	binary search
Eulerian path	$O(|V| + |E|)$	greedy
Chinese postman cycle	$O(\sqrt{|V|} \cdot |E|)$	minimal weigh perfect pairing
travelling salesman	$O(|V|2^{|V|})$	dynamic programming

7.1 Eulerian Tour

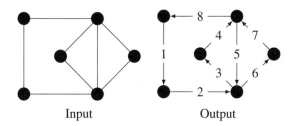

Input   Output

Application

You are in Kaliningrad—formerly Königsberg—and want to know if it is possible to take a walk that crosses each bridge exactly once and finishes back at the starting point. It is this situation that led Leonhard Euler to study the problem in 1759.

Definition

Given a connected graph $G(V,E)$ such that each vertex has even degree, we wish to find a cycle in this graph that traverses each edge exactly once. The same problem can be posed for directed and strongly connected graphs such that the out-degree of each vertex is equal to its in-degree.

Algorithm in Linear Time

A graph possesses an Eulerian cycle if and only if it is connected and every vertex is of even degree. This was shown by Euler in 1736. Similarly, a directed graph has an Eulerian cycle if and only if it is strongly connected and each vertex has the same in-degree and out-degree.

How do we find such a cycle? In 1873, Hierholzer and Wiener proposed the following algorithm. Take an arbitrary vertex v and start walking from v while marking the edges traversed as *forbidden*. The choice of edges taken can be arbitrary. This walk forcibly returns to the vertex v. This follows from the fact that the endpoints of the excursion are the only vertices incident to an odd number of allowed edges. The result is a cycle C that possibly only covers a portion of the graph. In this case, as the graph is connected, a vertex $v' \in C$ exists that still has allowed edges. We then start a new walk from v' and insert into C the cycle thus obtained. The procedure is repeated until we obtain a single Eulerian cycle.

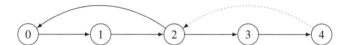

Figure 7.1 Hierholzer's algorithm running on an example. The first cycle detected is $0 \to 1 \to 2 \to 0$. Then along this cycle the vertices are explored to discover further attached cycles. The vertices 0 and 1 have been processed and are pushed onto the stack $P = [0,1]$. It remains to process the remaining vertices of this cycle, namely $Q = [0,2]$. The algorithm then explores a cycle starting from vertex 2 (*start*), which was popped from the stack Q, now reduced to [0]. The exploration discovers the path $2 \to 3 \to 4$ whose vertices are pushed onto the stack $R = [3,4]$. The extreme point of the path is *node* = 4. The final path is $0 \to 1 \to 2 \to 3 \to 4 \to 2 \to 0$.

For the algorithm to be in linear time, the search for the vertex v' must be efficient. For this, we decompose the cycle C into two portions P and Q. The vertices in P are those that have no more allowable edges; they will be part of the final tour. As long as Q is non-empty, we remove the vertex v from the head of Q and add it to the end of P, hence advancing the cycle. Next, we attempt to insert here a cycle passing through v. For this, if there is an allowable edge incident to v, we find by simple exploration a cycle R starting from v and returning to v. The cycle R is then added to the head of Q. The algorithm is in linear time, as each vertex is considered only once.

Implementation Details

We first describe the implementation for directed graphs. To ease the manipulation of the data, P, Q and R are represented by stacks, encoded by lists. The current cycle consists of the stack P, the vertex start, followed by the mirror list Q. The list R describes a path, which once completed as a cycle will be attached to the current cycle at the vertex start. To rapidly find an allowable outgoing arc of a vertex, we store in next[node] the number of outgoing arcs of a vertex node that have already been explored. It suffices to increment this counter when we traverse the arc towards the ith neighbour of node, where i=next[node].

```python
def eulerian_tour_directed(graph):
    P = []                              # resulting tour
    Q = [0]                             # vertices to be explored, start at 0
    R = []                              # path from start node
    next_ = [0] * len(graph)            # initialize next_ to 0 for each node
    while Q:
        start = Q.pop()                 # explore a cycle from start node
        node = start                    # current node on cycle
        while next_[node] < len(graph[node]):   # visit all allowable arcs
            neighbor = graph[node][next_[node]]  # traverse an arc
            next_[node] += 1            # mark arc traversed
            R.append(neighbor)          # append to path from start
            node = neighbor             # move on
        while R:
            Q.append(R.pop())           # add to Q the discovered cycle R
        P.append(start)                 # resulting path P is extended
    return P
```

The variant of this algorithm for non-directed graphs is a bit more subtle. Once an arc (u, v) is traversed, we must mark the arc (v, u) as forbidden. We have chosen to store in seen[v] the set of neighbours u of v such that (v, u) is no longer allowed. For more efficiency, v does not need to be added to seen[u] at the time of traversal of the arc (u, v), since at this same moment the counter next[u] is incremented and this arc will no longer be considered.

```python
def eulerian_tour_undirected(graph):
    P = []                              # resulting tour
    Q = [0]                             # vertices to be explored, start at 0
    R = []                              # path from start node
    next_ = [0] * len(graph)            # initialize next_ to 0 for each node
    seen = [set() for _ in graph]       # mark backward arcs
    while Q:
        start = Q.pop()                 # explore a cycle from start node
        node = start                    # current node on cycle
        while next_[node] < len(graph[node]):   # visit all allowable arcs
            neighbor = graph[node][next_[node]]  # traverse an arc
            next_[node] += 1            # mark arc traversed
            if neighbor not in seen[node]:   # not yet traversed
                seen[neighbor].add(node)     # mark backward arc
                R.append(neighbor)           # append to path from start
                node = neighbor              # move on
        while R:
            Q.append(R.pop())           # add to Q the discovered cycle R
        P.append(start)                 # resulting path P is extended
    return P
```

Variant: Eulerian Path

If a graph is connected and all its vertices are of even degree, except for two vertices u, v of odd degree, then a path exists that passes through each edge exactly once. This path begins at u and ends on v. It can be found with the same algorithm described above; it suffices to begin the path at u. To see why this works, just add a dummy edge (u, v) and look for a Eulerian cycle.

Problem

Goldbach graphs [spoj:GOLDG]

7.2   The Chinese Postman Problem

Application

In 1962, the mathematician Meigu Guan (or Kwan Mei-Ko) worked as a postman during the Chinese Cultural Revolution. He then posed the problem of finding the shortest cycle in a graph that visits each edge at least once. This is exactly the problem that a postman needs to solve to deliver the mail in each neighbourhood of a city.

Definition

Suppose we are given a connected undirected graph $G(V, E)$. The goal is to find a cycle in the graph that visits each edge at least once. When all the vertices are of even degree, this boils down to determining an Eulerian cycle, the problem treated in the preceding section. Note that in the original formulation of this problem, the graph was weighted.

Complexity

The algorithm executes in time $O(n^3)$, where n is the number of nodes of the graph (see Edmonds and Johnson, 1973).

Algorithm

The principle of the algorithm consists of working with a multigraph, i.e. a graph that may have several edges between the same two vertices. The idea is to add edges in order to render the graph Eulerian, and then to produce a Eulerian cycle.

The edges added must help link vertices of odd degree in order to make the graph Eulerian. As we wish to add as few edges as possible, these extra edges will form a collection of paths that will match edges of odd degree.

The central problem thus consists of computing a perfect matching in the complete graph of vertices in V of odd degree, where the weight of an edge (u, v) is equal to the distance between u and v in G.

The computation of all the distances costs $O(n^3)$ by the Floyd–Warshall algorithm. Then a perfect minimum weight matching can be computed in time $O(n^3)$ with Gabow's algorithm (1976). However, this sophisticated algorithm is beyond the scope of the present text.

Problem
Free Tour [spoj:FTOUR]

7.3   Cycles with Minimal Ratio of Weight to Length—Karp

A classic problem consists of detecting negative cycles in a graph. One application, known as *arbitrage*, is given as an exercise in Cormen et al. (2010, Ex. 24-3, p. 615): given n currencies with their exchange rates, we would like to determine a cycle that makes us rich by changing currencies along the cycle. However, in this section we will consider a somewhat different problem that admits an elegant solution.

Definition
Given a weighted directed graph, the goal is to find a cycle C that minimises the mean weight over the edges, i.e. that minimises the following

$$\frac{\sum_{e \in C} w(e)}{|C|}.$$

Application
Imagine a system modelled by a graph whose vertices represent states and whose arcs are the possible transitions between states. Each transition is labelled with its resource consumption. At each step in time, the system is in a particular state and must evolve to another state by following an outgoing arc. The goal is to minimise the long-term resource consumption, and an optimal solution is a minimal mean weight cycle.

Algorithm in $O(|V| \cdot |E|)$ by Karp (1978)
The algorithm supposes the existence of a source vertex s from which every vertex can be reached. If this is not the case, such a vertex can always be added to the graph.

As we are interested in the mean weight of the arcs of a cycle, the length of the cycles is also important. This is why, instead of simply computing the shortest paths, we would like to determine for each vertex v and each length $\ell = 0, \ldots, n$ a shortest path from the source s to v made up of exactly ℓ arcs. This part is implemented using dynamic programming. Assign $d[\ell][v]$ as the weight of the shortest path to v. Initially, $d[0][v]$ is 0 for $v = s$ and $+\infty$ for the other vertices. Then for each $\ell = 1, \ldots, n$,

$$d[\ell][v] = \min_{u} d[\ell - 1][u] + w_{uv}$$

where the minimum is taken over all incoming arcs (u, v) of weight w_{uv}. Let $d[v] = \min_{k \in \mathbb{N}} d[k][v]$ be the distance from the source s to v.

Key Observation
Let C be a cycle of minimal mean weight. Its weight λ satisfies the following

$$\lambda = \min_{v} \max_{k=0,\ldots,n-1} \frac{d[n][v] - d[k][v]}{n - k}. \tag{7.1}$$

To see this, it suffices to make a few observations, beginning with the case $\lambda = 0$. We must show that the right-hand side of (7.1) is zero, or equivalently,

$$\min_v \ \max_{k=0,\ldots,n-1} \ d[n][v] - d[k][v] = 0.$$

Since $\lambda = 0$, the graph does not have a negative weight cycle. For each vertex v, a shortest path exists from the source s to v which is acyclic, and hence

$$d[v] = \min_{k=0,\ldots,n-1} d[k][v].$$

Consequently,

$$\max_{k=0,\ldots,n-1} d[n][v] - d[k][v] = d[n][v] - d[v].$$

For each vertex v, we have $d[n][v] \geq d[v]$ and hence

$$\min_v d[n][v] - d[v] \geq 0.$$

It remains to exhibit a vertex v for which the equality $d[n][v] = d[v]$ holds. Let u be a vertex of C. As there is no negative weight cycle, a simple path P exists that is of minimal weight from the source s to u. We complete P by as many copies of C as required to obtain a path P' from s to u with length at least n. As C has weight zero, P' is again a minimal weight path to u. Let P'' be a prefix of P' of length exactly n and let v be the last vertex of P''. P'' is also a shortest path from the source to v, see Figure 7.2. Hence $d[n][v] = d[v]$ for this vertex, which proves the equality (7.1) for the case $\lambda = 0$.

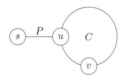

Figure 7.2 Illustration of the proof for the case $\lambda = 0$. P is a minimal weight path from the source to u, and adding copies of the cycle C with zero weight results in a minimal weight path; hence every vertex encountered on the cycle is itself reached by a minimal weight path.

For the case $\lambda \neq 0$, here is an interesting observation. If we subtract a value Δ from the weight of each arc, the value λ is also reduced by Δ. If we assign d' as the distances in the graph thus modified, the following equalities hold:

$$
\begin{aligned}
\frac{d'[n][v] - d'[k][v]}{n - k} &= \frac{d[n][v] - n\Delta - (d'[k][v] - k\Delta)}{n - k} \\
&= \frac{d[n][v]d[k][v]}{n - k} - \frac{n\Delta - k\Delta}{n - k} \\
&= \frac{d[n][v]d[k][v]}{n - k} - \Delta.
\end{aligned}
$$

This shows that the right-hand side of (7.1) is also reduced by Δ. By selecting for Δ the constant λ, we are reduced to the case $\lambda = 0$, which proves the equality (7.1).

Implementation Details

The matrix dist contains the distances as described above. There is also a variable prec which stores the predecessors on the shortest paths. Once these matrices are populated, the second step consists of finding the pair v, k optimising the expression (7.1), and a third step extracts a cycle. In the case where there are no cycles reachable from the source, the function returns None.

```python
def min_mean_cycle(graph, weight, start=0):
    INF = float('inf')
    n = len(graph)                    # compute distances
    dist = [[INF] * n]
    prec = [[None] * n]
    dist[0][start] = 0
    for ell in range(1, n + 1):
        dist.append([INF] * n)
        prec.append([None] * n)
        for node in range(n):
            for neighbor in graph[node]:
                alt = dist[ell - 1][node] + weight[node][neighbor]
                if alt < dist[ell][neighbor]:
                    dist[ell][neighbor] = alt
                    prec[ell][neighbor] = node
    #                                 -- find the optimal value
    valmin = INF
    argmin = None
    for node in range(n):
        valmax = -INF
        argmax = None
        for k in range(n):
            alt = (dist[n][node] - dist[k][node]) / float(n - k)
            # do not divide by float(n-k) => cycle of minimal total weight
            if alt >= valmax:     # with >= we get simple cycles
                valmax = alt
                argmax = k
        if argmax is not None and valmax < valmin:
            valmin = valmax
            argmin = (node, argmax)
    #                                 -- extract cycle
    if valmin == INF:             # -- there is no cycle
        return None
    C = []
    node, k = argmin
    for l in range(n, k, -1):
        C.append(node)
        node = prec[l][node]
    return C[::-1], valmin
```

Problem

Word Rings [spoj:WORDRING]

7.4   Cycles with Minimal Cost-to-Time Ratio

Definition
Let G be a directed graph, with two weights on its arcs—costs c and times t. The times are non-negative, while the costs are arbitrary. The goal is to find a cycle minimising the ratio between the total cost and the total time. This is known as the *tramp steamer problem*.

Application
The captain of a cargo vessel wants to determine a route that maximises his profit. For this, he has available a complete graph covering different ports, where each (u, v) is labelled by the travel time between u and v as well as the profit he can make by purchasing merchandise at the port u and selling it at the port v. The goal is to find a cycle that maximises the ratio of total profit to total time.

Algorithm Using Binary Search
See (Ahuja et al., 1993, sec. 5.7). Let C be a cycle. The objective value of C is at least δ if and only if

$$\frac{\sum_{a \in C} c(a)}{\sum_{a \in C} t(a)} \le \delta, \qquad \sum_{a \in C} c(a) \le \sum_{a \in C} \delta t(a), \qquad \sum_{a \in C} c(a) - \delta t(a) \le 0.$$

To detect a cycle C with a ratio strictly better than δ, it suffices to detect a negative cycle in the graph where the arcs a are weighted by $c(a) - \delta t(a)$. Hence, this test can be used in a binary search on δ to obtain a solution with the required precision. In the case of integer costs and times, a precision of $1 / \sum_a t(a)$ suffices to solve the problem exactly. The complexity is then $O(\log(\sum t(a)) \cdot |V| \cdot |A|)$, where V is the set of vertices and A the set of arcs.

    As initially we do not have an a priori upper bound on the optimum δ^*, we begin the test with $\delta = 1$. As long as the test fails, we multiply δ by 2, to finally obtain a δ' where the test is positive, thus providing upper and lower bounds on the optimum. In the case where the initial test is positive, we proceed in the same way, but instead divide by 2 until the test fails.

7.5   Travelling Salesman

Definition
Given a graph with weights on its arcs, we would like to compute a shortest path beginning at a given source and visiting each vertex exactly once: such a path is said to be *Hamiltonian*.

Complexity

The solution presented, using dynamic programming, executes in time $O(|V|^2 2^{|V|})$.

Algorithm

As the associated decision problem is NP-complete, we propose an acceptable solution for when the number of vertices is small, on the order of twenty or so. Suppose that the vertices are numbered from 0 to $n-1$, where for ease of notation we take $n-1$ as the source.

For each set $S \subseteq \{0, 1, \dots, n-2\}$, assign $O[S][v]$ as the minimal weight of a path from the source to v passing exactly once by all the vertices of S and terminating on v, with $v \notin S$.

For the base case, $O[\emptyset][v]$ is simply the length of the arc from $n-1$ to v. Otherwise, for non-empty S, $O[S][v]$ is the minimum of

$$O[S \setminus \{u\}][u] + w_{uv}$$

over all the vertices $u \in S$, where w_{uv} is the weight of the arc (u, v).

Problems

Small TSP [spoj:STSP]

Collecting Beepers [kattis:beepers]

7.6   Full Example: Menu Tour

See [spoj:MENUTOUR].

Rachid is in Barcelona for the first time, and wants to enjoy a truly fine dinner. The restaurant guides suggest that the ultimate dinner consists of C specialities, numbered from 1 to C, tasted in the specified order.

The streets of Barcelona form a regular grid: east–west oriented streets crossing north–south oriented streets. There are R restaurants in the city and they are located at the crossings. Walking from crossing (i_1, j_1) to crossing (i_2, j_2) takes exactly $|i_1 - i_2| + |j_1 - j_2|$ minutes, where $|x|$ denotes the absolute value of x. Here, (i, j) means the ith street from west to east and the jth street from south to north.

Unfortunately, none of the restaurants offer all C dishes. If a restaurant k offers dish c, then it costs $P[k, c]$ euros. Otherwise, the value $P[k, c] = 0$ indicates that the item is not offered. Rachid has B euros that he can spend on his dinner. He would like to choose a sequence of restaurants so that he can have his ultimate dinner without exceeding the available budget, while minimising the total travel time between restaurants. The tour can start and end at an arbitrary crossing, and can visit the same restaurant several times.

Example

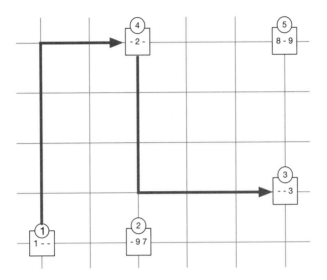

Figure 7.3 An instance of the Menu Tour problem.

In this example, there are three menu items, whose prices are displayed in order, for every restaurant (a '-' corresponds to a dish that is not offered, i.e. when $P[k, c] = 0$). If Rachid has a budget of 9 euros, the optimal tour consists of the restaurants 1–4–3 for a cost of 6 euros and a total travel time of 12 minutes. There is a shorter tour of 2 minutes consisting of the restaurant sequence 1–2, but its cost is 17 euros, exceeding the available budget of 9 euros.

Input

The input begins with a line consisting of the integers C, R, B, separated by a single space. Then R lines follow. The kth line describes the kth restaurant and consists of $2 + C$ integers separated by a single space, namely $i[k]$, $j[k]$, $P[k, 1]$, $\ldots$, $P[k, C]$, where $(i[k], j[k])$ defines the location of the restaurant.

Limits

- $1 \leq C \leq 20$;
- $1 \leq R \leq 100$;
- $0 \leq B \leq 100$;
- for every $1 \leq k \leq R$:

  - $1 \leq i[k] \leq 1\,000$;
  - $1 \leq j[k] \leq 1\,000$;
  - for every $1 \leq c \leq C, 0 \leq P[k, c] \leq 40$.

Output

The output should consist of a single integer y: the minimum total travel time of an optimal restaurant tour for Rachid. If there is no feasible tour, the value -1 should be returned.

Sample input	Sample output
3 5 9	12
1 1 1 0 0	
3 1 0 9 7	
6 2 0 0 3	
3 5 0 2 0	
6 5 8 0 9	

Solution

This problem sounds very much like a travelling salesman tour, but the order in which the dishes need to be consumed simplifies it a lot. It can be computed by dynamic programming. For any dish number c, restaurant r and budget b, let $A[c,r,b]$ be the minimum time for a tour that covers dishes from 0 to c, ends in restaurant r and costs exactly b euros. By convention denote $A[c,r,b] = +\infty$ if there is no such tour.

The base cases are for $c = 0$. For any restaurant r, if $P[r,0] > 0$ the tour could start in r and spend $P[r,0]$ on the first dish (numbered 0), without any travel time. Hence, $A[0,r,b] = 0$ for $b = P[r,0]$ in that case, and $A[0,r,b] = +\infty$ otherwise.

The induction step for $c > 0$ and any r,b follows the following recursion

$$A[c,r,b] = \begin{cases} +\infty & \text{if } b < P[r,c] \\ \min_i A[c-1,i,b-P[r,c]] + dist[i][r] & \text{otherwise,} \end{cases}$$

where the dist[i][r] denotes the distance between the restaurants i and r. These distances should be precomputed in order for the algorithm to be efficient. There are $O(NCB)$ variables, each is the minimisation over $O(N)$ alternatives, hence the total complexity is $O(N^2CB)$, which is acceptable given the upper bounds.

8   Shortest Paths

A classic problem on graphs consists of finding a shortest path between two vertices, a source s and a destination v. For the same cost we can obtain the shortest paths between the source s and all possible destinations v'; this is why the algorithms presented in this chapter solve this more general problem of the shortest paths from a unique source in a directed graph.

The length of a path is defined as the sum of its arc weights, and the distance from s to v is defined as the length of a shortest path between s and v. To simplify the presentation, in general we show only how to compute the distances. To obtain a path realising this distance, it suffices to maintain, in addition to the array of distances, an array of predecessors. Hence, if `dist[v]` is the distance from s to v with `dist[v]` = `dist[u]` + `w[u][v]` for a vertex u, we store `prec[v]` = `u` in the array of predecessors. By following the predecessors back to the source s, we can determine a shortest path in reverse order, leading from the source to a given destination.

8.1   Composition Property

The shortest paths exhibit a composition property, which is the key to the different shortest path algorithms. Richard Bellman called this the *Principal of Optimality*, which lies at the heart of problems of dynamic programming. Consider a path P from s to v (also known as an $s - v$ path), passing by a vertex u, see Figure 8.1. It is thus the concatenation of a path P_1 from s to u with a path P_2 from u to v. The length of P is the sum of the lengths of P_1 and P_2. Thus, if P is a shortest path from s to v, then P_1 must be a shortest path from s to u and P_2 a shortest path from u to v. This is obvious, as the replacement of P_1 by a shorter path would result in a shorter path from s to v.

Figure 8.1   A shortest path from s to v passing through u is the concatenation of a shortest path from s to u with a shortest path from u to v.

Black, Grey and White Vertices

This composition property is the basis of Dijkstra's algorithm and its variants, including on graphs with non-negative weights on its arcs. The algorithm maintains an array dist containing the distances from the source to the vertices; it is set to $+\infty$ for the vertices v for which no $s - v$ path has yet been found.

The vertices of the graph are thus divided into three groups, see Figure 8.2. The black vertices are those with an already-identified shortest path from the source, the grey vertices are the direct neighbours of the black vertices and the white vertices are those currently without a known shortest path.

Initially, only the source s is black, with dist[s] = 0. All the direct neighbours v of s are grey, and dist[v] is the weight of the arc (s, v). All the other vertices are for the moment white. The algorithm then repeatedly colours the grey vertices black, and their white neighbours grey, maintaining this invariant. Finally, all the vertices reachable from s will be black, whereas the others will remain white.

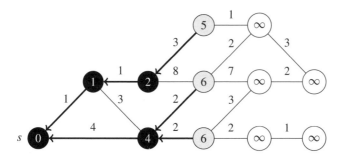

Figure 8.2 Example of the colouring of vertices by Dijkstra's algorithm. Each vertex v is labelled with dist[v], its current distance from the source, and the arcs specified by prec are highlighted in bold.

Key Observation

Which grey vertex should we select to colour black? The choice is made with a vertex v with the smallest dist[v]. Why is this the correct choice? Consider an arbitrary $s - v$ path P. Since s is black and v is grey, a first grey vertex u exists on this path. Hence, P can be decomposed into an $s - u$ path P_1 and a $u - v$ path P_2, where P_1 contains only intermediate black vertices, excluding u. By the choice of v, dist[u] $\geq$ dist[v], and by the hypothesis that the weights of the arcs are non-negative, the length of P_2 is also non-negative. Hence, the length of P is at least dist[v]. As the choice of P was arbitrary, this shows that the shortest $s - v$ path is of length dist[v]. Colouring v black is thus valid, and to maintain the invariant, for each vertex v' reachable from v by an arc, we must colour v' in grey if this is not already the case, and dist[v] + w[v][v'] becomes a new candidate for the distance dist[v'].

Data Structure for the Grey Vertices

As for every iteration we seek a grey vertex v with minimal dist[v], a priority queue holding the vertices v is well-suited, with the priority values being the values of dist. This is the implementation chosen for Dijkstra's algorithm. The removal of the vertex with the smallest distance can thus be done in time logarithmic in the number of vertices.

If the graph has a special structure, then a simpler structure could possibly be used. For example, in the case where the weights of the arcs are in $\{0, 1\}$, there will only be two types of grey vertices, those with a distance d and those with a distance $d+1$. This priority queue can then be implemented in a simpler manner using a *double-ended queue*, abbreviated *deque*. This queue contains the list of grey vertices in priority order, and it suffices to remove from the left in constant time a vertex v to be coloured black. The neighbours of v are added to the queue on the left or on the right, according to whether the weight on the corresponding arc is 0 or 1, see 8.2. Finally, all the operations of manipulation of the queue can be done in constant time, and we shave off a logarithmic factor compared to Dijkstra's algorithm.

If the graph is even simpler, with unit weights on all of its arcs—in a manner of speaking a non-weighted graph—then this double-ended queue can be replaced by a simple queue, and managed using the algorithm of breadth-first search described previously in Section 6.4 on page 93.

Shortest Path Algorithms		
Without weights	$O(|E|)$	breadth-first search (BFS)
Weights 0 or 1	$O(|E|)$	Dijkstra adapted with a double-ended queue
Weights non-negative	$O(|E| \log |V|)$	Dijkstra
Weights arbitrary	$O(|V| \cdot |E|)$	Bellman-Ford
Paths from all sources	$O(|V|^3)$	Floyd-Warshall

8.2   Graphs with Weights 0 or 1

Definition
Given a graph whose arcs are weighted by 0 or 1, and a source vertex s, we wish to compute the distances from s towards the other vertices.

Application
You are provided with a map of an $N \times M$ rectangular labyrinth containing obstructing walls and would like to exit while demolishing a minimum number of walls. The labyrinth can be seen as a directed graph whose arcs (from one cell to an adjacent cell) are weighted either by 0 (free access to the cell) or by 1 (access to a cell blocked by a wall). We seek to demolish as few walls as possible, which comes down to finding the shortest path in this graph from the entrance to the exit.

Algorithm
We return to the structure of a generic shortest path algorithm. At any moment, the vertices of the graph are divided into three groups: black, grey and white.

The algorithm maintains a double-ended queue containing all the grey vertices, as well as eventually some vertices that were grey at the time of their insertion, but that since have become black. The queue has the property that for a certain value x, all the black vertices v_b satisfy dist[v_b] = x, and up to a certain position all the grey vertices v_{g0} satisfy dist[v_{g0}] = x, whereas those after satisfy dist[v_{g1}] = x + 1.

As long as this queue is non-empty, the algorithm extracts a vertex v from the head of the queue, which hence has a minimal value dist[v]. If this vertex is already black, there is nothing to do. Otherwise, it is coloured black. In order to maintain the invariant, we must then add certain neighbours v' of v to the queue. Let $\ell = \text{dist}[v] + w[v][v']$. If v' is already black, or if dist[v'] $\leq \ell$, there is no reason to add v' to the queue. Otherwise, v' can be coloured grey, dist[v'] is lowered to ℓ and v' is added to the head or tail of the queue depending on whether $w[v][v'] = 0$ or $w[v][v'] = 1$.

```python
def dist01(graph, weight, source=0, target=None):
    n = len(graph)
    dist = [float('inf')] * n
    prec = [None] * n
    black = [False] * n
    dist[source] = 0
    gray = deque([source])
    while gray:
        node = gray.pop()
        if black[node]:
            continue
        black[node] = True
        if node == target:
            break
        for neighbor in graph[node]:
            ell = dist[node] + weight[node][neighbor]
            if black[neighbor] or dist[neighbor] <= ell:
                continue
            dist[neighbor] = ell
            prec[neighbor] = node
            if weight[node][neighbor] == 0:
                gray.append(neighbor)
            else:
                gray.appendleft(neighbor)
    return dist, prec
```

Problem
KATHTHI [spoj:KATHTHI]

8.3   Graphs with Non-negative Weights—Dijkstra

Definition
Given a directed graph with non-negative weights on its arcs, we seek the shortest path between a source and a destination.

Complexity

A brutal implementation is in $O(|V|^2)$, while the use of a priority queue lowers the complexity to $O(|E| \log |V|)$. By using a Fibonacci priority queue, we can obtain a complexity of $O(|E| + |V| \log |V|)$ (see Fredman and Tarjan, 1987); however, the improvement is perhaps not worth the implementation effort.

Algorithm

We continue with the formalism introduced in Section 8.1 on page 125. Dijkstra's algorithm maintains a set of vertices S for which a shortest path from the source has already been computed. Hence, S is precisely the set of black vertices. Initially, S contains only the source itself. In addition, the algorithm maintains a tree of shortest paths rooted at the source and covering S. We assign prec[v] as the predecessor of v in this tree and dist[v] as the distance computed, see Figure 8.3.

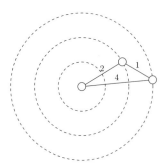

Figure 8.3 Dijkstra's algorithm captures the vertices via balls of increasing radius centred on the departure vertex. There are no vertices at distance 1, thus the algorithm leaps directly to the closest vertex, at distance 2, via the priority queue.

We then examine the edges at the boundary of S. More precisely, we consider the arcs (u, v) with u in S and v not in S. These arcs define paths composed of a shortest path from the source to u followed by the arc (u, v). This path has a weight that we assign as priority to the arc (u, v).

As explained in Section 8.1 on page 125, the algorithm extracts from the priority queue an arc (u, v) of minimal priority, thus defining a shortest $s - v$ path. We can then add the arc (u, v) to the tree of shortest paths, add v to S and iterate.

Priority Queues

The principal ingredient of this algorithm is a priority queue, which is a data structure containing a set of elements, allowing the addition of elements and the extraction of the one with the smallest priority.

Such a structure is, in general, implemented with a heap (here a min-heap, see Section 1.5.4 on page 22), where these operations have logarithmic cost in the size of the set.

A Slight Improvement

For more efficiency, we can ignore arcs already known to not lead to a shortest path, and not store them in the priority queue. For this, we update dist[v] whenever an arc to v is added to the queue. Hence, at the moment of considering an arc, we can decide if it improves the shortest path to v known up to this point.

Implementation Details

The code presented allows the computation of the shortest paths to each and every destination, if a particular destination is not specified when the function is invoked.

For each outgoing arc (u, v), we store in the queue the pair (d, v), where d is the length of the path associated with this arc.

It is possible for a vertex to be found several times in the queue with different weights (priorities). However, once the first occurrence of this vertex is extracted, it will be coloured black, and the further occurrences will be ignored at the time of their extraction.

```python
def dijkstra(graph, weight, source=0, target=None):
    n = len(graph)
    assert all(weight[u][v] >= 0 for u in range(n) for v in graph[u])
    prec = [None] * n
    black = [False] * n
    dist = [float('inf')] * n
    dist[source] = 0
    heap = [(0, source)]
    while heap:
        dist_node, node = heappop(heap)      # Closest node from source
        if not black[node]:
            black[node] = True
            if node == target:
                break
            for neighbor in graph[node]:
                dist_neighbor = dist_node + weight[node][neighbor]
                if dist_neighbor < dist[neighbor]:
                    dist[neighbor] = dist_neighbor
                    prec[neighbor] = node
                    heappush(heap, (dist_neighbor, neighbor))
    return dist, prec
```

Variant

The implementation of Dijkstra's algorithm can be slightly simplified with the use of a priority queue allowing the priority of an element to be changed, such as the queue presented in Section 1.5.4 on page 22. Instead of storing the arcs in the queue, we store the vertices, in fact all the vertices of the graph, and the priority of a vertex v is set to dist[v]. In practice, the queue contains pairs of the form (dist[v], v), and we compare them lexicographically. When a shorter path to v is discovered, we update the pair corresponding to v with the new shorter distance. The advantage of this variant is that we can skip marking the vertices black. For each vertex v, the queue contains only a single pair with v, and when (dist[v], v) is extracted from the priority queue, we know that we have discovered a shortest path towards v.

```
def dijkstra_update_heap(graph, weight, source=0, target=None):
    n = len(graph)
    assert all(weight[u][v] >= 0 for u in range(n) for v in graph[u])
    prec = [None] * n
    dist = [float('inf')] * n
    dist[source] = 0
    heap = OurHeap([(dist[node], node) for node in range(n)])
    while heap:
        dist_node, node = heap.pop()        # Closest node from source
        if node == target:
            break
        for neighbor in graph[node]:
            old = dist[neighbor]
            new = dist_node + weight[node][neighbor]
            if new < old:
                dist[neighbor] = new
                prec[neighbor] = node
                heap.update((old, neighbor), (new, neighbor))
    return dist, prec
```

Problems
Mice and Maze [spoj:MICEMAZE]
Almost Shortest Path [spoj:SAMER08A]
Dragon Maze [gcj:China2014roundB]
Potholers [spoj:POTHOLE]

8.4 Graphs with Arbitrary Weights—Bellman–Ford

Definition
For this problem, negative arc weights are allowed. If a cycle of negative total weight is reachable from the source, the distance from the source to the vertices of the cycle is $-\infty$. Indeed, by traversing this cycle an arbitrary number of times, we obtain a path from the source to a vertex in the cycle of negative weight with negative length and arbitrarily large magnitude. This bothersome situation is detected by the algorithm presented.

Complexity
Dynamic programming provides a solution in $O(|V| \cdot |E|)$; see Bellman (1958); Ford (1956) as well as Moore (1959), who independently discovered the same algorithm.

Algorithm
The central operation is the *relaxation* of the distances (see Figure 8.4), consisting for each arc (u, v) in testing if the use of this arc could diminish the distance from

the source to v. The value $d_u + w_{uv}$ is thus a candidate for the distance d_v. This is performed with two nested loops; the inner loop relaxes the distances via each arc, and the outer loop repeats this procedure a certain number of times. We show that after k iterations of the outer loop, we have computed for each vertex v the length of a shortest path from the source to v, using at most k arcs. This is true for $k = 0$, and if we assign $d_k[v]$ as this length for every $k = 1, \ldots, |V| - 1$, then

$$d_{k+1}[v] = \min_{u:(u,v)\in E} d_k[u] + w_{uv}.$$

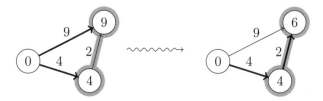

Figure 8.4 An example of relaxation via the greyed arc. Following this edge shortens the path to the destination vertex of the arc. The vertices are labelled with the distance from the source vertex, which has label 0. The shortest paths are shown in bold.

Detection of Negative Cycles

Consider the situation where the graph does not contain any negative cycles. In this case, all the shortest paths are simple and $|V| - 1$ iterations of the outer loop are sufficient to determine the distances towards each of the destinations. Hence, if we observe a change during the $|V|$th iteration, this indicates that a negative cycle exists that is reachable from the source. Our implementation returns a Boolean indicating the presence of such a cycle.

```
def bellman_ford(graph, weight, source=0):
    n = len(graph)
    dist = [float('inf')] * n
    prec = [None] * n
    dist[source] = 0
    for nb_iterations in range(n):
        changed = False
        for node in range(n):
            for neighbor in graph[node]:
                alt = dist[node] + weight[node][neighbor]
                if alt < dist[neighbor]:
                    dist[neighbor] = alt
                    prec[neighbor] = node
                    changed = True
        if not changed:                    # fixed point
            return dist, prec, False
    return dist, prec, True
```

Problem
Negative Cycles [spoj:NEGCYC]

8.5   All Source–Destination paths—Floyd–Warshall

Definition
Given a graph with weights on its arcs, we want to compute the shortest path between each pair of nodes. Once again, the problem is well-posed only in the absence of cycles with negative weight, and the algorithm detects this exception.

Complexity
The Floyd–Warshall algorithm executes in $O(n^3)$, where n is the number of vertices; see Floyd (1962); Warshall (1962) as well as Roy (1959), who independently discovered the same algorithm.

Algorithm
The distances between the vertices are computed by dynamic programming, see Figure 8.6. For each $k = 0, 1, \ldots, n$ a square matrix W_k is computed, containing in $W_k[u][v]$ the length of the shortest path from u to v using only the intermediate vertices of index strictly inferior to k, where the vertices are numbered from 0 to $n-1$. Hence, for $k = 0$, the matrix W_0 contains only the weights of the arcs, and $+\infty$ for the elements (u, v) not having an arc (u, v). The updating is simple using the composition principle: a shortest path from u to v passing through a vertex k is composed of a shortest path from u to k and a shortest path from k to v. We thus compute, for $k, u, v \in \{0, \ldots, n-1\}$:

$$W_{k+1}[u][v] = \min\{W_k[u][v], W_k[u][k] + W_k[k][v]\}.$$

It is indeed the same k as index of the vertices and as position in the array: for the computation of $W_{k+1}[u][v]$, we are allowed to consider the paths passing through the vertex k.

$$a_{uv} = \sum_{k=0}^{n-1} b_{uk} \times c_{kv} \qquad\qquad W_{uv}^{(\ell+1)} = \min_{k=0}^{n-1} W_{uk}^{(\ell)} + W_{kv}^{(\ell)}$$

$$A = BC \qquad\qquad W^{(\ell+1)} = W^{(\ell)} W^{(\ell)}$$

Figure 8.5 The Floyd–Warshall algorithm can be seen as a multiplication of matrices on the tropical algebra $(\mathbb{R}, \min, +)$. However, we cannot employ the usual algorithms of rapid multiplication since we are only operating in a semiring.

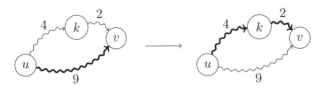

Figure 8.6 An example of relaxation via the vertex k. Passing through k shortens the path from u to v.

Implementation Details

The implementation maintains a unique matrix W, which plays the role of the successive W_k; it modifies the given weight matrix. It detects the presence of negative cycles and returns `False` in this case.

```
def floyd_warshall(weight):
    V = range(len(weight))
    for k in V:
        for u in V:
            for v in V:
                weight[u][v] = min(weight[u][v],
                                   weight[u][k] + weight[k][v])
        for v in V:
            if weight[v][v] < 0:       # negative cycle found
                return True
    return False
```

Detection of Negative Cycles

A negative cycle exists the passes through a vertex v if and only if $W_n[v][v] < 0$. However, as shown by Hougardy (2010), it is strongly advised to detect the negative cycles with the Bellman–Ford algorithm. In fact, in the presence of negative cycles, the values computed by the Floyd–Warshall algorithm can have an absolute value exponentially large in the number of vertices of the graph, causing an overflow in the capacity of the variables.

Example: Roads in Berland [spoj:CT25C]

Suppose we are given a strongly connected directed graph with non-negative weights on the arcs. These define a shortest distance $D[u, v]$ for every pair of vertices (u, v), which can be computed by the Floyd–Warshall algorithm. The score of the graph is defined as the sum of the shortest distances over all pairs of vertices. Now, suppose that an additional arc (u', v') with weight $w[u', v']$ is added to the graph. For example, a tunnel is constructed through a mountain from u' to v', much shorter than the old road going around the mountain between u' to v'. By how much will the total score be diminished in the presence of this new arc? For this, it suffices to compute the sum $\sum_{u,v} \max\{0, D[u, v] - (D[u, u'] + w[u', v'] + D[v', v])\}$. If n is the number of vertices of the graph and k the number of additional arcs, then the complexity is $O(n^3 + kn^2)$, quite acceptable for the limits $n, k \leq 300$.

8.6 Grid

Problem

Given a rectangular grid, where certain cells are inaccessible, find a shortest path between the entrance and the exit.

The Algorithm

This problem is easily solved with a breadth-first search on the graph determined by the grid. However, rather than explicitly constructing the graph, it is simpler to perform the search directly on the grid. The grid is given in the form of a 2-dimensional array containing the character # for the inaccessible cells and a space for the accessible cells. Our implementation uses this same array to mark the vertices already visited, and hence avoids an additional data structure. The cells visited will then contain symbols '→', '←', '↓', '↑', indicating the predecessor on the shortest path from the source.

```python
def dist_grid(grid, source, target=None):
    rows = len(grid)
    cols = len(grid[0])
    i, j = source
    grid[i][j] = 's'
    Q = deque()
    Q.append(source)
    while Q:
        i1, j1 = Q.popleft()
        for di, dj, symbol in [(0, +1, '>'),
                               (0, -1, '<'),
                               (+1, 0, 'v'),
                               (-1, 0, '^')]:    # explore all directions
            i2 = i1 + di
            j2 = j1 + dj
            if not (0 <= i2 < rows and 0 <= j2 < cols):
                continue                      # reached the bounds of the grid
            if grid[i2][j2] != ' ':   # inaccessible or already visited
                continue
            grid[i2][j2] = symbol     # mark visit
            if (i2, j2) == target:
                grid[i2][j2] = 't'    # goal is reached
                return
            Q.append((i2, j2))
```

Variants

The proposed implementation is easy to modify to permit diagonal steps on the grid, between cells sharing only a corner. A hexagonal grid can be treated in a similar manner by transforming it into a grid with square cells, but with a particular neighbourhood. Figure 8.7 illustrates this transformation.

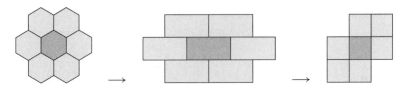

Figure 8.7 Representation of a hexagonal grid by a square grid.

Problem
A Famous Grid [spoj:SPIRALGR]

8.7   Variants

Given the importance of the shortest path problem, we present a number of classic variants.

8.7.1   Non-Weighted Graphs

In a non-weighted graph, a breadth-first search is sufficient to determine the shortest paths.

8.7.2   Directed Acyclic Graphs

A topological sort, see Section 6.7 on page 102, allows the vertices to be processed in an appropriate order: to compute the distance from the source to a vertex v, we can benefit from the distances to all the predecessors of v computed beforehand and apply a simple dynamic programming recursion.

Application
This problem is given as an exercise in Cormen et al. (2010, Ex. 24-6, p. 618). We wish to determine a route from home to work that starts by ascending and finishes by descending, in order to first get some exercise and then cool down. For this, we model the city as a graph, where the vertices represent the intersections with their elevation, and the edges represent the roads with their lengths. Using the previous algorithm, we can compute for each vertex v the distance from the source using only ascending arcs, and at the same time compute the distance from v to the target using only descending arcs. The answer is the sum of these distances minimised over all vertices v.

8.7.3   Longest Path

The dynamic programming mentioned above can be adapted to compute efficiently the longest paths in a directed acyclic graph (DAG for short). For a general graph, the problem consists in finding the longest path from the source to the destination which passes through each vertex at most once. This problem is *NP-hard*—we do not know of an algorithm to solve it in polynomial time. If the number of vertices is small, on the order of twenty or so, then we can use the method of dynamic programming on the subsets S of vertices and compute $D[S][v]$, the length of the longest path from the source to v using only the intermediate vertices from S. Then, for every non-empty S, we have the relation

$$D[S][v] = \max_{u \in S} D[S \setminus u][u] + w[u][v],$$

where $S \setminus u$ is the set S with the vertex u removed, and $w[u][v]$ is the weight of the arc (u, v). The base case is then

$$D[\emptyset][v] = \begin{cases} w[u][v] & \text{if the arc } (u, v) \text{ exists} \\ -\infty & \text{otherwise.} \end{cases}$$

8.7.4   Longest Path in a Tree

Often, the problems that are difficult in general become easy on trees, as the notion of subtree may allow a solution by dynamic programming. This is indeed the case for the problem of the longest path in a tree, whose linear algorithm is presented in Section 10.3 on page 178.

8.7.5   Path Minimising the Maximal Weight Over the Arcs

In the case where the goal is not to minimise the *sum* of the edge weights of a path, but rather the *maximum*, a simple solution is to build on Kruskal's algorithm, which uses a union-find structure. We begin with an empty graph, and add the edges in order of increasing weight, up until the source and the destination are joined in the same connected component. For directed graph, a similar approach can be made to work, but the simplest solution might be to adapt Dijkstra's algorithm, replacing additions of distances with the maximum of arc weights over a path.

8.7.6   Graph Weighted on the Vertices

Consider a graph whose *vertices* carry weights, rather than the arcs. The goal is to find a path from the source to the destination minimising the sum of the weights of the vertices traversed. This situation can be reduced to the case described previously. We replace each vertex v by two vertices v^- and v^+ linked by an arc with the weight of v, and replace each arc (u, v) by an arc (u^+, v^-) of weight zero.

8.7.7   Path Minimising the Maximal Weight on the Vertices

In the case where the weight of a path is defined as the maximum of the weights of the intermediate vertices of the path, we can use the Floyd–Warshall algorithm. It suffices to order the vertices by increasing weight and terminate the iteration as soon as a path from the source to the destination is found.

It suffices to maintain a Boolean array of connectivity $C_k[u][v]$ indicating if a path from u to v exists that uses only the intermediate vertices with indices strictly inferior to k. The update thus becomes

$$C_k[u][v] = C_{k-1}[u][v] \vee (C_{k-1}[u][k] \wedge C_{k-1}[k][v]).$$

8.7.8   All Edges Belonging to a Shortest Path

Given a weighted graph G, a source s and a destination t, several shortest paths between s and t can exist. The goal is to determine *all* the edges belonging to these shortest paths. To accomplish this, we make two invocations of Dijkstra's algorithm, one with s and the other with t as source, to compute for each vertex v the distance $d[s,v]$ from the source and the distance $d[v,t]$ towards the destination. An edge (u,v) of weight $w[u,v]$ will belong to a shortest path if and only if

$$d[s,u] + w[u,v] + d[v,t] = d[s,t].$$

Variant for a Directed Graph

Dijkstra's algorithm admits only a given *source*, and not a specific *destination*. Thus, for the computation of all the distances $d[v,t]$ towards t, it is necessary to temporarily reverse the arcs.

Problems
Almost Shortest Path [spoj:SAMER08A]
Flowery Trails [kattis:flowerytrails]

9 Matchings and Flows

Traditionally, the heart of combinatorial optimisation lies in the matching and flow problems. These problems are related and exist with several variants. The principle underlying most of these algorithms is the repeated improvement of a solution, initially empty, leading to an optimal solution.

Suppose that in the bipartite graph of Figure 9.1 we wish to determine a *perfect matching*, i.e. a pairing of each vertex on the left with a distinct vertex on the right. The edges of the graph indicate the authorised pairings. If we begin by matching u_0 to v_0, then we immediately find ourselves blocked. To obtain a perfect matching, we are forced to backtrack and undo this pairing. This principle is illustrated in the following sections.

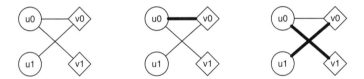

Figure 9.1 Progressive construction of a perfect matching.

The flow algorithms presented here require that for every arc (u, v), the reverse arc (v, u) also exists. Thus, beforehand they invoke the following function, which as necessary completes the graph with reverse arcs of capacity 0. For every arc (u, v), it tests if u is present in the adjacency list of v. This executes with complexity $O(|E| \cdot |V|)$, negligible in our cases.

```python
def add_reverse_arcs(graph, capac=None):
    for u, _ in enumerate(graph):
        for v in graph[u]:
            if u not in graph[v]:
                if type(graph[v]) is list:
                    graph[v].append(u)
                    if capac:
                        capac[v][u] = 0
                else:
                    assert type(graph[v]) is dict
                    graph[v][u] = 0
```

Complexity of the Algorithms Presented

In the following table, for bipartite graphs $G(U, V, E)$ we assume $|U| \leq |V|$. C denotes the maximal capacity of the arcs.

	Matchings	
bipartite without weights	$O(|V| \cdot |E|)$	augmenting paths
bipartite with weights	$O(|V|^3)$	Kuhn-Munkres
bipartite with preferences	$O(|V|^2)$	Gale-Shapley
	Flows	
bounded capacities	$O(|V| \cdot |E| \cdot C)$	Ford-Fulkerson
bounded capacities	$O(|V| \cdot |E| \cdot \log C)$	binary blocking flows
arbitrary capacities	$O(|V| \cdot |E|^2)$	Edmonds-Karp
arbitrary capacities	$O(|V|^2 \cdot |E|)$	Dinic
	Cuts	
arbitrary graph	$O(|V|^2 \cdot |E|)$	Dinic
planar graph	$O(|E| \log |V|)$	Dijkstra

9.1 Maximum Bipartite Matching

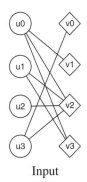

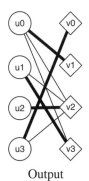

Input   Output

Application

Assigning n courses to n classrooms, assigning n tasks to n workers—the applications of the problem of maximum bipartite matching are widespread. A weighted version of this problem exists that is described in Section 9.2 on page 145. As the applications are most of the time modelled with bipartite graphs, we limit ourselves here to this case, but the problem can also be solved for general graphs.

Definition

Let $G(U, V, E)$ be a bipartite graph with $E \subseteq U \times V$. A *matching* is a set $M \subseteq E$ such that no two edges in M have the same endpoint. Clearly, any subset of a matching is also a matching. A matching M is said to be maximal if there is no matching M' that is a superset of M. In other words, M is maximal if it is not possible to add an edge to M and still obtain a matching. Clearly, a maximal matching can be found by a greedy algorithm. In contrast, a matching M is said to be *maximum* if there is no matching M' with strictly larger cardinality than M. In this section, we consider the problem of finding a maximum matching, also called the maximal cardinality matching problem, or simply matching problem. For simplicity, we restrict ourselves to bipartite graphs.

Our goal is to find a maximal cardinality matching. For fixed M, a vertex is said to be *matched* if it is the endpoint of an edge in M, otherwise the vertex is *free*.

Key Observation

A natural approach to tackle an optimisation problem is to begin with a naive solution and attempt to improve it iteratively until eventually it becomes optimal. To understand how we might improve a matching, take a look at the *symmetric difference* between matchings. Given a *blue* matching M (shown as solid lines) and a *red* matching M' (shown as dashed lines), the symmetric difference $M \oplus M'$ is defined as $M \setminus M' \cup M' \setminus M$. It is composed of cycles and paths of alternating colours, red and blue, along the edges. By a counting argument, we see that if $|M'| > |M|$, then an *alternating* path P always exists that begins and ends with a red edge, see Figure 9.2.

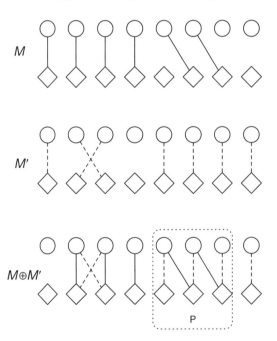

Figure 9.2 The symmetric difference $M \oplus M'$ is made up of an alternating cycle, and a path P augmenting for M' and two paths augmenting for M.

With respect to M, this path P starts and ends on a free vertex and alternates between edges that are not in M and edges in M. Such a path is said to be *augmenting*, as the difference $M \oplus P$ is a matching with one edge more than M.

Hence, if M is not yet a matching of maximal cardinality, then an augmenting path for M exists. More precisely, if there is a matching M' with $|M'| > |M|$ and a vertex $u \in U$ matched in M' but free in M, then there is an augmenting path P for M starting at u.

Algorithm in $O(|U| \cdot |E|)$

This observation leads to our first algorithm. Starting with the empty matching M, while still possible, we look for a path P augmenting for M, and replace M with $M \oplus P$. Such an augmenting path can easily be found with a depth-first search. It suffices to start from a free vertex of U, and consider all its neighbours v not already visited. If v is not yet matched, the path from the root to v is an augmenting path. If v is matched with a vertex u', then we continue the exploration from u'.

Finding and then applying an augmenting path thus costs $O(|E|)$, and this step must be taken for at most $|U|$ vertices, hence the complexity of this algorithm is $O(|U| \cdot |E|)$.

Technical Details

In the following implementation,[1] the matching is encoded by an array `match` associating with each vertex $v \in V$ the matching vertex in U, where `match[v]` = None if v is free.

The graph is represented by an array `E` such that `E[u]` is the list of neighbours of u. The sets of vertices U, V must be given in the form `[0,1,...,|U|-1]` and `[0,1,...,|V|-1]`.

Note that this implementation uses Python's lazy evaluation of boolean expressions, a technique common to almost all programming languages. This means that in the OR expression, the function `augment` is called if and only if the first term is false.

```
def augment(u, bigraph, visit, match):
    for v in bigraph[u]:
        if not visit[v]:
            visit[v] = True
            if match[v] is None or augment(match[v], bigraph,
                                        visit, match):
                match[v] = u       # found an augmenting path
                return True
    return False


def max_bipartite_matching(bigraph):
    n = len(bigraph)                # same domain for U and V
    match = [None] * n
    for u in range(n):
        augment(u, bigraph, [False] * n, match)
    return match
```

---

[1] Do you understand why only the vertices of V are marked when visited?

Other Algorithms

An algorithm from Hopcroft and Karp (1972) allows the resolution of the maximum matching problem in a bipartite graph in time $O(\sqrt{|V|} \cdot |E|)$. Its principle is to discover several augmenting paths with the same traversal, and to privilege the short augmenting paths. Alt et al. (1991) found an algorithm in $O(|V|^{1.5}\sqrt{|E|/\log|V|})$ which is interesting for dense graphs (with many edges). However, these algorithms are complicated to implement and not that much faster in practice than the algorithm presented in this section.

Problem of Minimal Covering by Vertices in a Bipartite Graph

Given a bipartite graph $G(U, V, E)$, we want to find a set $S \subseteq U \cup V$ of minimal cardinality such that every edge $(u, v) \in E$ is *covered* by S, in the sense that at least one of the vertices u, v is in S. Such a set is called a *vertex cover*; however, at times, the terms *traversal* or *nodal cover* are used.

Application

Consider a city the map of which consists of n north–south streets and n east–west streets, crossing in n^2 intersections. We would like to monitor a number of the most important intersections. A camera can monitor all of the intersections of any given street. What is the minimum number of cameras that need to be installed in order to monitor the given set of critical intersections?

Kőnig's Theorem

Since each edge in a matching must have at least one endpoint in S, the size of the maximal matching is a lower bound on the minimal size of the smallest covering. Kőnig's theorem states that there is, in fact, equality between these optimal values.

The proof is constructive and provides an algorithm for finding a minimal covering from a maximal matching M of the graph $G(U, V, E)$. Let Z be the set of vertices unmatched by M, and that are in U. We add to Z all the vertices reachable from Z by alternating paths, see Figure 9.3. We define the set

$$S = (U \backslash Z) \cup (V \cap Z).$$

The construction of Z implies that for each edge $(u, v) \in M$, if $v \in Z$, then $u \in Z$ also. Conversely, since u was not initially in Z with the free vertices of U, u was added to Z thanks to a matching edge; hence $v \in Z$.

This implies that for each matching edge $(u, v) \in M$, either both its endpoints are in Z or neither of them are. Hence, every matching edge has exactly one endpoint in S, and $|S| \geq |M|$.

We now show that S covers all of the edges of the graph. Let (u, v) be an edge of the graph. If $u \notin Z$, then the edge is covered, so suppose that $u \in Z$. If (u, v) is not a matching edge, then the maximal character of Z means that v must also be in Z, and hence in S. If (u, v) is in M, then by the preceding observation $v \in Z$, and hence

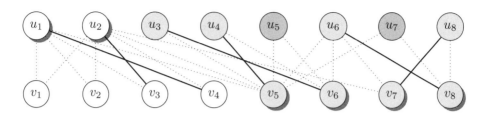

Figure 9.3 Computation of a minimal covering by vertices. First, a maximum matching is computed, the edges of which are shown with thick lines. The set Z is composed of unmatched vertices in U (in dark grey), completed by vertices reachable from Z by alternating paths (in light grey). Finally, the solution produced is the set $S = (U \setminus Z) \cup (V \cap Z)$, the vertices of which are shown with a shadow.

$v \in S$. This shows that S is a covering of the vertices, implying $|S| \leq |M|$, hence we can conclude that $|S| = |M|$.

Problems
Crime Wave [icpcarchive:5584]
Dungeon of Death [spoj:QUEST4]
Muddy Fields [spoj:MUDDY]

Problem of Minimal Covering by Edges in a Bipartite Graph
This time, the goal is to find the smallest set of edges $S \subseteq E$ covering all of the vertices of a given bipartite graph $G(U, V, E)$, such that each vertex of $U \cup V$ is incident to at least one edge of S. This problem is a bit simpler than the preceding one. In fact, it suffices to start with a maximum matching in G, and for each unmatched vertex we add an arbitrary incident edge, see Figure 9.4. Indeed, for a given covering by edges $S \subseteq E$ we can arbitrarily associate each vertex v to an incident edge $e \in S$, and say that e is *responsible* for the covering of v. Then, every edge of S is responsible for one or two vertices. The edges responsible for two vertices form a matching M. Then, M is optimal if and only if S is optimal.

Example: Mission Improbable [kattis:improbable]
Your mission is to rob a warehouse containing large cubical crates, all of the same size. These crates are stacked in piles, forming a square grid. The grid is monitored by three cameras. The first camera, in front, determines for each row the height of the tallest pile, while the second camera, on the side, does the same for each column. The third camera, overhead, shows whether or not each pile is empty.

   The input to the problem is a square matrix M of integers indicating the height of each pile in the grid. Your goal is to steal away with the maximum number of crates without the surveillance cameras detecting a change.

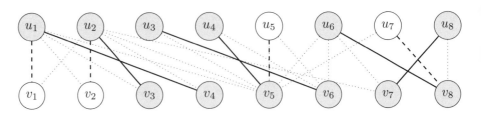

Figure 9.4 Computation of a minimal covering by edges. First, a maximum matching is computed, whose edges are shown with thick lines. For each unmatched vertex, shown in white, an arbitrary incident edge is added, shown with dashed lines.

A Solution

First, observe that if we can diminish the height of a pile without getting caught, then we can shrink it down to a single crate. So—which piles are ripe for the taking? To fix the notation, the *height* of a row or column is defined as the maximal height of its piles.

Consider a stack of height $h > 1$ at the intersection of a row and column the heights of which are strictly greater than h. Then, we can safely make off with all but one of the crates in this stack, as there are other piles in the same row and same column that will be higher.

Now, fix a height $h > 1$ and consider the bipartite graph the vertices of which are the rows on one hand, and the columns on the other, and for which there is an edge for each stack of height exactly h. We ignore the isolated vertices in this graph and mark the vertices corresponding to the rows and columns with maximal height exactly h. The non-isolated unmarked vertices have a value strictly greater than h. We must find a minimal set S of edges in this graph covering all the marked vertices. These edges correspond to piles that we must preserve in order to go undetected by the cameras.

If an edge is between two unmarked vertices, it will not be part of an optimal solution S, since it cannot be used to cover a marked vertex. Now consider two edges (u, v) and (u, v') with u, v marked and v' unmarked. Then, an optimal solution exists without the edge (u, v'), as we can always exchange it with the edge (u, v). Hence, for each marked vertex u in this graph, if it has at least one marked neighbour, then we can suppress all the edges incident to u leading to unmarked neighbours.

Similarly, if a marked vertex exists without unmarked neighbours, we can choose an arbitrary incident edge for the optimal solution S. The result of these rules is the classic problem of the covering by edges in a bipartite graph, since all the remaining edges are between marked vertices. Note that from a practical point of view, it is not necessary to construct such a graph for each height h; instead, we can construct the union of these graphs and invoke one single time an algorithm to find a minimal covering by edges.

9.2   Maximal-Weight Perfect Matching—Kuhn–Munkres

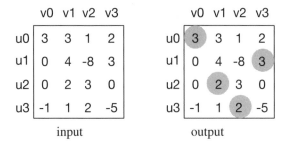

input   output

Application

In a teaching department there are n courses to distribute amongst n teachers. Each teacher has provided preferences in the form of weights for each course. The problem does not need normalisation, as some teachers might have more influence than others. No one ever said that life had to be fair! The goal is to find a bijection between courses and teachers maximising the total weights of the preferences over all of the assignments. This is the problem of perfect maximum-weighted matching in a bipartite graph.

Definition

Let $G(U, V, E)$ be a bipartite graph with weights $w : E \to \mathbb{R}$ on the edges. Without loss of generality, we can suppose $|U| = |V|$ and that the graph is complete, i.e. $E = U \times V$. The goal is to find a perfect matching $M \subseteq E$ maximising the weight $\sum_{e \in M} w(e)$ (also called *profit*).

Variants

A variant of this problem is to compute a perfect matching of minimal cost. In this case, it suffices to change the signs of the weights and then solve the problem of maximal profit. If $|U| > |V|$, it suffices to add new vertices to V, linked to all the vertices of U with weight 0. There is then a correspondence between the perfect matchings of this new graph with the maximum matchings of the original graph. If the graph is not complete, it suffices to complete it with edges of weight $-\infty$; these will never be selected for an optimal solution.

Complexity

The Kuhn–Munkres algorithm, also known as the *Hungarian method*, has complexity in time of $O(|V|^3)$. This name is a reference to the Hungarian mathematicians Denes Kőnig and Jenő Egerváry, who inspired the American Harold Kuhn to discover this method in 1955. James Munkres then proved, in 1957, its polynomial complexity (see Kuhn, 1955; Munkres, 1957). In 2006, it was found that the German mathematician Carl Gustav Jacob Jacobi had, in fact, discovered this algorithm in 1840, published posthumously only in 1890, see Ollivier (2009a,b)!

Algorithm

This is an algorithm belonging to the class of what is known as *primal-dual algorithms*, so named because they are modelled using linear programming. The description given here is quite simple, and will not use the vocabulary of linear programming.

The principal idea consists of considering a related problem, that of *minimal valid labels*. The labels are weights ℓ on the vertices, and they are *valid* if for every edge (u, v)

$$\ell(u) + \ell(v) \geq w(u, v). \tag{9.1}$$

The dual problem consists of finding valid labels with minimal total weight. By summing the inequality over all of the edges (u, v) of a matching we easily see that the total weight of any valid labelling is equal to or greater than the weight of any perfect matching.

The labels ℓ define a set E_ℓ made up of all the edges (u, v) such that

$$\ell(u) + \ell(v) = w(u, v).$$

The graph restricted to these edges is called the *equality subgraph*.

If ever we could find valid labels ℓ and a perfect matching $M \subseteq E_\ell$ then the value of $\sum_{E_\ell} \ell$ is equal to the value of $|M|$. Since the value of $\sum_{E_\ell} \ell$ bounds above that of any perfect matching, this shows that M is of maximal weight.

The goal is thus to produce such a couple ℓ, M. At any moment, the algorithm has valid labels ℓ as well as a matching $M \subseteq E_\ell$. Then repeatedly, the algorithm will attempt to augment the matching M, or if this is not possible, to improve the labels (diminish their total value).

Extend the Matching

To extend the matching, we must look for an augmenting path in the equality subgraph. For this, we construct an alternating tree. We begin by choosing a free vertex in $u_i \in U$, i.e. not yet coupled by M. This vertex will be the root of the tree. The tree alternates between vertices of U and of V. It also alternates from one level to another between the edges of $E_\ell \backslash M$ and the edges of M. Such a tree can be constructed with, for example, a depth-first search. If ever one of the leaves of v is itself free, then the path from u_i to v is an augmenting path, and it is possible to augment M along this path and increment $|M|$ by 1. In this case, the construction of the alternating tree can be interrupted.

Properties of the Alternating Tree

Consider the situation where the matching could not be extended. We have thus constructed an alternating tree A rooted at a free vertex u_i, with the property that none of the vertices of $V \cap A$ are free. Denote A_U the vertices of U covered by A and A_V the vertices of V covered by A. We then have $|A_U| = 1 + |A_V|$. In other words, A_U is composed of the root of A plus the vertices matched with each vertex of A_V.

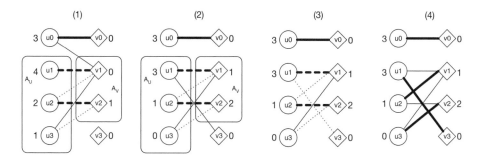

Figure 9.5 The steps of the Kuhn–Munkres algorithm. (1) The bipartite graph described by the weight matrix given at the start of the section, with the labels of the vertices, the edges of the equality subgraph and in thick lines the edges of a matching. The edges of a maximal alternating tree rooted at u_3 are shown in dotted lines. This tree covers the sets of vertices A_U, A_V and can no longer be extended. (2) The improvement of the labels reveals a new (u_1, v_3). (3) The alternating tree includes the free vertex v_3. (4) The matching can be extended along the path from u_3 to v_3.

Improving the Labelling

We must be cautious when improving the labelling. On one hand, the labels must remain valid, and on the other hand, the tree A must remain an equality subgraph. Hence, if ever we diminish the label of the root u_i by a value $\Delta > 0$, then we must increase by the same value its descendants in the tree, which allows us to in turn diminish by Δ all their descendants. Finally, the improvement consists of diminishing by Δ the labels of all the vertices of A_U and increasing by Δ the labels of the vertices in A_V. The total value of the labelling will thus diminish strictly, since $|A_U| > |A_V|$. Observe that the difference between the left and right sides of the expression (9.1)— known as the *slack*—is preserved when $u, v \in A$ or $u, v \notin A$, hence the tree A remains in the equality subgraph. For the validity of the labels, it suffices to consider the edges (u, v) with $u \in A_U$ and $v \notin A_V$. Hence, we can choose Δ as the minimal slack over these edges, see Figure 9.5.

Progress

This procedure has the advantage that an additional edge between A_U and $V \setminus A_V$ will be introduced into the equality graph. This is notably the case of the edge determining the minimal slack Δ, since its slack then becomes 0. Note that other edges of this graph might disappear, but this is of no importance for this algorithm.

Initialisation

To initiate the algorithm, we begin with a valid labelling ℓ and an empty matching M. To keep things simple, we choose $\ell(v) = 0$ for every $v \in V$, and $\ell(u) = \max_{v \in V} w(u, v)$ for every $u \in U$.

An Implementation in Time $O(|V|^4)$

Our implementation features an outer loop over the vertices $u_i \in U$, the invariant of which claims that the vertices already seen are all matched by M. This loop has for complexity a factor of $O(|V|)$. Then, for each free vertex u_i, we attempt to extend the matching by constructing an alternating tree, or improving the labels if necessary. The construction of the alternating tree costs $O(|V|^2)$.

After each improvement of the labels, the alternating tree expands, and in particular $|A_V|$ increases strictly. However, $|A_V|$ is bounded by $|U|$, hence the expansion of the matching costs $O(|V|^3)$, and the total complexity is $O(|V|^4)$.

```python
def improve_matching(G, u, mu, mv, au, av, lu, lv):
    assert not au[u]
    au[u] = True
    for v in range(len(G)):
        if not av[v] and G[u][v] == lu[u] + lv[v]:
            av[v] = True
            if mv[v] is None or \
                improve_matching(G, mv[v], mu, mv, au, av, lu, lv):
                mv[v] = u
                mu[u] = v
                return True
    return False


def improve_labels(G, au, av, lu, lv):
    U = V = range(len(G))
    delta = min(min(lu[u] + lv[v] - G[u][v]
                    for v in V if not av[v]) for u in U if au[u])
    for u in U:
        if (au[u]):
            lu[u] -= delta
    for v in V:
        if (av[v]):
            lv[v] += delta


def kuhn_munkres(G):        # maximum profit bipartite matching in O(n^4)
    assert len(G) == len(G[0])
    n = len(G)
    mu = [None] * n                      # Empty matching
    mv = [None] * n
    lu = [max(row) for row in G]         # Trivial labels
    lv = [0] * n
    for u0 in range(n):
        if mu[u0] is None:               # Free node
            while True:
                au = [False] * n         # Empty alternating tree
                av = [False] * n
                if improve_matching(G, u0, mu, mv, au, av, lu, lv):
                    break
                improve_labels(G, au, av, lu, lv)
    return (mu, sum(lu) + sum(lv))
```

Implementation Details

The vertices of U are encoded by the integers 0 to $n - 1$, as are those of V. This leads us to encode ℓ in two arrays lu and lv, one for each set U, V. Similarly, mu and mv hold the matching, where mu[u] = v, mv[u] = v if $u \in U$ is matched with $v \in V$.

The free vertices are indicated by mu[u] = None or mv[v] = None. Finally, the Boolean arrays au and av indicate whether a vertex is covered by an alternating tree.

An Implementation in Time $O(|V|^3)$

To obtain a cubic execution time, we must maintain an array slackVal to ease the computation of Δ in the improvement of the labelling. For each vertex $v \in V \setminus A_V$ we will thus have

$$\text{slackVal}_v = \min_{u \in A_U} \ell(u) + \ell(v) - w(u, v).$$

Another array slackArg holds the vertex u minimising the expression.

With these arrays, it is easier to augment the tree, as it is no longer necessary to reconstruct it from the root at each change of labels. The tree is thus no longer constructed with a depth-first search, but by selecting new edges in the following manner.

We select an edge (u, v) minimising the slack with $u \in A$ and $v \notin A$. If the slack is not zero, then the labels can be updated as explained above, resulting in the reduction of the slack of (u, v) to zero. In every case, (u, v) is an edge that can be attached to the tree. Two cases must be considered. Either v is not matched, and we have detected an augmenting path. Or v is already matched to some vertex u': in this case, we can also add (u', v) to the tree A, and hence u' to A_U, then update the slacks in linear time, and iterate. Thus, an augmenting path is found in quadratic time. Once a vertex of U becomes matched, it stays so forever; thus there are only $|V|$ augmenting paths to be found. The final complexity is indeed $O(|V|^3)$.

Implementation Details

This time, we would like to know for each vertex in V if it belongs to the tree, and if so, what is its predecessor. As the tree is not constructed by a depth-first search, this information must be stored in an array. It will allow us to climb back to the root when we need to update the matching. We assign Av[v] as the predecessor of $v \in A_V$, and set Av[v] = None for every vertex $v \in V \setminus A_V$ outside of the tree. The name of the array begins with a capital letter to distinguish it from the Boolean array encoding A_U.

The arrays slackVal and slackArg will be represented by a single array slack, containing the pairs (val, arg). This implementation accepts graphs $G(U, V, E)$ with $|U| \neq |V|$.

```
def kuhn_munkres(G, TOLERANCE=1e-6):
    nU = len(G)
    U = range(nU)
    nV = len(G[0])
    V = range(nV)
    assert nU <= nV
    mu = [None] * nU                       # empty matching
    mv = [None] * nV
    lu = [max(row) for row in G]     # trivial labels
    lv = [0] * nV
    for root in U:                         # build an alternate tree
        au = [False] * nU              # au, av mark nodes...
        au[root] = True                # ... covered by the tree
        Av = [None] * nV               # Av[v] successor of v in the tree
        # for every vertex u, slack[u] := (val, v) such that
        # val is the smallest slack on the constraints (*)
        # with fixed u and v being the corresponding vertex
        slack = [(lu[root] + lv[v] - G[root][v], root) for v in V]
        while True:
            (delta, u), v = min((slack[v], v) for v in V if Av[v] is None)
            assert au[u]
            if delta > TOLERANCE:      # tree is full
                for u0 in U:               # improve labels
                    if au[u0]:
                        lu[u0] -= delta
                for v0 in V:
                    if Av[v0] is not None:
                        lv[v0] += delta
                    else:
                        (val, arg) = slack[v0]
                        slack[v0] = (val - delta, arg)
            assert abs(lu[u] + lv[v] - G[u][v]) <= TOLERANCE  # equality
            Av[v] = u                  # add (u, v) to A
            if mv[v] is None:
                break                  # alternating path found
            u1 = mv[v]
            assert not au[u1]
            au[u1] = True              # add (u1, v) to A
            for v1 in V:
                if Av[v1] is None:     # update margins
                    alt = (lu[u1] + lv[v1] - G[u1][v1], u1)
                    if slack[v1] > alt:
                        slack[v1] = alt
        while v is not None:           # ... alternating path found
            u = Av[v]                  # along path to root
            prec = mu[u]
            mv[v] = u                  # augment matching
            mu[u] = v
            v = prec
    return (mu, sum(lu) + sum(lv))
```

Perfect Matching Minimising the Edge of Maximal Weight

Definition
Given a bipartite graph $G(U, V, E)$ weighted on the edges $w : E \to \mathbb{Z}$, once again the goal is to find a perfect matching M. However, instead of maximising the total edge weight of M, we would like to minimise the maximum of an edge of M, hence compute $\min_M \max_{e \in M} w(e)$ over all perfect matchings.

Reduction to the Problem of Maximal Matching
Suppose that the edges are ordered by increasing weight. For a given threshold k, we could test whether a perfect matching exists in the graph restricted to the first k edges. As this property is monotone in k, it is possible to solve the problem by binary search on the interval $[|V|, |E|]$.

However, by exploiting the particular behaviour of the algorithm seeking a perfect matching, we can avoid the binary search and save a factor of $O(\log |E|)$ in the complexity.

The algorithm seeks to construct a perfect matching by extending the current matching with an augmenting path, found by constructing a forest of alternating trees. We initialise the variable k to 0; and maintain a matching M and an alternating tree for M in the graph restricted to the first k edges. Whenever the tree becomes complete without resulting in an augmenting path, we increment k and add the kth edge to the graph while eventually augmenting the alternating tree. Each extension of the matching M has a cost linear in the current number of edges, hence finding the smallest k such that the graph admits a perfect matching has a complexity of $O(|V| \cdot |E|)$.

Problem
Selfish Cities [spoj:SCITIES]

9.3   Planar Matching without Crossings

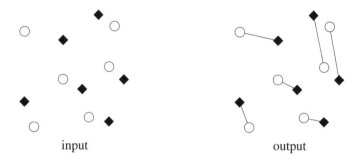

input   output

Definition
We are given n white points and n black points in the plane. We suppose that these are non-degenerate, in the sense that no three of the points are collinear. The goal is to

find a perfect matching between the white points and the black points, such that if we link all of the matched pairs with line segments, none of these intersect.

Key Observation
Imagine for an instant that the points are matched but some segments cross each other. Consider two matched pairs $u - v$ and $u' - v'$ the segments of which cross, see Figure 9.6. If we change their assignments to $u - v'$ and $u' - v$, their segments no longer intersect. Does this operation improve matters somewhat?

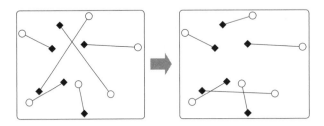

Figure 9.6 Uncross two matching segments.

Note that the total number of crossings can increase with this 'un-crossing', as in Figure 9.6. Hence, this is not the correct measure of progress. However, the total length of the segments has diminished! This observation leads us to a first algorithm.

Algorithm without Guarantee of Performance
Start by arbitrarily matching black and white points. As long two matched pairs exist with segments that cross uncross them. By the preceding observation, this algorithm is guaranteed to find a solution. Moreover, our experiments have shown that, in fact, the performance is quite good in practice!

Algorithm in $O(n^3)$ by Reduction to a Minimal-Cost Perfect Matching
We define a complete bipartite graph $G(U, V, E)$, where U are the white points, V black points and for every $u \in U$ and $v \in V$ the cost of the edge (u, v) is the Euclidean distance between the two points. The preceding observation shows that a perfect matching with minimal cost is necessarily without crossings. Thus, it suffices to apply the Kuhn–Munkres algorithm to the graph to solve the problem. However, we can suspect that too much work is being done here, since a matching without crossings is not necessarily of minimal cost.

Algorithm in $O(n \log n)$
Indeed, a much better algorithm exists that is based on the *ham sandwich* theorem, proved by Banach in 1938. This theorem states that given n black points and n white points in the plane in a non-degenerate configuration, then a line exists such that on either side of it there are as many black points as white (exactly $\lfloor n/2 \rfloor$ of each). More precisely, if n is odd, the line passes by a white point and a black point, while if n is even, the line does not cross any of the points.

An algorithm from Matousek, Lo and Steiger (1994) computes this line in time $O(n)$. However, it is complex to implement.

How does this help us? With the guarantee that there are no three collinear points, we obtain the following property. Either n is even, so that the separating line contains none of the points, or n is odd and the separating line contains exactly one white point and one black point. In the latter case, it is correct to match them. And in any case, we can iterate on the two independent sub-instances separated by the line. This recursive decomposition has a depth $O(\log_2 n)$, hence the final algorithm is indeed in $O(n \log n)$.

9.4 Stable Marriages—Gale–Shapley

Definition
Suppose there are n women and n men. Each man ranks the women in order of preference, and the women rank the men in the same way. A *marriage* is a perfect matching in a complete bipartite graph between the men and the women. It is called *stable* if a man i and a woman j do not exist such that the man prefers j to his current wife, and the woman prefers i to her current husband. The goal is to compute a *stable marriage* from the $2n$ stated preferences. The solution is not necessarily unique.

Complexity
The Gale–Shapley algorithm (1962) solves this problem in time $O(n^2)$.

Algorithm
The algorithm starts with no married couples. Then, as long as there are single men, the algorithm selects a bachelor i and the woman j that i likes best among the women who have not yet been considered. The algorithm then seeks to marry i with j. The wedding will take place if j is still single, or if j is married to a man k but prefers i to k. In this case, k is summarily divorced and sent off to continue partying with the group of single men.

Analysis
For the complexity, every couple i, j is considered at most once by the algorithm, and the work to do for each couple takes constant time. For the validity, it suffices to observe that as the algorithm proceeds, (1) a given woman is married to men that she prefers more and more, while (2) a given man is married to women that he prefers less and less. Hence, for a proof by contradiction of the algorithm's validity, suppose that at the end a man i married to a woman j' and a woman j married to a man i' exist such that i prefers j to j' and j prefers i to i'. By observation (2), at some point in time the algorithm examined the couple i, j. However, by (1), the algorithm never married i with j. This means that at the moment the couple (i, j) was considered, j must have

been married with a man k that she preferred to i. This contradicts the fact that she ends up being married to a man she likes less than i.

Implementation Details

In our implementation, the men are numbered from 0 to $n - 1$, as are the women. The input consists of two arrays. The array men contains for each man his list of n preferred women, in decreasing order. The array women contains the women's corresponding lists of preferences. The array women is first transformed into a array rank containing for each woman j and man i the rank of preference that j has for i. For example, if rank[j][i] = 0, then i is the preferred man of j, and if rank[j][i'] = 1, then i' is the second on the list for j, etc.

Finally, the array spouse associates with each woman the man with whom she is *currently*[2] married. The queue singles contains the single men, and for each man i, current_suitor[i] indicates the index of the next woman to be wooed in his list of preferences.

```python
from collections import deque


def gale_shapley(men, women):
    n = len(men)
    assert n == len(women)
    current_suitor = [0] * n
    spouse = [None] * n
    rank = [[0] * n for j in range(n)]  # build rank
    for j in range(n):
        for r in range(n):
            rank[j][women[j][r]] = r
    singles = deque(range(n))  # all men are single and get in the queue
    while singles:
        i = singles.popleft()
        j = men[i][current_suitor[i]]
        current_suitor[i] += 1
        if spouse[j] is None:
            spouse[j] = i
        elif rank[j][spouse[j]] < rank[j][i]:
            singles.append(i)
        else:
            singles.put(spouse[j])  # sorry for spouse[j]
            spouse[j] = i
    return spouse
```

Problem

Stable Marriage Problem [spoj:STABLEMP]

---

[2] Note from the translator: the divorce lawyers must be rubbing their hands with glee!

9.5   Maximum Flow by Ford–Fulkerson

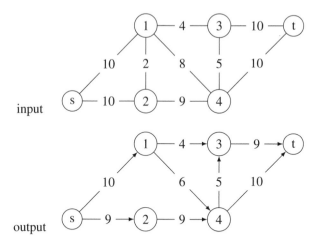

Application

This algorithm can be used to find the bottlenecks in the evacuation of passengers from an aircraft, or the resistance of an electrical network. In fact, numerous problems can be modelled as a maximum flow in a graph.

Much of the pioneering work in this domain was done in the 1950s, in the context of the Cold War. The original paper by Ford and Fulkerson was in fact a memorandum of the RAND corporation, and was motivated by ... studies of the Soviet Railway system[3]! A top-secret report, 'Fundamentals of a Method for Evaluating Rail Net Capacities', unclassified only in 1999, describes how this algorithm, and the related minimum-cut algorithms (see Section 9.8), could be used to evaluate the capacity of the Soviet railway system, and the optimal way to disable it! A fascinating article on this topic is Schrijver (2002).

Definition

Formally, we are given a directed graph $G(V, A)$ with capacities on the arcs $c : A \to \mathbb{R}^+$ and two distinct vertices: a *source* $s \in V$ and a *sink* $t \in V$. Without loss of generality, we can suppose that for each arc (u, v) the arc (v, u) is also present in the graph, since we can always add arcs of capacity zero without modifying the optimal solution.

A *flow* is a function $f : A \to \mathbb{R}$, satisfying that:

$$\forall (u, v) \in A : f(u, v) = -f(v, u), \tag{9.2}$$

while respecting the capacities

$$\forall e \in A : f(e) \le c(e), \tag{9.3}$$

---

[3] Thanks to Maxim Berman for bringing this to our attention.

and respecting the conservation of flows at each vertex, other than at the source and the sink:

$$\forall v \in V \setminus \{s,t\} : \sum_{u:(u,v) \in A} f(u,v) = 0. \tag{9.4}$$

The interpretation of $f(u,v) > 0$ is that $f(u,v)$ units are flowing through the arc (u,v). However, if $f(u,v) < 0$, then no flow is traversing the arc (u,v). The skew symmetric condition (9.2) has been imposed to simplify the notation in (9.4).

The value of the flow is the quantity emanating from the source, $\sum_v f(s,v)$. The goal is to find the flow of maximal value.

Non-Directed Graphs

In a non-directed graph, we replace each edge (u,v) by the two arcs (u,v) and (v,u) with the same capacity.

Residual Graph and Augmenting Paths

For a given flow f, we consider the *residual* graph consisting of all the arcs (u,v) with positive *residual capacity* $c(u,v) - f(u,v)$. In this graph, a path P from s to t is called an *augmenting* path, as we can augment the flow along the edges of this path by a value Δ, which is the minimal residual capacity along the arcs of P. To preserve (9.2) as we augment $f(u,v)$, we must diminish $f(v,u)$ by the same amount.

The Ford–Fulkerson Algorithm

The Ford–Fulkerson algorithm has complexity $O(|V| \cdot |A| \cdot C)$ where $C = \max_{a \in A} c(a)$. For this algorithm to terminate, the capacities must be integers. It repeatedly seeks an augmenting path P and augments the flow along P. The search for a path is performed using a depth-first search, and the only guarantee is that at each iteration the flow increases strictly. The value of a flow is bounded by the total capacities of the arcs leaving the source, hence by $|A| \cdot C$. This proves the announced complexity.

Implementation Details

In our implementation, the graph is described with an adjacency list; however, to ease the manipulation of the flows, the flow is represented by a two-dimensional matrix F. The procedure augment attempts to augment the flow along a path from u to target with a value at most val. The procedure returns the amount of the augmentation of the flow in the case of success and zero otherwise. It looks for this path via a depth-first search and for this uses the marker visit.

```
def _augment(graph, capacity, flow, val, u, target, visit):
    visit[u] = True
    if u == target:
        return val
    for v in graph[u]:
        cuv = capacity[u][v]
        if not visit[v] and cuv > flow[u][v]:  # reachable arc
            res = min(val, cuv - flow[u][v])
            delta = _augment(graph, capacity, flow, res, v, target, visit)
            if delta > 0:
                flow[u][v] += delta               # augment flow
                flow[v][u] -= delta
                return delta
    return 0


def ford_fulkerson(graph, capacity, s, t):
    add_reverse_arcs(graph, capacity)
    n = len(graph)
    flow = [[0] * n for _ in range(n)]
    INF = float('inf')
    while _augment(graph, capacity, flow, INF, s, t, [False] * n) > 0:
        pass                             # work already done in _augment
    return (flow, sum(flow[s]))          # flow network, amount of flow
```

Doubling Flow Algorithm

A potential improvement to this algorithm was proposed by Goldberg and Rao (1998) and has complexity $O(|V| \cdot |A| \cdot \log C)$. Rather then blindly augmenting the first path found, it attempts to improve the flow by a large value each time. More precisely, let C be the largest capacity on the arcs of the graph, and Δ the largest power of 2 equal to or less than C. Then we could repeatedly seek to augment the flow with paths augmenting the residual capacity by at least Δ. When this is no longer possible, we continue with a value of Δ a factor of two smaller, and so on. The last step with $\Delta = 1$ finishes when s and t are disconnected in the residual graph, hence the algorithm indeed computes a maximum flow.

For the first step, by the definition of C, we know that the maximum flow is bounded above by $|V| \cdot C$. Hence, the first step involves at most n augmenting paths. The search for such a path costs $O(|V| + |A|)$. Since there are only $\log_2 C$ steps, the total complexity of this algorithm is $O(|V| \cdot |A| \cdot \log C)$.

Problems
Potholers [spoj:POTHOLE]
Maximum Flow [spoj:FLOW]

9.6   Maximum Flow by Edmonds–Karp

Observation

The Ford–Fulkerson and Goldberg–Rao algorithms have the annoying property that their complexities depend on the given capacities. Happily, a small transformation exists that renders the complexity independent of C (see Edmonds and Karp, 1972).

Surprisingly, applying the same algorithm, but first to the shortest augmenting paths, results in a complexity that is independent of the maximal capacity. The idea is that the length of the shortest augmenting path increases strictly for at most $|E|$ iterations. This is due to the following observations:

- Let L_f be the *level graph* of G, where s is at level 0, all the vertices reachable from s by a *non-saturated* arc[4] form the level 1, and so on. It is hence an acyclic subgraph of the residual graph.
- An arc (u, v) is *admissible* if its flow is strictly below its capacity and if v is on the next level after u.
- A shortest path from s to t in the residual graph is necessarily a path in the level graph. If we augment the flow along this path, one of its arcs must become saturated.
- An augmentation along a path can render certain arcs non-saturated, but only arcs towards lower levels. Hence, the arcs that become admissible cannot decrease the distance from s to v counted in number of arcs. By symmetry, the distance from v to t cannot decrease either.
- After at most $|E| + 1$ iterations, an arc (u, v) and its inverse (v, u) must have been saturated. This proves that at some point the vertex u has changed level, and by the preceding observation the distance from s to t has strictly increased.
- As there are only n levels, there are at most $|V| \cdot |E|$ iterations in all.
- The search for a shortest path is done with breadth-first search in time $O(|V|)$. The total complexity is thus $O(|V| \cdot |E|^2)$.

Edmonds–Karp Algorithm in $O(|V| \cdot |E|^2)$

Starting with an empty flow, as long as augmenting paths exist, augment along a shortest augmenting path.

Implementation Details

The shortest augmenting paths are found with a breadth-first search (BFS), with the help of a queue Q. The array augm_path has two functions. First, it serves to mark the vertices already visited by the BFS traversal.[5] Then, rather than simply marking the vertices with a Boolean, we store the predecessor on the path from the source to the vertex in question. Thus, we can trace back to the source by following the values of augm_path to augment the flow along this path. The array A contains for each visited vertex v the minimal residual capacity along the path from the source to v. With this array, we can determine by how much the flow can be augmented along the augmenting path found.

---

[4] An arc is saturated if the flow equals the capacity of the arc.
[5] Do you understand why it is necessary to mark augm_path[source]?

```
def _augment(graph, capacity, flow, source, target):
    n = len(graph)
    A = [0] * n                     # A[v] = min residual cap. on path source->v
    augm_path = [None] * n          # None = node was not visited yet
    Q = deque()                     # BFS
    Q.append(source)
    augm_path[source] = source
    A[source] = float('inf')
    while Q:
        u = Q.popleft()
        for v in graph[u]:
            cuv = capacity[u][v]
            residual = cuv - flow[u][v]
            if residual > 0 and augm_path[v] is None:
                augm_path[v] = u    # store predecessor
                A[v] = min(A[u], residual)
                if v == target:
                    break
                Q.append(v)
    return (augm_path, A[target])   # augmenting path, min residual cap.


def edmonds_karp(graph, capacity, source, target):
    add_reverse_arcs(graph, capacity)
    V = range(len(graph))
    flow = [[0 for v in V] for u in V]
    while True:
        augm_path, delta = _augment(graph, capacity, flow, source, target)
        if delta == 0:
            break
        v = target                  # go back to source
        while v != source:
            u = augm_path[v]        # augment flow
            flow[u][v] += delta
            flow[v][u] -= delta
            v = u
    return (flow, sum(flow[source])) # flow network, amount of flow
```

9.7 Maximum Flow by Dinic

The idea of Dinic's algorithm, discovered at the same time as the preceding algorithm, is the following. Rather than seeking a set of augmenting paths one by one, up until the distance between s and t increases, we find such a flow with a single traversal. This reduces the complexity to $O(|V|^2 \cdot |E|)$ (see Dinitz, 2006).

Imagine a function dinic(u,val) that attempts to pass a flow from u to t in the level graph. The restriction is that the flow is not greater than val. The function then returns the value of this flow, which can be improved along the path from s to u, by the successive invocations that led to u. More precisely, to *push* a flow with value val from u to t, we visit all the neighbours v of u in the level graph, and recursively attempt to pass a maximum flow from v to t. The sum is then the maximum flow that we can *push* from u to t.

The function `dinic(u,val)` then detects if no additional flow can pass from u to t, and t thus becomes inaccessible from u. In this case, it removes u from the level graph, simply by indicating a dummy level -1. Hence, the subsequent calls will no longer attempt to pass flow through u. Clearly, after $O(n)$ iterations, s and t are disconnected, and we compute a new level graph, see Figure 9.7.

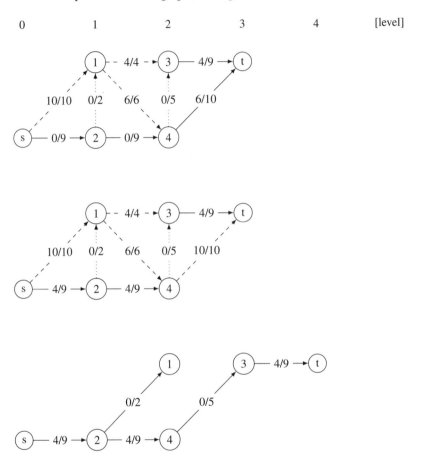

Figure 9.7 The evolution of the level graph during the execution of Dinic's algorithm. Only the arcs from one level to the next are shown, labelled by f/c where f is the flow and c the capacity. The dashed lines show the saturated, hence non-passable, arcs, while the dotted lines show the arcs that will later become part of the level graph. After having augmented the flow of value 4 along the path $s - 2 - 4 - t$, the vertex t becomes disconnected. It is thus necessary to reconstruct the level graph, shown on the bottom.

Even if an adjacency list is used to represent the graph, it is more practical to use matrices for the residual capacity and the flow. We must pay attention that each operation preserves the symmetry $f(u,v) = -f(v,u)$.

Implementation Details
The array `level` contains the level of a vertex in the level graph. This graph is recomputed as soon as the sink is no longer accessible from the source. The function

dinic_step pushes as much flow as possible from *u* to the sink, without exceeding the given limit. For this, it pushes a maximum of flow to its neighbours *v* in the level graph, and accumulates in val the quantity of flow already pushed. When no further flow can be sent, the vertex *v* can be removed from the level graph, by setting its level to None.

Problem
Fast Maximum Flow [spoj:FASTFLOW]

```
def dinic(graph, capacity, source, target):
    assert source != target
    add_reverse_arcs(graph, capacity)
    Q = deque()
    total = 0
    n = len(graph)
    flow = [[0] * n for u in range(n)]   # flow initially empty
    while True:                          # repeat while we can increase
        Q.appendleft(source)
        level = [None] * n               # build levels, None = inaccessible
        level[source] = 0                # by BFS
        while Q:
            u = Q.pop()
            for v in graph[u]:
                if level[v] is None and capacity[u][v] > flow[u][v]:
                    level[v] = level[u] + 1
                    Q.appendleft(v)

        if level[target] is None:   # stop if sink is not reachable
            return flow, total
        up_bound = sum(capacity[source][v] for v in graph[source]) - total
        total += _dinic_step(graph, capacity, level, flow, source, target,
                             up_bound)


def _dinic_step(graph, capacity, level, flow, u, target, limit):
    if limit <= 0:
        return 0
    if u == target:
        return limit
    val = 0
    for v in graph[u]:
        residual = capacity[u][v] - flow[u][v]
        if level[v] == level[u] + 1 and residual > 0:
            z = min(limit, residual)
            aug = _dinic_step(graph, capacity, level, flow, v, target, z)
            flow[u][v] += aug
            flow[v][u] -= aug
            val += aug
            limit -= aug
    if val == 0:
        level[u] = None          # remove unreachable node
    return val
```

9.8   Minimum $s - t$ Cut

Application

In a country, there are several roads linking various cities. A railway company wants to attract customers to its new train line connecting city s with city t, and wishes to place billboard advertisements along certain of these roads, so that every trip from s to t must traverse one of these roads. The goal is to minimise the number of billboards for this task.

Definition

An instance of this problem consists of a directed graph $G(V, A)$ with two distinct vertices s, t and a cost for each arc $c : A \to \mathbb{R}^+$. An $s - t$ *cut* is a set $S \in V$ containing s but not t. Equivalently, the cut S is sometimes identified by the arcs leaving S, i.e. the arcs (u, v) with $u \in S$ and $v \notin S$, see Figure 9.8. The value of the cut is the total cost of these arcs. The goal is to find the cut with minimal cost.

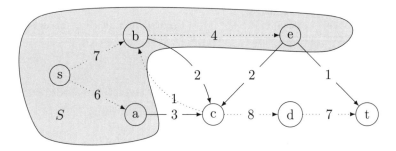

Figure 9.8 A minimum $s - t$ cut S of cost $3 + 2 + 2 + 1 = 8$. The arcs leaving S are drawn with solid lines.

Link with the Maximum Flow Problem

Suppose we identify the capacities c of a maximum flow problem with the costs c of a minimum cut problem. Every flow must traverse the cut, hence the value of any cut is an upper bound for the value of any flow. But we can do even better:

The MAX-FLOW-MIN-CUT theorem states that the value of the maximum flow is equal to the value of the minimum cut.

This theorem was shown independently by Elias, Feinstein and Shannon (1956) on one hand and by Ford and Fulkerson (1956) on the other. The proof follows from a sequence of several simple observations.

1. For a flow f the quantity of the flow leaving a cut S, i.e. $f(S) = \sum_{u \in S, v \notin S} f(u, v)$, is the same for every S. This is simply because for any $w \notin S, w \neq t$, we have (by (9.4) and then by (9.2))

$$f(S) = \sum_{u \in S, v \notin S} f(u,v) = \sum_{u \in S, v \notin S} f(u,v) + \sum_{v} f(w,v)$$

$$= \sum_{u \in S, v \notin S, v \neq w} f(u,v) + \sum_{u \in S} f(u,w) + \sum_{v \in S} f(w,v) + \sum_{v \notin S} f(w,v)$$

$$= \sum_{u \in S \cup w, v \notin S \cup w} f(u,v) = f(S \cup w).$$

2. By (9.3), we have $f(S) \leq c(S)$, i.e. the flow leaving S is never greater than that of S. This already proves half of the theorem—the value of the maximum flow is at most the value of the minimum cut.

3. Now, if for a given flow f, we have $f(S) < c(S)$ for every cut S, then an augmenting path exists. For this, we start with $S = \{s\}$ and $A = \emptyset$. Since $f(S) < c(S)$, an arc (u,v) exists with $u \in S, v \notin S, f(u,v) < c(u,v)$. We add (u,v) to A and v to S, and repeat while $t \notin S$. During this process, A is a spanning tree of S rooted at the source, using only non-saturated arcs. Eventually, A will reach the sink t and contain an augmenting path.

Algorithm

This observation leads us to an algorithm to solve the minimum cut problem. First, we compute a maximum flow. Then, in the residual graph, we determine the set S of vertices v reachable from s by arcs with positive residual capacity. Then, S does not contain t, as the existence of an augmenting path contradicts the optimality of the flow. The maximal character of S means that every arc leaving S is saturated by the flow, and its residual capacity is zero. Hence, S is a cut of minimal value.

9.9   *s* − *t* Minimum Cut for Planar Graphs

Planar Graphs

The $s - t$ minimum cut problem can be solved more efficiently in the case of a planar graph[6] where the embedding in the plane is given. To simplify the presentation, we suppose that the graph is a planar grid. This grid is made up of vertices linked by arcs, which decompose the plane into areas known as *faces*. Imagine that the grid is rectangular, that the source is the vertex on the bottom left and the sink is the vertex on the top right.

Dual Graphs

In the *dual* graph, each face becomes a vertex, and there are two additional vertices s' and t'. The vertex s' represents the left and top boundary of the grid and the vertex t' the right and bottom boundary. In this new graph, two vertices are connected if the

---

[6] A graph is *planar* if it is possible to draw it in the plane without edges crossing each other. Formally, a mapping of the vertices to some points must exist (embedding) such that the arcs (segments) intersect only at their endpoints.

corresponding faces are adjacent. The edge between the dual vertices has the same weight as the primal edge at the contact line between the faces.

Key Observation
Every $s' - t'$ path in the dual graph of length w corresponds to an $s - t$ cut in the primal graph with the same value w, and vice-versa.

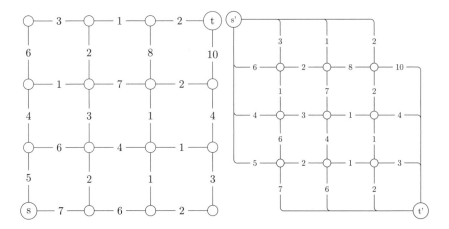

Figure 9.9 On the left, the primal graph. On the right, the dual graph: a minimal-length $s' - t'$-path corresponds to an $s - t$ minimum cut.

Algorithm in $O((|V| + |E|) \log |V|)$
Hence to compute a minimum cut in this grid, it suffices to find a shortest path in the dual graph, for example, with Dijkstra's algorithm.

Variants
An important problem is to find a minimum cut which disconnects the graph, i.e. to find the smallest $s - t$ cut over all pairs s, t of vertices. This problem can be solved with the Stoer–Wagner algorithm in time $O(|V| \cdot |E| + |V|^2 \log |V|)$, which is more interesting than solving the $\Theta(|V|^2)$ $s - t$ cuts for each pair s, t of vertices, see (Stoer and Wagner, 1997).

Problem
Landscaping [kattis:landscaping]

Example: Coconuts [spoj:COCONUTS]
We are given a graph $G(V, E)$ the vertices of which are coloured white or black. The goal is to produce a set $S \subseteq V$ of minimal cost in the following sense. First, you change the colour of each vertex in S; this costs $1 per vertex. Then, there is a fine of $1 for each arc the vertices of which have a different colour. What is the least amount we have to pay? This problem can be reduced to a minimal cut problem. First, add

two vertices s,t to the graph, and then link s to all the black vertices and t to all the white vertices. Then, an $s - t$ cut in this graph is a set $S \cup \{s\}$ and the value of the cut is exactly the cost of S as described above, see Figure 9.10.

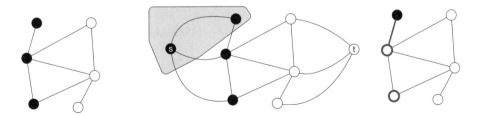

Figure 9.10 From left to right: the given graph; the instance of the min-cut problem with its optimal solution shaded; and the corresponding solution of cost \$3, where two vertices are coloured white and one edge has endpoints with distinct colours.

9.10 A Transport Problem

A generalisation of the flow problem is the *transport problem*, where several sources and sinks exist. Here, each vertex v has a value d_v, representing the supply when it is positive and the demand when it is negative. The instance must satisfy $\sum_{v \in V} d_v = 0$ in order to have a solution. The goal is to find a flow transporting the quantities proposed to the customers, hence a flow respecting the capacities and such that for each vertex v the flow entering minus the flow leaving is equal to d_v. This problem can easily be reduced to a flow problem by adding a source and a sink vertex and linking the source to all vertices with a supply, linking all vertices with a demand to the sink and setting the appropriate capacities to these new arcs.

There is a generalisation of the flow problem, where arcs have costs per unit flow in addition to capacities. For example, if an arc e has a flow $f_e = 3$ and a cost $w_e = 4$, the cost generated by the flow on this arc is 12. The goal is then to find a flow minimising the total cost. The flow can either be a maximum flow or a flow respecting all the demands in the case of a transport problem. The latter is known as a *minimal cost transport problem*.

For this problem, algorithms exist that are similar to the Kuhn–Munkres Hungarian algorithm (see Ahuja et al., 1993). A first approach could be to start with a maximum flow, and then try to repeatedly augment the flow along negative-cost cycles.

9.11 Reductions between Matchings and Flows

Two interesting links exist between the maximum bipartite matching problem and the maximum flow problem.

From Flows to Matchings

On one hand, we can use a maximum flow algorithm to compute a maximum matching in a bipartite graph $G(U, V, E)$. For this, it suffices to construct a new graph $G'(V', E')$ in which the vertices $V' = U \cup V \cup \{s, t\}$ contain two new vertices s, t. The *source* vertex s is linked to all of the vertices of U and every vertex of V is linked to the *sink* vertex t. Moreover, each arc $(u, v) \in E$ corresponds to an arc $(u, v) \in E'$. All the arcs in G' have unit capacity.

We represent this graph by levels. The first level contains s, the second U, the third V and the last t. The flow produced by the algorithm will have the property[7] that on every arc the flow has value either 0 or 1. Hence, a flow of value k in G' corresponds to k paths that traverse each level, without ever returning to a preceding level. Consequently, since the capacities are unitary, a vertex $u \in U$ cannot be crossed by more than one path and neither nor can the vertices of V. Hence, the arcs between the levels 2 and 3 traversed by the flow form a matching of size k.

From Matchings to Flows

On the other hand, we can use a maximum bipartite matching algorithm in order to solve a transport problem with capacities $c(e) = 1$ for all edges e. Let $G(V, E), (d_v)_{v \in V}$ be an instance of a transport problem.

The first step is to add a source s and a sink t, and then for every vertex v, to add $\max\{0, -d_v\}$ edges (s, v) and $\max\{0, d_v\}$ edges (v, t). The result is a graph G' with eventually multiple edges between two vertices, in which case we speak of a *multigraph*. The initial instance of the transport problem has a solution if and only if the new multigraph G' has an $s - t$ flow of value $\Delta = \sum_{v:d_v>0} d_v$.

The second step is to construct a bipartite graph $H(V^+, V^-, E')$ admitting a perfect matching, if and only if G' has an $s - t$ flow with value Δ.

For each edge of G' of the form $e = (s, v)$, we generate the vertex $e^+ \in V^+$. For each edge of G' of the form $e = (v, t)$, we generate the vertex $e^- \in V^-$. For the other edges e of G', we generate two vertices $e^- \in V^-$ and $e^+ \in V^+$ and link them with an edge. Moreover, for every pair of edges e, f such that the destination of e coincides with the origin of f, an edge (e^+, f^-) is generated.

Consider a perfect matching in H of size k. An edge in the matching of the form (e^-, e^+) corresponds to the absence of the flow traversing the edge e of G'. An edge in the matching of the form (e^+, f^-) with $e \neq f$ corresponds to a unit of flow traversing the edge e and then the edge f. By construction, all edges incident to the source or the sink are traversed by the flow. The matching corresponds to an $s - t$ flow of value k, as illustrated in Figure 9.11.

---

[7] In principle, fractional flows are possible, but all reasonable flow algorithms produce an integer flow if the capacities are integers.

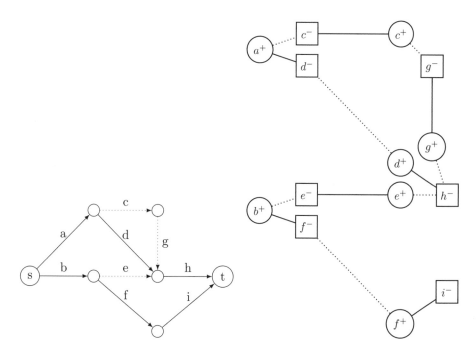

Figure 9.11 Reduction of the unit-capacity $s - t$ flow problem to a maximal bipartite matching problem. The maximum flow and corresponding maximum matching are depicted with solid lines.

9.12 Width of a Partial Order—Dilworth

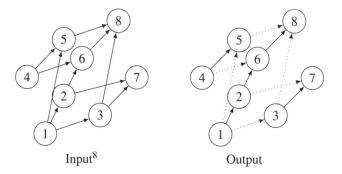

Input[8]   Output

Definition

Suppose we are given a partial order, i.e. an acyclic and transitive directed graph $G(V, A)$. A *chain* in G is a directed path and by extension the set of vertices it covers. A chain decomposition is a set of chains such that every vertex is covered by exactly one chain. Its size is defined as the number of its chains. An *antichain* in G is a set S

of vertices such that $u, v \in S$ with $(u, v) \in A$ does not exist. The *width* of the partial order is defined as the size of the largest antichain. The problem is to compute this width.

An important relation between chains and antichains is given by Dilworth's theorem (1950):

The size of the largest antichain equals the size of the smallest chain decomposition.

Showing that the size of the largest antichain is at most the size of the smallest chain decomposition is straightforward. Assume that there is an antichain longer than a smallest decomposition in chains. Then, according to the pigeonhole principle, at least two elements of the antichain should be in the same chain, which is a contradiction.

It is possible to prove the other direction either by induction on the size of the graph, or as a reduction to Kőnig's theorem (see Section 9.1 on page 142): we construct a bipartite graph $H(V, V', E)$ such that V' is a copy of V and for each arc $(u, v) \in A$ in the original graph, there is $(u, v') \in E$, where v' is a copy of v.

Let M be a maximum matching in the new graph H. By Kőnig's theorem, a set S of vertices exists that touches every edge of H, and $|M| = |S|$.

Every matching in H corresponds to a decomposition in chains: following the edges of the matching, we can recover chains in G. Every unmatched node in V corresponds to an endpoint of a chain. Hence, the size of the decomposition is the number of endpoints $|V| - |M|$, which is minimum because M is maximum.

We now want to build a longest antichain from S. If we select the nodes v in V such that neither v nor v' is in S, then we have at least $|V| - |S|$ elements. If there was an edge between any pair (v, v') of these elements, then either v or v' would be in S, which is a contradiction. Thus, the selected elements form an antichain, and we have proved Dilworth's theorem.

Algorithm in $O(|V| \cdot |E|)$

This problem can be reduced to a maximum matching problem, see Figure 9.12.

- Construct a bipartite graph $H(V, V', E)$ where V' is a copy of V and $(u, v') \in E$ if and only if $(u, v) \in A$.
- Compute a maximal bipartite matching M in H.
- Count the number of unmatched vertices in V. This is the size of the largest antichain in G, hence the width of the partial order G.
- Consider the set of arcs C in G such that $(u, v) \in C$ if and only if $(u, v) \in M$. Then C is a decomposition of V into a minimal number of chains.

Application: Reservations of Taxis [kattis:taxicab]

Imagine the following situation. A taxi company has gathered reservations for tomorrow's trajectories. During the night, it must assign the taxis in its fleet to the reservations and minimise the number of taxis employed. Each reservation starts from

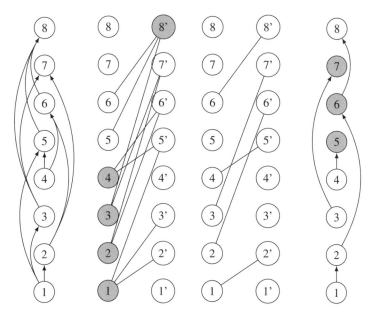

Figure 9.12 From left to right: a partial order G, the associated bipartite graph H with a covering of the vertices S marked in grey, a maximum matching in H, the decomposition into minimum chains in G associated with an antichain marked in grey.

a precise location in the city at a certain time, in order to reach a given destination. We suppose that all the source–destination travel times are known. We can thus decide if the same taxi can honour the reservation j after having completed the reservation i. In this case, we denote $i \preceq j$, and the relation $\preceq$ is a partial order on the day's reservations. The solution to the problem is simply the width of this partial order.

Generalisation

If the graph is weighted, we can look for a minimal decomposition into chains which also minimises the total weight of the arcs. This problem can be solved in time $O(|V|^3)$ by reduction to the problem of minimal-cost perfect matching in a bipartite graph.

Implementation Details

Our implementation returns an array p encoding an optimal partition, where $p[u]$ is the index of the chain containing the vertex u, where the chains are numbered starting with 0. The input is a square matrix M indicating for each pair of vertices u, v the cost of the arc (u, v) or None if there is no such arc. This implementation supposes that the vertices are given in topological order, otherwise a topological sort must be done first, see 6.7. Hence, if the arc (u, v) exists, then $u < v$.

```
def dilworth(graph):
    n = len(graph)
    match = max_bipartite_matching(graph)    # maximum matching
    part = [None] * n                        # partition into chains
    nb_chains = 0
    for v in range(n - 1, -1, -1):           # in inverse topological order
        if part[v] is None:                  # start of chain
            u = v
            while u is not None:             # follow the chain
                part[u] = nb_chains          # mark
                u = match[u]
            nb_chains += 1
    return part
```

Problems
Stock Charts [gcj:2009round2C]
Taxi Cab Scheme [icpcarchive:3126] [poj:2060]

10 Trees

Rooted trees are combinatorial structures which appear naturally when considering objects with a structure of recursive decomposition. This is the case, for example, for classifications, hierarchies or genealogies. The recursive nature of trees is an invitation to recursive algorithms, and the key to an algorithm is to find the appropriate method of exploration. In this section, we review certain classic problems concerning trees.

Formally, a tree is a connected acyclic graph. One of its vertices can be designated as the *root*, and in this case we generally speak of a *rooted tree*. This root provides the tree with an orientation from parent to child. Starting from a vertex and climbing up the links, we arrive at the root. The vertices without children are called *leaf nodes*. A tree with n vertices contains exactly $n - 1$ edges. For proof, it suffices to observe that if we repeatedly remove a leaf from the tree, along with its incident edge, we end up with an isolated vertex, i.e. a tree with 1 vertex and 0 edges.

The vertices of a rooted tree are partitioned into levels. The root is the unique vertex at level 0, its child nodes are at level 1 and so on. The largest non-empty level number defines the depth of the tree, which is also the maximum distance from the root to a leaf. The subtree rooted at vertex v consists of all vertices and edges reachable from the root of the original tree only through vertex v. A disjoint union of trees is called a forest, as the reader might have guessed.

There are numerous dynamic data structures based on trees, such as binary red-black search trees or interval trees. These structures invoke rebalancing operations on the trees in order to guarantee logarithmic-time insert, delete and query operations. However, in programming competitions, the inputs are given only once, and thus it is often possible to skip the insert/delete operations by directly constructing balanced structures.

A tree can be represented by essentially one of two methods. The first is the classic representation of a graph with an adjacency list, which does not distinguish any particular vertex as the root of the tree. Another representation commonly used is that of an *array of predecessors*. For a rooted tree (often with vertex 0 as the root), each vertex other than the root has a unique predecessor, encoded in the array. Based on the context, one or the other of the representations will be best suited, while translating between them can easily be done in linear time.

```
def tree_prec_to_adj(prec, root=0):
    n = len(prec)
    graph = [[prec[u]] for u in range(n)]   # add predecessors
    graph[root] = []
    for u in range(n):                       # add successors
        if u != root:
            graph[prec[u]].append(u)
    return graph


def tree_adj_to_prec(graph, root=0):
    prec = [None] * len(graph)
    prec[root] = root            # mark to visit root only once
    to_visit = [root]
    while to_visit:              # DFS
        node = to_visit.pop()
        for neighbor in graph[node]:
            if prec[neighbor] is None:
                prec[neighbor] = node
                to_visit.append(neighbor)
    prec[root] = None            # put the standard mark for root
    return prec
```

10.1   Huffman Coding

Definition

Let Σ be a finite alphabet. We denote by Σ^* the set of all words on Σ. Let $S \subseteq \Sigma^*$ be a finite set of words. A *binary code* for an alphabet Σ of n characters is a function $c : \Sigma \to \{0,1\}^*$ such that no word $c(a)$ of the code is a prefix of another word $c(b)$ for $a, b \in S$. This code applied to each of the letters transforms a word from S into a word in $\{0,1\}^*$, and the property for the prefixes allows an unambiguous decoding of the original. In general, we would like the encoding to be as short as possible, hence the more frequent letters should be encoded by shorter words. Formally, given a frequency function $f : S \to \mathbb{R}^+$, we seek a code minimising the cost

$$\sum_{a \in S} f(a) \cdot |c(a)|.$$

Algorithm in $O(n \log n)$

A Huffman code can be seen as a binary tree, the leaves of which are the letters of the alphabet and each node is labelled with the sum of the frequencies of the letters of the leaves of the subtree rooted at this node. Every inner node is connected to exactly two child nodes with edges labelled, respectively, by 0 and 1. The concatenation of the labels along the path from the root to a leaf vertex constitutes the code word c of the corresponding word from S. As such, the cost of c can be expressed as the sum over $a \in S$, of f_a multiplied by the depth of the leaf a in the tree. To construct the tree, we begin with a forest, where each word from S is a tree consisting of a single node, labelled by its frequency. Then, as long as there are multiple trees, we merge the two trees with minimal frequency by attaching them under a new root, and label the new root with the sum of the frequencies of the two subtrees, see Figure 10.1. The arcs connecting the root to the merged subtrees are labelled, respectively and arbitrarily, with 0 and 1. By an exchange argument, we can show that the encoding thus produced is optimal (see Huffman, 1952).

To manipulate the trees, we place them in a data structure allowing efficient insertion of elements and retraction of the minimal element: a priority queue. These operations have a logarithmic cost in the number of objects in the structure. In general, this structure is implemented with a *heap*. In Python, such a structure can be found in the module heapq.

The elements stored in the priority queue are pairs (f_A, A) where A is a binary tree and f_A is the total frequency of the letters stored under A. A tree is encoded in two ways. A letter a represents a tree consisting of a unique leaf (and root) a. A tree composed of a left subtree ℓ and a right subtree r is represented by the pair (ℓ, r), which must be a list instead of a tuple to avoid deep copies of the structure.

```python
def huffman(freq):
    forest = []                              # build forest with singletons
    for item in freq:
        heappush(forest, (freq[item], item))
    while len(forest) > 1:
        (f_l, left) = heappop(forest)        # merge two trees
        (f_r, right) = heappop(forest)
        heappush(forest, (f_l + f_r, [left, right]))
    code = {}                                # build code from unique tree
    extract(code, forest[0][1], [])
    return code


def extract(code, tree, prefix):
    if isinstance(tree, list):       # inner node
        left, right = tree
        prefix.append('0')
        extract(code, left, prefix)    # build code recursively
        prefix.pop()
        prefix.append('1')
        extract(code, right, prefix)   # ... on both subtrees
        prefix.pop()
    else:
        code[tree] = ''.join(prefix)   # extract codeword from prefix
```

Problems

Huffman Trees [poj:1261]

Variable Radix Huffman Encoding [spoj:VHUFFM]

10.2   Lowest Common Ancestor

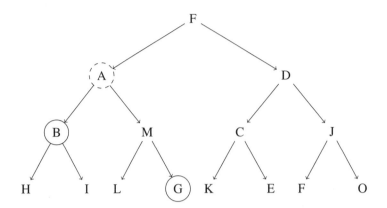

```
Input: B, G
Output: A
```

Definition
Given a tree with n nodes, we would like to answer, in time $O(\log n)$, queries for the *lowest common ancestor* or LCA of two given nodes u, v, i.e. the unique node u' such that u and v are contained in the subtree rooted at u' and with no direct descendant of u' having this property.

Structure in $O(\log n)$ per Query
The idea is to store with each node u a level, defined as its distance to the root. In addition, we maintain an array anc, where anc[k,u] is the ancestor of u at the level level[u]-2^k if it exists and -1 otherwise. Then, we can use these pointers to quickly climb to the ancestors.

Consider the query LCA(u,v): '*what is the closest ancestor of u and v?*', where without loss of generality we can suppose level[u] $\leq$ level[v]. First, we choose an ancestor v' of v at the same level as u, and set $u' = u$. Then, iteratively for each k from $\log_2 n$ down to 0, if anc[k,u'] $\neq$ anc[k,v'], then u', v' are replaced by their ancestors anc[k,u'], anc[k,v']. At the end, $u' = v'$, and this is the common ancestor we seek. To simplify the code, we use the same variables u,v for u',v', once the input parameters are no longer useful.

Implementation Details
We suppose that the tree is given in the form of an array parent, indicating the parent node parent[u] for each node $u \in \{0, 1, \ldots, n - 1\}$ in the tree. We also suppose that a parent has a smaller index than its children, and that the root is the vertex 0.

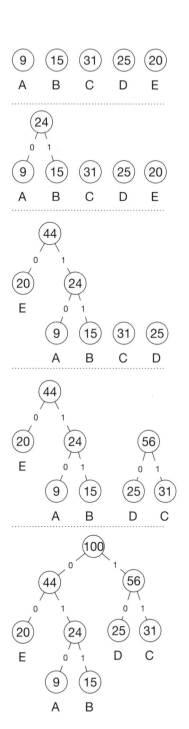

Letter	Frequency Input	Code Output
A	7	00
B	7	01
C	7	10
D	7	11
A	40	1
B	5	01
C	2	001
D	1	000

Figure 10.1 Construction of a Huffman code. Each node is labelled by the sum of the frequencies of the letters at the leaves of the subtrees rooted at this node. On the right, two examples of Huffman codes resulting from two different inputs.

```
class LowestCommonAncestorShortcuts:
    def __init__(self, prec):
        n = len(prec)
        self.level = [None] * n          # build levels
        self.level[0] = 0
        for u in range(1, n):
            self.level[u] = 1 + self.level[prec[u]]
        depth = log2ceil(max(self.level[u] for u in range(n))) + 1
        self.anc = [[0] * n for _ in range(depth)]
        for u in range(n):
            self.anc[0][u] = prec[u]
        for k in range(1, depth):
            for u in range(n):
                self.anc[k][u] = self.anc[k - 1][self.anc[k - 1][u]]

    def query(self, u, v):
        # -- assume w.l.o.g. that v is not higher than u in the tree
        if self.level[u] > self.level[v]:
            u, v = v, u
        # -- put v at the same level as u
        depth = len(self.anc)
        for k in range(depth-1, -1, -1):
            if self.level[u] <= self.level[v] - (1 << k):
                v = self.anc[k][v]
        assert self.level[u] == self.level[v]
        if u == v:
            return u
        # -- climb until the lowest common ancestor
        for k in range(depth-1, -1, -1):
            if self.anc[k][u] != self.anc[k][v]:
                u = self.anc[k][u]
                v = self.anc[k][v]
        assert self.anc[0][u] == self.anc[0][v]
        return self.anc[0][u]
```

Alternative Solution by Reduction to a Minimum Over a Range

Consider a depth-first traversal of the tree, as in Figure 10.2. Suppose for simplicity that the vertices are numbered such that for every vertex u, its number is higher than that of its parent. We store in the table t the trace of the traversal, adding the vertex u at the time it was first visited, when it was last visited and between two recursive descendants. Informally, if we draw a line clockwise around the tree embedded in the plane, the table t contains the vertices in the order they appear under the pen. We denote by $f[u]$ the time of the end of processing of the vertex u. Clearly, t contains between $f[u]$ and $f[v]$ all of the intermediate vertices visited by the traversal between u and v. Hence, the minimal vertex in this interval is the lowest common ancestor of u and v. It suffices then to generate in linear time the table t of the depth-first traversal of the tree and to use a segment tree to answer queries, see Section 4.5 on page 75. The construction of this structure requires time $O(n \log n)$, and the complexity of a query is $O(\log n)$.

Implementation Details

The input to this implementation is the graph in the form of an adjacency list. It makes no hypothesis as to the numbering of the vertices. Consequently, the trace `dfs_trace` contains not only the vertices but the couple (depth, vertex). As the input could be very large, the DFS traversal is implemented iteratively using a stack `to_visit`. The array `next` indicates for each vertex how many descendants have already been explored.

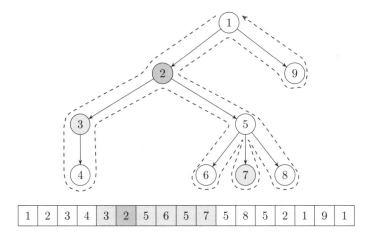

Figure 10.2 Reduction of the problem of lowest common ancestor to the problem of the minimum over a range of the trace of a depth-first traversal. The query illustrated is LCA(3,7), which returns the node 2.

```
class LowestCommonAncestorRMQ:
    def __init__(self, graph):
        n = len(graph)
        dfs_trace = []
        self.last = [None] * n
        to_visit = [(0, 0, None)]                # node 0 is root
        succ = [0] * n
        while to_visit:
            level, node, father = to_visit[-1]
            self.last[node] = len(dfs_trace)
            dfs_trace.append((level, node))
            if succ[node] < len(graph[node]) and \
               graph[node][succ[node]] == father:
                succ[node] += 1
            if succ[node] == len(graph[node]):
                to_visit.pop()
            else:
                neighbor = graph[node][succ[node]]
                succ[node] += 1
                to_visit.append((level + 1, neighbor, node))
        self.rmq = RangeMinQuery(dfs_trace, (float('inf'), None))
    def query(self, u, v):
        lu = self.last[u]
        lv = self.last[v]
        if lu > lv:
            lu, lv = lv, lu
        return self.rmq.range_min(lu, lv + 1)[1]
```

Variant
This structure also permits the computation of the distance between two nodes of the tree, as the shortest path must pass through the lowest common ancestor.

Problem
Lowest Common Ancestor [spoj:LCA]

10.3   Longest Path in a Tree

Definition
Given a tree, we want to compute the longest path in this tree.

Complexity
The following algorithm is linear in the size of the tree.

Algorithm by Dynamic Programming
As with many problems involving trees, we can here apply dynamic programming by reasoning on the subtrees. We distinguish a root, thus orienting the edges of the tree.

For every vertex v, consider the subtree with v as root. We assign $b[v]$ as the length of the longest path in this subtree with endpoint v and $t[v]$ the length of the longest path in this subtree without restriction. The length $b[v]$ is also known as the *depth* of the subtree rooted at v.

If v has no children, then $b[v] = t[v] = 0$. Otherwise, the following relations hold:

$b[v] = 1 + \max b[u]$ maximised over the children u of v

$t[v] = \max\{\max t[u_1],\ \max b[u_1] + 2 + b[u_2]\}$ and over the pairs of children u_1, u_2 of v

The program can dispense with tests on the number of children by using -1 as the default value. Note that it is not necessary to sort the children of a node to obtain the two children maximising their b-value.

Some Observations
Let r be an arbitrary vertex of the tree and u a vertex at the maximal distance from r. Then, a longest path exists in the tree with endpoint u. To be convinced, suppose we have a longest path with endpoints v_1, v_2. Let u' be a vertex on the path from r to u and v' a vertex on the path from v_1 to v_2 that minimises the distance from u' to v'. If the two paths intersect, we can choose any vertex in the intersection, see Figure 10.3.

Assign d as the distance in the tree. By the choice of u we have

$$d(u', u) \geq d(u', v') + d(v', v_1)$$

and by the optimality of the path from v_1 to v_2,

$$d(v_1, v') \geq d(v', u') + d(u', u).$$

This implies $d(u',v') = 0$, i.e. $u' = v'$, and $d(v',v_1) = d(v',u)$, thus the path from v_2 to u is also a longest path in the tree.

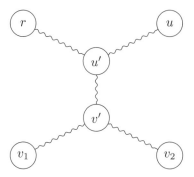

Figure 10.3 An exchange argument shows that if u is a vertex at a maximal distance from r then a longest path exists starting from u.

Algorithm by Depth-First Search

The preceding observation implies the existence of an alternative algorithm. A depth-first search (DFS) allows us to identify a vertex at a maximal distance from a given vertex. Hence, we can choose an arbitrary vertex r, find a vertex v_1 at a maximal distance from r and then again find a vertex v_2 at a maximal distance from v_1. The path from v_1 to v_2 is a path of maximal length.

Variant

We wish to remove the fewest possible edges in a tree so that in the remaining forest no path is longer than R. To solve this problem, it suffices to remove the critical edges determined in the dynamic programming solution above.

Consider the processing of a vertex v with its children $u_1, \ldots, u_d$ ordered such that $b[u_1] \leq \ldots \leq b[u_d]$. For every i from d down to 1, we must remove the edge (v, u_i) if $b[u_i] + 1 > R$ or if $i > 1$ and $b[u_{i-1}] + 2 + b[u_i] > R$.

Problems

Labyrinth [spoj:LABYR1]
Longest path in a tree [spoj:PT07Z]
SpeedCameras [codility:calcium2015]

10.4 Minimum Weight Spanning Tree—Kruskal

Definition

Given an undirected connected graph, we would like to find a set of edges T such that every pair of vertices is linked by a path through these edges. In this case, T is called a *spanning tree*. The edges have weights, and we want the total weight of our set of edges to be minimal. Note that such a set is acyclic—and hence a tree—since the deletion of an edge of a cycle preserves the connectedness. We thus seek what is known as a *minimum weight spanning tree*, see Figure 10.4.

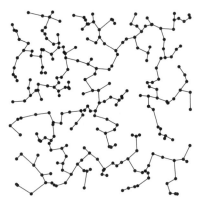

Figure 10.4 Minimum weight spanning tree in a complete graph of 256 vertices where the weight of each edge is the Euclidean distance separating its endpoints.

Application
The edges of a graph are given with a cost (or weight) w, and we need to purchase at least cost some edges to render the resulting subgraph connected. Thus, we must find a set $T \subset E$ such that $G(V, T)$ is connected with $\sum_{e \in T} w(e)$ minimal.

Algorithm in $O(|E| \log |E|)$
Kruskal's algorithm (1956) solves this problem in a greedy manner by considering the edges (u, v) in order of increasing weight and adding an edge (u, v) to the solution set T if it does not introduce a cycle. The optimality of the algorithm can be shown by an exchange argument. Let T be the solution produced by the algorithm and let B be an arbitrary optimal solution. Let e be the first edge chosen by the algorithm that does not belong to B. Then $B \cup \{e\}$ must contain a cycle C. By the choice of e, all the edges of the cycle C have weight at least as large as e. Hence, replacing one of these edges by e in B preserves the connectivity of B without increasing the cost, while decreasing a certain distance between T and B, namely $|T \setminus B| + |B \setminus T|$. By selecting B as the optimal solution closest to T, we conclude $B = T$.

Implementation Details
To visit the edges in order of increasing weight, we create a list of couples (weight, edge). This list is sorted lexicographically on the couples, then processed in order. We use a union-find structure (see Section 1.5.5 on page 26) in order to maintain a forest and efficiently detect if adding an edge forms a cycle.

```
def kruskal(graph, weight):
    u_f = UnionFind(len(graph))
    edges = []
    for u, _ in enumerate(graph):
        for v in graph[u]:
            edges.append((weight[u][v], u, v))
    edges.sort()
    min_span_tree = []
    for w_idx, u_idx, v_idx in edges:
        if u_f.union(u_idx, v_idx):
            min_span_tree.append((u_idx, v_idx))
    return min_span_tree
```

Prim's Algorithm

Another algorithm for this problem exists, namely Prim's algorithm. It works in a similar manner to Dijkstra's algorithm. It maintains for a set of vertices S a priority queue Q containing all the edges leaving S. Initially, S contains a single arbitrary vertex u. Then, while S does not contain all the vertices, an edge (u, v) with minimal weight is extracted from Q with $u \in S, v \notin S$. The vertex v is then added to S and Q updated accordingly. The complexity of this algorithm is again $O(|E| \log |E|)$.

Problems
Cobbled streets [spoj:CSTREET]
Minimum Spanning Tree [spoj:MST]

11 Sets

This chapter extends the chapter on sequences. It illustrates how a single method, specifically dynamic programming, allows the resolution of a large variety of problems. We begin with the presentation of two classic problems—the knapsack and making change.

11.1 The Knapsack Problem

Definition
Given n objects with weights $p_0, \ldots, p_{n-1}$ and values $v_0, \ldots, v_{n-1}$, and given a knapsack with a capacity C, where C is an integer, the problem is to find a subset of the objects with maximal total value, the total weight of which does not exceed the capacity C. This problem is NP-hard.

Key Observation
For $i \in \{0, \ldots, n-1\}$ and $c \in \{0, \ldots, C\}$, assign $\mathrm{Opt}[i][c]$ as the largest value obtainable among objects with index 0 to i without their weight exceeding the capacity c. For the base case $i = 0$, we have $\mathrm{Opt}[0][c] = 0$ if $p_0 > c$ and $\mathrm{Opt}[0][c] = v_0$ otherwise.

For larger values of i, at most two possible choices appear for the object of index i: we can take it or we can leave it. In the first case, the available capacity is reduced by p_i. We thus have the relation:

$$\mathrm{Opt}[i][c] = \max \begin{cases} \mathrm{Opt}[i-1][c-p_i] + v_i & \text{case where we take the object,} \\ & \text{provided } c \geq p_i \\ \mathrm{Opt}[i-1][c] & \text{case where we leave the object.} \end{cases}$$

Algorithm in $O(nC)$
An algorithm with such a complexity is said to be *pseudo-polynomial*.[1] A Boolean matrix Sel is maintained in parallel with the dynamic programming matrix Opt.

---

[1] A pseudo-polynomial algorithm is one that is polynomial in the *value* of the inputs but not in their *size*. Here, adding an extra bit to the size of C doubles the running time.

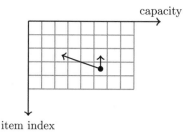

item index

Figure 11.1 A representation of the array `Opt`. The computation of each element requires at most two elements in the preceding row, including the one immediately above. This is a special case of the problem of the longest path in a grid, described in Section 3.1 on page 62.

It allows us to remember the choices made leading to the values stored in `Opt`. Once these matrices are populated following the recurrence formula described above, a traversal of the elements in reverse order allows the extraction from the matrix `Sel` the set of elements providing the optimal total value.

```python
def knapsack(p, v, cmax):
    n = len(p)
    opt = [[0] * (cmax + 1) for _ in range(n + 1)]
    sel = [[False] * (cmax + 1) for _ in range(n + 1)]
    #                           --- basic case
    for cap in range(p[0], cmax + 1):
        opt[0][cap] = v[0]
        sel[0][cap] = True
    #                           --- induction case
    for i in range(1, n):
        for cap in range(cmax + 1):
            if cap >= p[i] and opt[i-1][cap - p[i]] + v[i] > opt[i-1][cap]:
                opt[i][cap] = opt[i-1][cap - p[i]] + v[i]
                sel[i][cap] = True
            else:
                opt[i][cap] = opt[i-1][cap]
                sel[i][cap] = False
    #                           --- reading solution
    cap = cmax
    solution = []
    for i in range(n-1, -1, -1):
        if sel[i][cap]:
            solution.append(i)
            cap -= p[i]
    return (opt[n - 1][cmax], solution)
```

Problems

The Knapsack Problem [spoj:KNAPSACK]

Knapsack [spoj:KNPSACK]

11.2   Making Change

Suppose we need to make change for a customer, of value R—the difference between the purchase price and the amount tendered. We have coins or banknotes at our disposal, of respective value $x_0, \ldots, x_{n-1}$ cents (or whatever!). The problem thus consists of determining the existence of a positive linear combination of $x_0, \ldots, x_{n-1}$ that equals R. You might laugh, as this seems so simple, but in Burma (now known as Myanmar), there used to be banknotes of 15, 25, 35, 45, 75 and 90 kyats (see Figure 11.2).

For this problem, banknotes or coins of value x_i can contribute multiple times to the sum (or at least until the merchant runs out …). We compute a Boolean array b, with $b[i, s]$ indicating whether a combination exists of the coins indexed from 0 to i, of value exactly s. Clearly, $b[-1, 0] = True$, corresponding to the empty coin set, and $b[-1, s] = False$ for all $s > 0$. As a solution either does contain a coin of value x_i or does not, we have the recursion $b[i, s] = b[i, s - x_i] \vee b[i - 1, s]$. The implementation below avoids the use of index i on b by processing its elements in the right order.

```
def coin_change(x, R):
    b = [False] * (R + 1)
    b[0] = True
    for xi in x:
        for s in range(xi, R + 1):
            b[s] |= b[s - xi]
    return b[R]
```

Figure 11.2 A 45 kyat banknote.

Variant
In the case where a solution exists, we can try to determine a solution using a minimal number of banknotes or coins.

Observation
You might think that it suffices to consider the currency by decreasing value and provide at each step the largest banknote or coin that does not exceed the remaining sum due. This realises a minimal amount of currency for most monetary systems.

However, if we consider a system with values 1, 3, 4 and 10 and wish to make change for a sum of 6, the greedy approach results in a solution with the three values $4+1+1$, whereas the unique optimal solution is $3+3$.

Algorithm in $O(nR)$

Let $A[i][m]$ be the minimal number of coins to return for an amount $0 \le m \le R$ using the monetary system $x_0, \ldots, x_{i-1}$, with $A[i][m] = \infty$ if there is no such solution. We can derive a recurrence relation similar to that obtained for the knapsack problem: for any amount m, $A[0][m]$ is m/x_0 if x_0 divides m and ∞ otherwise. For $i = 1, \ldots, n-1$ we have the relation:

$$A[i][m] = \min \begin{cases} A[i][m - x_i] + 1 & \text{case where we can use the coin,} \\ & \text{provided } m \ge x_i \\ A[i-1][m] & \text{case where we cannot use the coin.} \end{cases}$$

11.3 Subset Sum

input   output

Definition

Given n positive integers $x_0, \ldots, x_{n-1}$, we would like to know if a subset exists the sum of which is exactly a given value R. This problem is NP-hard. This problem has the flavour of the change-making problem, with the twist that every coin can be used at most once.

Algorithm in $O(nR)$

We maintain a Boolean array indicating for each index i and every $0 \le s \le R$ whether a subset of the integers $x_0, x_1, \ldots, x_i$ exists the sum of which is s.

Initially, the entries in this array are true only for the index 0 and the empty set. Then, for every $i \in \{0, \ldots, n-1\}$ and every $s \in \{0, \ldots, R\}$, we can produce a subset of sum s with the integers $x_0, \ldots, x_i$, if and only if a subset exists of $x_0, \ldots, x_{i-1}$ of sum either s or $s - x_i$. We proceed as for change-making, with a slightly different recursion, namely $b[i,s] = b[i-1, s - x_i] | b[i-1, s]$.

Again using a carefully chosen loop order for s, our implementation avoids the use of index i on the array b.

```
def subset_sum(x, R):
    b = [False] * (R + 1)
    b[0] = True
    for xi in x:
        for s in range(R, xi - 1, -1):
            b[s] |= b[s - xi]
    return b[R]
```

Algorithm in $O(2^{\lceil n/2 \rceil})$

This algorithm is interesting when R is large and n small. We split the input $X = \{x_0, \ldots, x_{n-1}\}$ into two disjoint subsets A and B of size at most $\lceil n/2 \rceil$. If S_A (respectively, S_B) is the set of sums of each subset of A (respectively, B), we construct the set $Y = S_A$, and then the set $Z = R - S_B$ containing the values of the form $R - v$ where v runs over S_B. It hence suffices to test if Y and Z have a non-empty intersection.

```
def part_sum(x_table, i=0):
    if i == len(x_table):
        yield 0
    else:
        for s_idx in part_sum(x_table, i + 1):
            yield s_idx
            yield s_idx + x_table[i]


def subset_sum(x_table, r_target):
    k = len(x_table) // 2                # divide input
    y_value = list(part_sum(x_table[:k]))
    z_value = [r_target - v for v in part_sum(x_table[k:])]
    y_value.sort()        # test of intersection between y_value and z_value
    z_value.sort()
    i = 0
    j = 0
    while i < len(y_value) and j < len(z_value):
        if y_value[i] == z_value[j]:
            return True
        if y_value[i] < z_value[j]:  # increment index of smallest element
            i += 1
        else:
            j += 1
    return False
```

Variant: Partition into Two Subsets as Fairly as Possible

Given $x_0, \ldots, x_{n-1}$, we want to produce $S \subseteq \{0, \ldots, n-1\}$ such that $|\sum_{i \in S} x_i - \sum_{i \notin S} x_i|$ is the smallest possible.

There is a simple algorithm with time complexity in $O(n \sum x_i)$. We proceed as for the partial sum problem, and then search in the Boolean array b for an index s such that

$b[s]$ is true and s is as close as possible to $(\sum x_i)/2$. Hence, for every $a = 0, 1, 2, \ldots$ and $d = +1, -1$, consider $b[(\sum x_i)/2 + a \cdot d]$.

Problem
Boat Burglary [spoj:BURGLARY]

11.4 The *k*-sum Problem

Definition
Given a set of n integers $x_0, \ldots, x_{n-1}$, we want to know if it is possible to select k of them the sum of which is zero. Without loss of generality, we assume that no element has value 0, because a solution using 0 is also a solution using only $k - 1$ elements; a simpler problem.

Application
For $k = 3$, this problem is important for discrete geometry, as numerous classic problems can be reduced to the 3-sum problem. For example, given n triangles, do they entirely cover another target triangle? Or, given n points, does a line exist that intersects at least three of these points? For all these problems, algorithms exist in $O(n^2)$. This is essentially optimal, as it is conjectured that an algorithm does not exist with time complexity $O(n^{2-\Omega(1)})$ (Gajentaan and Overmars, 1995). For larger values of k, this problem is important for cryptography.

Algorithm in $O(n^{k-1})$
First, an observation for the case $k = 2$—the problem reduces to deciding if i, j with $x_i = -x_j$ exists. If x is sorted, a parallel run-through—as in the merge of two sorted lists—allows the resolution of the problem (see Section 4.1 on page 73). Otherwise, we can store the input in a hash table and then for each x_i see if $-x_i$ can be found in the table.

For $k = 3$, we propose an algorithm in time $O(n^2)$. We start by sorting x. Then, for each x_j, we look to see if the lists $x + x_j$ and $-x$ have an element in common. Such an element would be of the form $x_i + x_j$ and $-x_k$ with $x_i + x_j + x_k = 0$, with i, j, k necessarily being distinct indices because of the absence of zero in the input. This approach can be generalised for larger values of k, but is less efficient than the following algorithm.

Algorithm in $O(n^{\lceil k/2 \rceil})$
We construct a multiset A of integers obtained by summing exactly $\lfloor k/2 \rfloor$ integers of the input. Similarly, we construct a multiset B obtained by summing exactly $\lceil k/2 \rceil$ integers of the input.

Then, it suffices to test if the sets A and $-B = \{-x | x \in B\}$ have a non-empty intersection. For this, we sort A and $-B$, and then proceed as in the merge of two sorted lists by conjointly running through the two lists. The complexity is $O(n^{\lceil k/2 \rceil})$.

Implementation Details

To avoid taking several times the same indices, we store in A, B not only the sums but also couples consisting of each sum as well as the indices realising it. Thus, we can verify for each couple in A and B with sum 0 if the indices are disjoint.

Problem

4 Values whose Sum is 0 [poj:2785]

12 Points and Polygons

The main object at the heart of computational geometry is the point, representing a position in some space. A number of classic problems concerning sets of points in the plane are presented in this chapter.

Points in the plane are naturally represented by their pair of coordinates. An important basic operation on points is the orientation test, see Figure 12.1: given three points a, b, c, are they aligned, i.e. all contained in some line, and if not, will the transformation $a \rightarrow b \rightarrow c$ move the points counter-clockwise (to the left) or clockwise (to the right)? Formally, we look at the sign of the z-component of the vector cross product $\vec{ab} \times \vec{bc}$. If this is positive, then the transformation moves the points counter-clockwise, if negative then clockwise, and if zero, the points are aligned.

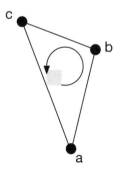

Figure 12.1 The test `left_turn(a,b,c)` returns `True` for these points.

```
def left_turn(a, b, c):
    return ((a[0] - c[0]) * (b[1] - c[1]) -
            (a[1] - c[1]) * (b[0] - c[0]) > 0)
```

Whenever the points have non-integer coordinates it is recommended to perform computations expecting equality with a small tolerance, say 10^{-7}, rather than comparing to 0, in order to protect from rounding errors.

12.1   Convex Hull

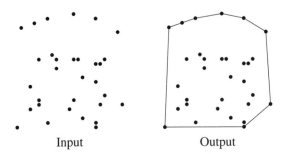

Input   Output

Definition
Given a set of n points, the *convex hull* is defined as the smallest convex polygon that encloses all of the points of the set. This polygon is also the polygon of smallest perimeter containing all of these points.

Imagine a wooden board covered with nails. A rubber band enclosing these nails represents the convex hull of the nail positions.

Lower Bound on the Time Complexity
In general, it is not possible to compute the convex hull in time $o(n \log n)$[1]. To convince yourself, consider a sequence of n numbers $a_1, \ldots, a_n$. The computation of the convex hull of the points $(a_1, a_1^2), \ldots, (a_n, a_n^2)$ returns them in an order corresponding to the natural order of the numbers $a_1, \ldots, a_n$. This means that if we could compute the convex hull using only $o(n \log n)$ operations, we would obtain a sort algorithm of the same complexity. However, sorting is known to have complexity $\Theta(n \log n)$, in general.

An Algorithm in $O(n \log n)$
The best known algorithm for this problem is due to Ronald Graham. We present a variant, proposed by A. M. Andrew, which does not process the points in the order of their angle around some fixed point, but in the order of their x-coordinate (see Andrew, 1979). Most implementations of Graham's algorithm make use of trigonometric functions, while Andrew's algorithm is based solely on the orientation test mentioned above. As a result, it is slightly easier to implement and can avoid rounding errors.

First, we describe how to obtain the upper part of the convex hull. Points are processed from left to right, in the order of their x coordinates. A list top contains the convex hull of the points already processed. When processing some point p, it is first appended to top. Then, for as long as the second-last point of top renders the sequence non-convex, it is removed from the list.

---

[1] Yes, this is the little o of Landau's notation.

Implementation Details

The lower part bot of the convex hull is obtained in the same manner. The result is the concatenation of the two lists, reversing the list top in order to obtain the points of the convex hull in the 'normal' order. This is defined as the reverse direction of the hands of an analogue clock (a quaint object used by preceding generations to keep track of time, extremely accurate twice each day if perchance it was not wound up). Note that the first and last elements of the lists are identical, and would therefore be duplicated in the resulting concatenation. Hence, it is important to remove these endpoints.

In order to simplify the code presented, the point *p* is added to the lists top and bot only after the deletion of elements that would make the sequence non-convex.

```
def andrew(S):
    S.sort()
    top = []
    bot = []
    for p in S:
        while len(top) >= 2 and not left_turn(p, top[-1], top[-2]):
            top.pop()
        top.append(p)
        while len(bot) >= 2 and not left_turn(bot[-2], bot[-1], p):
            bot.pop()
        bot.append(p)
    return bot[:-1] + top[:0:-1]
```

Problems

Doors and Penguins [spoj:DOORSPEN]

Build the Fence [spoj:BSHEEP]

Full Example: Blowing out Candles

See [icpcarchive:8155].

As Jacques-Édouard really likes birthday cakes, he celebrates his birthday every hour, instead of every year. His friends ordered him a round cake from a famous pastry shop and placed candles on its top surface. The number of candles equals the age of Jacques-Édouard in hours. As a result, there is a huge amount of candles burning on the top of the cake. Jacques-Édouard wants to blow out all of the candles with a single breath.

You can think of the flames of the candles as being points in a same plane, all within a disk of radius R (in nanometers) centred at the origin. On that same plane, the air blown by Jacques-Édouard follows a trajectory that can be described by a straight strip of width W, which comprises the area between two parallel lines at distance W, the lines themselves being included in that area. What is the minimum width W such that Jacques-Édouard can blow out all of the candles if he chooses the best orientation to blow?

Input

The first line consists of the integers N and R, separated with a space, where N is Jacques-Édouard's age in hours. Then N lines follow, each of them consisting of the two integer coordinates x_i and y_i of the ith candle in nanometers, separated with a space.

Limits

- $3 \leq N \leq 2 \cdot 10^5$;
- $10 \leq R \leq 2 \cdot 10^8$;
- for $1 \leq i \leq N$, $x_i^2 + y_i^2 \leq R^2$;
- all points have distinct coordinates.

Output

Print the value W as a floating point number. An additive or multiplicative error of 10^{-5} is tolerated: if y is the answer, any number either within $[y - 10^{-5}; y + 10^{-5}]$ or within $[(1 - 10^{-5})y; (1 + 10^{-5})y]$ is accepted.

Sample input	Sample output
3 10	7.0710678118654755
0 0	
10 0	
0 10	

Solution

Without loss of generality, an optimal solution consists of a strip which touches two of the given points on one border of the strip and another single point on the opposite border of the strip, see Figure 12.2. Clearly all three points belong to the convex hull of the given input points and without loss of generality, the two points on the first border of the strip are consecutive on the convex hull. With this observation done, the algorithm is quite easy to find. First compute the convex hull. Then loop over all successive pairs of points p_i, p_{i+1} along the hull, and at every step maintain a point p_k which is furthest from the line going through the points p_i, p_{i+1}. This means that while the pairs of points loop in counter-clockwise order over the convex hull, the opposite point also moves in counter-clockwise order over the convex hull. But when the pair makes one step on the hull, the opposite point might remain the same or take several steps. Nevertheless, the overall complexity of this part of the algorithm is only $O(n)$ in total. The minimum distance observed for all of these triplets p_i, p_{i+1}, p_k is the solution to the problem.

The bottleneck in the overall running time is the computation of the convex hull, which takes time $O(n \log n)$, acceptable complexity given the upper bounds of the problem.

12.2 Measures of a Polygon

Given a simple polygon[2] p in the form of a list of n points in normal orientation[3], there are several measures of interest, see Figure 12.3.

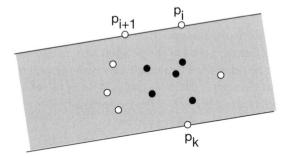

Figure 12.2 The structure of an optimal solution. The points of the convex hull are shown in white.

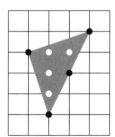

Figure 12.3 The number of integer points on the boundary (in black) is 4 the number of integer points inside (in white) is 4, and the area is $4 + 4/2 - 1 = 5$.

Area

We can compute the area A in linear time via the formula

$$A = \frac{1}{2} \sum_{i=0}^{n-1} (x_i y_{i+1} - x_{i+1} y_i),$$

where the index $i + 1$ is taken modulo n. The ith term corresponds to the signed area of the triangle $(0, p_i, p_{i+1})$, whose sign depends on the orientation of the triangle. Removing this triangle reduces the problem to the computation of the area of a polygon having one less point on the boundary, hence the area of a polygon can be expressed as a sequence of additions and subtractions of areas of triangles.

---

[2] A polygon is simple if its edges do not cross.
[3] Normal orientation means counter-clockwise.

```
def area(p):
    A = 0
    for i, _ in enumerate(p):
        A += p[i - 1][0] * p[i][1] - p[i][0] * p[i - 1][1]
    return A / 2.
```

Number of Integer Points on the Boundary
To simplify, we suppose that the points of the polygon have integer coordinates. In this case, the answer can be determined by summing for each segment $[a, b]$ of p, the number of integer points between a and b, excluding a so as to not count it twice. If x is the absolute value of the difference of the x-coordinates of a and b and y the equivalent for the y-coordinates, then this is equal to:

$$\begin{cases} y & \text{if } x = 0 \\ x & \text{if } y = 0 \\ \text{the LCD of } x \text{ and } y & \text{otherwise.} \end{cases}$$

Number of Integer Points in the Interior
This number is obtained by Pick's theorem, which relates the area A of a polygon with the number of interior points n_i and the number of boundary points n_b (with integer coordinates) by the equation:

$$A = n_i + \frac{n_b}{2} - 1.$$

Minimal Triangulation of a Convex Polygon
Given a convex polygon, we would like to link its points by segments, such that each segment between two successive points p_i, p_{i+1} of the polygon forms a triangle with a point p_k. We want to minimise the total length of these additional segments. This problem can be solved with dynamic programming. If in an optimal triangulation two successive points p_i, p_{i+1} of the polygon are joined to a point p_k, then this triangle divides the polygon into two pieces, one composed of the points from p_k to p_i and the other composed of the points from p_{i+1} to p_k. Each piece forms an independent problem and can be triangulated in an optimal manner. We can in this way describe a dynamic program of $O(n^2)$ variables, each being the optimum over $O(n)$ alternatives, and hence with final complexity $O(n^3)$.

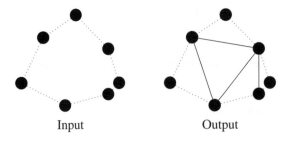

Input   Output

Problem
Toil for Oil [spoj:OIL]

12.3   Closest Pair of Points

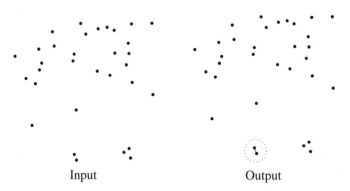

Input   Output

Application
In a campground, tents are pitched arbitrarily, and each is occupied by someone with a radio. We would like to impose a common threshold for the noise level not to be exceeded, giving a minimum distance between tents, so that nobody is bothered by the music of their neighbours.

Definition
Given n points $p_1, \ldots, p_n$, we want to find the pair of points p_i, p_j minimising the Euclidean distance between p_i and p_j.

Randomised Algorithm in Linear Time
Several algorithms in time $O(n \log n)$ have been proposed for this classic problem, using a sweep line or divide and conquer. We present a randomised algorithm in linear time, i.e. the *expected* computation time of which is linear. Based on our experiments, in practice it is only slightly more efficient than an algorithm using sweep line, but is much easier to implement.

The algorithm works in phases. The idea is that at each phase, we have already discovered a pair of points at a distance d and we can question whether another pair exists at a smaller distance. For this, we divide the space into a grid with step $d/2$ in both directions. Choosing a grid step of $d/2$ instead of d guarantees the presence of at most one element per cell, easing the processing. Each point thus belongs to some cell of the grid. Let P be the set of points for which we have already verified that the distances between each pair of points of P is at least d. Then, each cell of the grid contains at most one point of P.

The grid is represented by a dictionary G associating with each non-empty cell the point of P that it contains. At the time of adding a point p to P and to G, it suffices to test its distance with the points q contained in the 5×5 cells around p's cell,

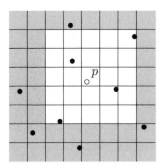

Figure 12.4 Each cell of the grid contains at most one point. At the time a new point p is considered, it suffices to measure its distance with the points contained in the neighbouring cells (white).

see Figure 12.4. If a pair of points at distance $d' < d$ is discovered, the procedure is restarted from the beginning with a new grid of step $d'/2$.

Complexity

We suppose that the access to G takes constant time, as does the computation of the cell containing a given point. The key argument is that if the points given as input are chosen in a uniformly random order, then when the ith point is processed ($3 \le i \le n$), we improve the distance d with probability $1/(i-1)$. Hence, the expected complexity is on the order of $\sum_{i=3}^{n} i/(i-1)$, hence linear in n.

Implementation Details

To compute the cell associated with a point (x, y) in the grid with a given step, it suffices to divide each coordinate by step and then round down. In Python, the integer division by the operator `//` returns the required value, but as a floating point number. We must convert it to integer type in order to loop over the neighbouring cells, as the function `range` admits only integer parameters. In other languages, particular attention must be paid to negative coordinates. For example, in `C++`, the expression `(int)(-1.1 / 2)` returns 0 rather than the -1 required, and hence the function `floor`[4] of the standard math library should be used.

---

[4] The floor of a real number x is the greatest integer equal to or less than x.

```
from math import hypot    # hypot(dx, dy) = sqrt(dx * dx + dy * dy)
from random import shuffle



def dist(p, q):
    return hypot(p[0] - q[0], p[1] - q[1])   # Euclidean dist.


def cell(point, size):
    x, y = point                         # size = grid cell side length
    return (int(x // size), int(y // size))
def improve(S, d):
    G = {}                               # maps grid cell to its point
    for p in S:                          # for every point
        a, b = cell(p, d / 2)            # determine its grid cell
        for a1 in range(a - 2, a + 3):
            for b1 in range(b - 2, b + 3):
                if (a1, b1) in G:        # compare with points
                    q = G[a1, b1]        # in surrounding cells
                    pq = dist(p, q)
                    if pq < d:           # improvement found
                        return pq, p, q
        G[a, b] = p
    return None



def closest_points(S):
    shuffle(S)
    assert len(S) >= 2
    p = S[0]                 # start with distance between
    q = S[1]                 # first two points
    d = dist(p, q)
    while d > 0:             # distance 0 cannot be improved
        r = improve(S, d)
        if r:               # distance improved
            d, p, q = r
        else:               # r is None: could not improve
            break
    return p, q
```

Problems
Closest Point Pair [spoj:CLOPPAIR]
Closest Triplet [spoj:CLOSEST]

12.4   Simple Rectilinear Polygon

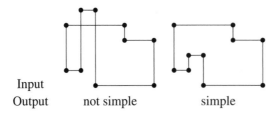

Input
Output   not simple   simple

Definition
A polygon is *rectilinear* if its edges alternate between vertical and horizontal orientations. It is *simple* if its edges do not cross each other. The goal is to test whether a given rectilinear polygon is simple.

Observation
If a polygon is rectilinear, then each of its vertices has a vertical neighbour as well as a horizontal neighbour among those that precede or follow it. Hence, the vertices of the polygon can be of type 'left' or 'right', and also of type 'top' or 'bottom'; a simple test of the neighbours suffices to label them, see Figure 12.5.

Algorithm
The algorithm, based on the sweep line technique, is of complexity $O(n \log n)$.

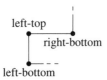

Figure 12.5 The types of points of a rectilinear polygon.

The algorithm will sweep the vertices of the polygon in lexicographical order of the coordinates, and maintain in a structure S the set of y-coordinates of the left vertices the right neighbours of which have not yet been visited. Initially, S is empty, and for each vertex met, we process it as follows:

- If (x, y) is identical to the last vertex processed, there is an intersection of vertices of the polygon.
- If (x, y) is a left vertex, we check to see if y is already in S: this would mean that a left vertex with the same y-coordinate has already been visited, hence two horizontal edges are superposed.
- If (x, y) is a right vertex, then necessarily y is in S, as its left neighbour has already been visited. Thus y can be removed from S.
- If (x, y) is a bottom vertex, then there is nothing to do.
- If (x, y) is a top vertex, then let (x, y') be its bottom neighbour. If this is not the vertex processed just before, then the segment $(x, y') - (x, y)$ and another vertical segment are superposed. Otherwise, we inspect S to see if eventually there are values y'' such that $y' < y'' < y$: this would mean that a horizontal segment with

y-coordinate y'' crosses the current vertical segment $(x, y') - (x, y)$, and hence once again the polygon is not simple.

Complexity

For good performance, the following operations on S must be performed efficiently:

- adding and removing elements from S ;
- testing if S contains an element in a given interval $[a, b]$.

If we encode S as an array t such that $t[y] = -1$ if $y \in S$ and $t[y] = 0$ otherwise, then determining whether an element of S exists in an interval $[a, b]$ reduces to looking for a -1 in the range between $t[a]$ and $t[b]$. We thus represent t using a segment tree, see Section 4.5 on page 75, so that the requests for the minimum in a range as well as the updates to t can be performed in logarithmic time, guaranteeing a complexity of $O(n \log n)$ for this algorithm.

Implementation Details

Rather than working with the coordinates of the vertices, which are not bounded, we consider their rank. Let $y_0 < \cdots, < y_k$ be the list of distinct y-coordinates of vertices ($k \leq n/2$ since the polygon is rectilinear). Hence, $y_i \in S$ if and only if $t[i] = -1$. To determine if S contains an element y_j in the interval $[y_i, y_k]$, it suffices to determine if the minimum of t between $t[i + 1]$ and $t[k - 1]$ is -1.

```python
def is_simple(polygon):
    n = len(polygon)
    order = list(range(n))
    order.sort(key=lambda i: polygon[i])      # lexicographic order
    rank_to_y = list(set(p[1] for p in polygon))
    rank_to_y.sort()
    y_to_rank = {y: rank for rank, y in enumerate(rank_to_y)}
    S = RangeMinQuery([0] * len(rank_to_y))      # sweep structure
    last_y = None
    for i in order:
        x, y = polygon[i]
        rank = y_to_rank[y]
        #                            -- type of point
        right_x = max(polygon[i - 1][0], polygon[(i + 1) % n][0])
        left = x < right_x
        below_y = min(polygon[i - 1][1], polygon[(i + 1) % n][1])
        high = y > below_y
        if left:                     # y does not need to be in S yet
            if S[rank]:
                return False         # two horizontal segments intersect
            S[rank] = -1             # add y to S
        else:
            S[rank] = 0              # remove y from S
        if high:
            lo = y_to_rank[below_y]   # check S between [lo + 1, rank - 1]
            if (below_y != last_y or last_y == y or
                    rank - lo >= 2 and S.range_min(lo + 1, rank)):
                return False          # horiz. & vert. segments intersect
        last_y = y                    # remember for next iteration
    return True
```

13 Rectangles

Numerous problems involving geometrical figures are concerned with rectangles, for example when they arise from drawing house plans or from computer graphics. Often, the rectangles are *rectilinear*, i.e. with their sides parallel to the axes, thus easing their handling. An important algorithmic technique in geometry is the *sweep line*, already described in Section 13.5 on page 205.

13.1 Forming Rectangles

Definition
Given a set S of n points in the plane, we would like to determine all of the rectangles with their four corners in S. These rectangles do not necessarily have to be rectilinear.

Algorithm
The complexity is $O(n^2 + m)$ where m is the size of the solution. The key observation is that the two pairs of diagonally opposed corners of a rectangle have a common signature. This consists of their midpoint and the distance between them. It then suffices to store in a dictionary all pairs of points p, q with key (c, d) where $c = (p + q)/2$ is the midpoint between p and q and $d = |q - p|$ is the distance. The couples having the same signature are those forming the rectangles of S, see Figure 13.1.

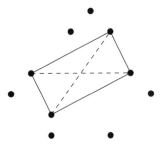

Figure 13.1 A common signature between pairs of opposing corners: the diagonals intersect at their midpoint and are of the same length.

Implementation Details
Often in programming contests the input consists of integers. For improved efficiency, one should in these cases avoid the use of floating point numbers whenever possible. Hence, in this implementation, when calculating c, the division by 2 is skipped, as is the square root for the calculation of d.

```
def rectangles_from_points(S):
    answ = 0
    pairs = {}
    for j, _ in enumerate(S):
        for i in range(j):      # loop over point pairs (p,q)
            px, py = S[i]
            qx, qy = S[j]
            center = (px + qx, py + qy)
            dist = (px - qx) ** 2 + (py - qy) ** 2
            signature = (center, dist)
            if signature in pairs:
                answ += len(pairs[signature])
                pairs[signature].append((i, j))
            else:
                pairs[signature] = [(i, j)]
    return answ
```

Problem
Rectangle [spoj:HMSRECT]

13.2   Largest Square in a Grid

Definition
Given a black and white image in the form of an $n \times m$ array of pixels, we would like to determine the largest completely black square, see Figure 13.2.

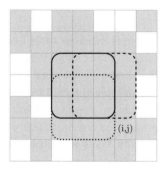

Figure 13.2 The black square of maximal size k having for bottom right-hand corner (i, j) contains three black squares of size $k - 1$ finishing on the corners $(i, j - 1)$, $(i - 1, j - 1)$ and $(i - 1, j)$.

Algorithm in Linear Time

This problem can easily be solved with dynamic programming. Suppose the rows are numbered from top to bottom and the columns from left to right. A square is said to *finish* at (i, j) if its bottom right-hand corner is (i, j). If the square is of size k, it is made up of cells (i', j') for $i - k < i' \leq i$ and $j - k < j' \leq j$.

For each cell (i, j) of the grid, we seek the largest integer k such that the square of size k finishing on (i, j) is completely black. Assign $A[i, j]$ as this value. If the cell (i, j) is white, then $A[i, j] = 0$, which corresponds to the absence of a black square.

Every black square of size k contains four black square of size $k - 1$. Hence, $A[i, j] = k$ for $k \geq 1$ if and only if each of the three values $A[i - 1, j]$, $A[i - 1, j - 1], A[i, j - 1]$ is at least $k - 1$. Conversely, if the cell (i, j) is white and these three values are at least ℓ, then the union of the corresponding squares together with the cell (i, j) contain a square of size $\ell + 1$ finishing at (i, j).

These observations lead to the following recurrence formula:

$$A[i, j]$$
$$= \begin{cases} 0 & \text{if the cell } (i, j) \text{ is white,} \\ 1 + \min\{A[i - 1, j], A[i - 1, j - 1], A[i, j - 1]\} & \text{otherwise.} \end{cases}$$

Problem

Making Chess Boards [spoj:CT101CC]

13.3   Largest Rectangle in a Histogram

Definition

Given a histogram in the form of an array of non-negative integers $x_0, \ldots, x_{n-1}$, the goal is to place a rectangle of maximal area within this histogram. This means finding an interval $[\ell, r)$ that maximises the area $(r - \ell) \times h$, where the height h is $h = \min_{\ell \leq i < r} x_i$.

Application

At the bottom of the Atlantic Ocean lies a telecommunications cable linking Europe and North America. The technical characteristics of this cable vary with time, as a function of the movements of the ocean, fluctuations of temperature, etc. Hence, at each moment there is a maximal bandwidth possible for transmission defining a function max bandwidth vs. time. Changing the transmission bandwidth for a connection is possible but requires an exchange between the terminals that prohibits any communication for a short time. Imagine that you know in advance the maximal bandwidths possibles for each of the 60×24 minutes of a day. You would like to find an interval of time and a bandwidth allowing the transmission of a maximal quantity of information without a disconnection. This problem reduces to finding a rectangle with maximal area within a histogram.

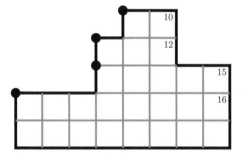

Figure 13.3 As long as the histogram is increasing, the corners are pushed onto the stack. When the histogram decreases, the higher corners must be popped, the corresponding candidate rectangles tested and then the last popped corner is pushed again but with the smaller height.

Algorithm in Linear Time

The algorithm is based on the sweep line technique. For each prefix $x_0, \ldots, x_{i-1}$ of the array, we maintain a collection of rectangles whose right-hand side has not yet been encountered. They are defined by a pair of integers (ℓ, h), where ℓ is the left-hand side and h is the height. It thus suffices to consider the rectangles maximal for inclusion, hence h is the minimum over $x_\ell, x_{\ell+1}, \ldots, x_{i-1}$ and $\ell = 0$ or $x_{\ell-1} < h$. Thus, the rectangle cannot be enlarged to the left or upwards without leaving the histogram. We store these pairs of integers in a stack ordered by h. An interesting observation: the pairs are also ordered by ℓ.

Now, for each value x_i, it is possible that the right side of certain rectangles has been found. This is notably the case for all of the rectangles encoded (ℓ, h) on the stack with $h > x_i$. The width of such a rectangle is $i - \ell$. However, the value x_i will also create a new pair (ℓ', x_i). The left side ℓ' is either the value ℓ of the last rectangle popped, or $\ell' = i$ if no element was popped, see Figure 13.3. To simplify the implementation, we pop a pair (ℓ, h) even when $h = x_i$.

```python
def rectangles_from_histogram(H):
    best = (float('-inf'), 0, 0, 0)
    S = []
    H2 = H + [float('-inf')]   # extra element to empty the queue
    for right, _ in enumerate(H2):
        x = H2[right]
        left = right
        while len(S) > 0 and S[-1][1] >= x:
            left, height = S.pop()
            # first element is area of candidate
            rect = (height * (right - left), left, height, right)
            if rect > best:
                best = rect
        S.append((left, x))
    return best
```

Problems
Largest Rectangle in a Histogram [spoj:HISTOGRA]
Galerie d'art [prologin:2012:galerie]

13.4   Largest Rectangle in a Grid

Application
Given a building site with trees scattered about the lot, we wish to find a maximal rectangular area on which to build a house without cutting any trees.

Definition
Given a black and white image in the form of an array of $n \times m$ pixels, we want to determine the largest completely black rectangle. Here, a rectangle is the intersection between a set of contiguous rows and a set of contiguous columns, see Figure 13.4.

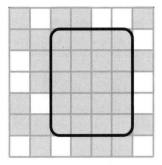

Figure 13.4 A black rectangle of maximal area in a grid.

Algorithm in Linear Time
The solution is based on the reduction to the search of the largest rectangle within a histogram. For each row i, we look for the largest black rectangle with its base on row i. For this, we maintain an array t which for each column j gives the maximal number k such that between (i, j) and $(i, j - k + 1)$ all the pixels are black. Then, t defines a histogram under which we seek the largest rectangle. The array t is easily updated from one row to the next, as a function of the colours of the pixels in each column.

```
def rectangles_from_grid(P, black=1):
    rows = len(P)
    cols = len(P[0])
    t = [0] * cols
    best = None
    for i in range(rows):
        for j in range(cols):
            if P[i][j] == black:
                t[j] += 1
            else:
                t[j] = 0
        (area, left, height, right) = rectangles_from_histogram(t)
        alt = (area, left, i, right, i-height)
        if best is None or alt > best:
            best = alt
    return best
```

13.5   Union of Rectangles

We now introduce a simple problem for which a plethora of interesting solutions exist.

Definition

Given n rectilinear rectangles, we would like to compute the area of their union. The same techniques could be used to compute the perimeter or the number of connected regions.

Key Observation

A first step is to make the complexity of our algorithms independent of the coordinates of the rectangles: these coordinates span at most $2n$ points on each axis. Therefore, they lie on a grid made up of $O(n^2)$ cells, which are either entirely covered by a rectangle or disjoint from every rectangle, see Figure 13.5.

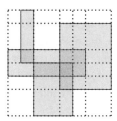

Figure 13.5 Grid with $O(n)$ rows and $O(n)$ columns. Each cell is either included in the union of rectangles or is disjoint from it.

Algorithm in $O(n^3)$

A first simple solution consists then of determining a Boolean array indicating for each cell if it is contained in the union of rectangles. The area of the union can then be computed by a simple sum of the areas of the cells. The work performed for each rectangle is $O(n^2)$, which leads to the announced complexity of $O(n^3)$.

```python
def rectangles_contains_point(R, x, y):
    for x1, y1, x2, y2 in R:
        if x1 <= x < x2 and y1 <= y < y2:
            return True
    return False


def union_rectangles_naive(R):
    X = set()          # set of all x coordinates in the input
    Y = set()          # same for y
    for x1, y1, x2, y2 in R:
        assert x1 <= x2 and y1 <= y2
        X.add(x1)
        X.add(x2)
        Y.add(y1)
        Y.add(y2)
    j_to_x = list(sorted(X))
    i_to_y = list(sorted(Y))
    # X and Y partition space into a grid
    area = 0
    for j in range(len(j_to_x) - 1):       # loop over columns in grid
        x1 = j_to_x[j]
        x2 = j_to_x[j + 1]
        for i in range(len(i_to_y) - 1):   # loop over rows
            y1 = i_to_y[i]                  # (x1,...,y2) is the grid cell
            y2 = i_to_y[i + 1]
            if rectangles_contains_point(R, x1, y1):
                area += (y2 - y1) * (x2 - x1)   # cell is covered
    return area
```

Key Observations and Skeleton

When dealing with a problem posed in two dimensions, it is often interesting to reduce it to the one-dimensional version. In this case, the one-dimensional analogue consists of computing the total length spanned by the union of a set of intervals. Let union_intervals be a function solving this problem. It can be implemented in time $O(n \log n)$ by processing the endpoints of the given intervals from left to right. Whenever a left endpoint is encountered, a counter opened is incremented, and whenever a right endpoint is encountered, the counter is decremented. The size of the union is cumulated in a variable union_size, to which we add the difference between the current and the previous endpoint in case opened is positive (*before* it is updated). For technical reasons, the function union_intervals needs to be able to process multisets of intervals. These can easily be implemented in Python using the Counter class.

```
from collections import Counter
OPENING = +1  # constants for events
CLOSING = -1  # -1 has higher priority
def union_intervals(intervals):
    union_size = 0
    events = []
    for x1, x2 in intervals:
        for _ in range(intervals[x1, x2]):
            assert x1 <= x2
            events.append((x1, OPENING))
            events.append((x2, CLOSING))
    previous_x = 0    # arbitrary initial value
    #                   ok, because opened == 0 at first event
    opened = 0
    for x, offset in sorted(events):
        if opened > 0:
            union_size += x - previous_x
        previous_x = x
        opened += offset
    return union_size
```

Algorithm in $O(n^2 \log n)$

How can the function union_intervals help us to solve the two-dimensional problem? Imagine a horizontal line, sweeping over the plane from bottom to top. Its intersection with the given rectangles at any given time consists of a set of intervals. Whenever the line reaches the bottom of a rectangle, a corresponding interval is added to the set, which is later removed when the sweep line reaches the top of the rectangle. The algorithm maintains the set of these intervals in a variable current_intervals. Similar to the one-dimensional version, the sweep line progresses by following a sorted event list. This list stores instructions for adding or removing intervals from the set current_intervals. Every instruction comes with a y-coordinate, which is used to define the order of their processing. The total area of the union of the rectangles is stored in a variable area. When processing an event, the sweep line is moved vertically by the difference between the y-coordinate of the current event and the previous event. This difference multiplied by union_intervals(current_intervals) is the area we need to add to the variable area.

The event list can be sorted in time $O(n \log n)$, before the events are processed. The bottleneck in processing an event is the running time of union_intervals, which is also $O(n \log n)$. This leads to a total time complexity of $O(n^2 \log n)$.

As a first structure, we can maintain a set of intervals: adding and removing intervals is done in constant time. Computing the total length spanned by their union can be done in $O(n \log n)$ by scanning them in increasing (left, right) coordinates, so the total complexity is $O(n^2 \log n)$.

```
def union_rectangles(R):
    events = []
    for x1, y1, x2, y2 in R:                        # initialize events
        assert x1 <= x2 and y1 <= y2
        events.append((y1, OPENING, x1, x2))
        events.append((y2, CLOSING, x1, x2))
    current_intervals = Counter()
    area = 0
    previous_y = 0   # arbitrary initial value,
    #                   ok, because union_intervals is 0 at first event
    for y, offset, x1, x2 in sorted(events):        # sweep top down
        area += (y - previous_y) * union_intervals(current_intervals)
        previous_y = y
        current_intervals[x1, x2] += offset
    return area
```

Algorithm in $O(n^2)$

There is an easy trick to shave off the logarithmic factor. The bottleneck in the function union_intervals is sorting the endpoints of the given intervals. To avoid this operation, we consider the set of all x-coordinates in the input (left or right borders of the rectangles) and use it to divide the horizontal axis into $O(n)$ elementary segments. We maintain an array of integers indicating for each segment how many rectangles cover it. Then adding or removing a new interval takes $O(n)$ time, as we must modify the counters of segments covered by the current interval. Computing the total length spanned by their union also takes $O(n)$, so the total complexity is $O(n^2)$.

```
def union_rectangles_fast(R):
    X = set()                      # set of all x coordinates in the input
    events = []                    # events for the sweep line
    for x1, y1, x2, y2 in R:
        assert x1 <= x2 and y1 <= y2
        X.add(x1)
        X.add(x2)
        events.append((y1, OPENING, x1, x2))
        events.append((y2, CLOSING, x1, x2))
    # array of x coordinates in left to right order
    i_to_x = list(sorted(X))
    # inverse dictionary maps x coordinate to its rank
    x_to_i = {xi: i for i, xi in enumerate(i_to_x)}
    # nb_current_rectangles[i] = number of rectangles intersected
    # by the sweepline in interval [i_to_x[i], i_to_x[i + 1]]
    nb_current_rectangles = [0] * (len(i_to_x) - 1)
    area = 0
    length_union_intervals = 0
    previous_y = 0  # arbitrary initial value,
    #                 because length is 0 at first iteration
    for y, offset, x1, x2 in sorted(events):
        area += (y - previous_y) * length_union_intervals
        i1 = x_to_i[x1]
        i2 = x_to_i[x2]            # update nb_current_rectangles
        for j in range(i1, i2):
            length_interval = i_to_x[j + 1] - i_to_x[j]
            if nb_current_rectangles[j] == 0:
                length_union_intervals += length_interval
            nb_current_rectangles[j] += offset
            if nb_current_rectangles[j] == 0:
                length_union_intervals -= length_interval
        previous_y = y
    return area
```

Algorithm in $O(n \log n)$

Is it possible to do even better by using a segment tree, a data structure used for queries for a minimum over a range of indices (see Section 4.5 on page 75). Indeed, the previous algorithm involves adding 1 or removing 1 over a range of indices, and computing a sum over indices with nonzero values. Our segment tree is initialised with two arrays L and t of size $2n - 1$. The ith segment is of length $L[i]$, and t plays the role of the array described in the previous algorithm: $t[i]$ counts how many rectangles cover the ith segment.

This segment tree allows the following operations:

- change(i, k, d) adds the value d to the elements $t[j]$ for $i \leq j < k$;
- cover() returns the sum $\sum L[j]$ taken over the indices j such that $t[j] \neq 0$.

The operation change is called whenever the sweep line encounters the bottom side of a rectangle ($d = 1$) or its top side ($d = -1$). The method cover() returns the total length spanned by the current intervals.

The data structure consists of a binary tree, where each node p is responsible for a range of indices I in t (and hence also in L). It possesses three attributes:

- $w[p]$ is the sum of $L[j]$ over $j \in I$.
- $c[p]$ is a quantity added to every $t[j]$ for $j \in I$.
- $s[p]$ is the sum of $L[j]$ over every $j \in I$ such that $t[j] \neq 0$.

The root of the tree is node 1 and the result of cover() is stored in $s[1]$. The array t is stored implicitly in the attribute c. The value $t[j]$ is the sum of $c[p]$ over all of the nodes p along the path from the root to the leaf node corresponding to j. As is the case for the structure for the minimum over a range (*minimum range query*), the update can be done in logarithmic time. See Figure 13.6 on the next page for an example of usage of such a segment tree.

The complexity of $O(n \log n)$ is justified by the required sort of the events.

```
class CoverQuery:
    def __init__(self, L):
        assert L != []                    # L is assumed sorted
        self.N = 1
        while self.N < len(L):
            self.N *= 2
        self.c = [0] * (2 * self.N)       # --- covered
        self.s = [0] * (2 * self.N)       # --- score
        self.w = [0] * (2 * self.N)       # --- length
        for i, _ in enumerate(L):
            self.w[self.N + i] = L[i]
        for p in range(self.N - 1, 0, -1):
            self.w[p] = self.w[2 * p] + self.w[2 * p + 1]
    def cover(self):
        return self.s[1]


    def change(self, i, k, offset):
        self._change(1, 0, self.N, i, k, offset)


    def _change(self, p, start, span, i, k, offset):
        if start + span <= i or k <= start:    # --- disjoint
            return
        if i <= start and start + span <= k:   # --- included
            self.c[p] += offset
        else:
            self._change(2 * p, start, span // 2, i, k, offset)
            self._change(2 * p + 1, start + span // 2, span // 2,
                         i, k, offset)
        if self.c[p] == 0:
            if p >= self.N:                    # --- leaf
                self.s[p] = 0
            else:
                self.s[p] = self.s[2 * p] + self.s[2 * p + 1]
        else:
            self.s[p] = self.w[p]
```

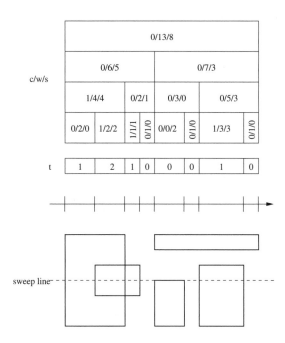

Figure 13.6 Illustration of the sweep and the data structure.

```
def union_rectangles_fastest(R):
    if R == []:                     # segment tree would fail on an empty list
        return 0
    X = set()                       # set of all x coordinates in the input
    events = []                     # events for the sweep line
    for Rj in R:
        (x1, y1, x2, y2) = Rj
        assert x1 <= x2 and y1 <= y2
        X.add(x1)
        X.add(x2)
        events.append((y1, OPENING, x1, x2))
        events.append((y2, CLOSING, x1, x2))
    i_to_x = list(sorted(X))
    # inverse dictionary
    x_to_i = {i_to_x[i]: i for i in range(len(i_to_x))}
    L = [i_to_x[i + 1] - i_to_x[i] for i in range(len(i_to_x) - 1)]
    C = CoverQuery(L)
    area = 0
    previous_y = 0  # arbitrary initial value,
    #                  because C.cover() is 0 at first iteration
    for y, offset, x1, x2 in sorted(events):
        area += (y - previous_y) * C.cover()
        i1 = x_to_i[x1]
        i2 = x_to_i[x2]
        C.change(i1, i2, offset)
        previous_y = y
    return area
```

13.6   Union of Disjoint Rectangles

Definition
Given n disjoint rectilinear rectangles, we wish to determine all pairs of adjacent rectangles.

Application
This can serve to compute the perimeter of the union, for example, by subtracting from the total of the perimeters of the rectangles the length of the contacts between all the adjacent rectangles. This last value must be taken with a factor of 2, as a unit of contact removes a unit of perimeter from each rectangle. Another application is to determine the connected components formed by the adjacent rectangles, see Figure 13.7.

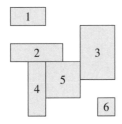

Figure 13.7 Detect the adjacency between the rectangles $(2,4), (2,5), (3,5)$ and $(4,5)$.

Algorithm in $O(n \log n)$
The algorithm uses the sweep line technique. We first explain how to determine the pairs of rectangles having their left or right sides touching. The case for the top and bottom sides is identical. A list of events is made up of the four corners of each of the n rectangles. Each event is an n-tuple (x, y, i, c), where (x, y) are the coordinates of the corner c of the ith rectangle, and c takes on the values $0, 1, 2, 3$ for bottom-right, top-right, bottom-left and top-left, respectively. The events are then processed in lexicographical order, which comes down to a sweep of the corners from left to right, and within a single column from bottom to top. In the case of identical corners, we consider first the top corners of the rectangles.

It then suffices to maintain the list of rectangles for which we have already seen a bottom corner in the column, but not yet the top corner. To guarantee that the rectangles are disjoint, this list contains at most two rectangles, a rectangle to the left of the column and one to the right. A bottom corner adds a rectangle to this list, whereas a top corner removes one. Finally, two rectangles are adjacent if and only if they are found in this list at the same time.

Variant

If in the problem statement, we consider two rectangles to be adjacent if even only a corner is shared, then it suffices to change the priorities and, for two identical points, first process the bottom corners and then the top corners.

Problem

City Park [icpcarchive:6889]

14 Numbers and Matrices

This short chapter presents a few efficient implementations of classic manipulations of numbers: arithmetical operations, evaluation of expressions, resolution of linear systems, and sequences of multiplication of matrices.

14.1 GCD

Definition
Given two integers a, b we seek the largest integer p such that a and b can be expressed as integer multiples of p; this is their *greatest common divisor* (GCD).

The calculation of the GCD can be implemented recursively to be very efficient. A mnemonic trick: from the second iteration on, we arrange to always have the second argument smaller than the first: a mod $b < b$.

```
def pgcd(a, b):
    return a if b == 0 else pgcd(b, a % b)
```

The complexity of this division version of Euclid's algorithm is $O(\log a + \log b)$. Indeed, the first parameter diminishes by at least a factor of two every second iteration.

14.2 Bézout Coefficients

Definition
For two integers a and b, we would like to find two integers u and v such that $au + bv = d$ where d is the GCD of a and b.

This calculation is based on an observation similar to the above. If $a = qb + r$, then $au + bv = d$ corresponds to $(qb + r)u + bv = d$, or $bu' + rv' = d$ for

$$\begin{cases} u' = qu + v \\ v' = u \end{cases} \quad \Leftrightarrow \quad \begin{cases} u = v' \\ v = u' - qv' \end{cases} .$$

This calculation also terminates in $O(\log a + \log b)$ steps.

Variant

Certain problems involve the calculation of extremely large numbers, and consequently require a response modulo a large prime number p in order to test if the solution is correct. Since p is prime, we can easily divide by an integer a non-multiple of p: a and p are relatively prime, hence their Bézout coefficients satisfy $au + pv = 1$, hence au is equal to 1 modulo p and u is the inverse of a. Hence, to divide by a, we can instead multiply by u (mod p).

```python
def bezout(a, b):
    if b == 0:
        return (1, 0)
    u, v = bezout(b, a % b)
    return (v, u - (a // b) * v)


def inv(a, p):
    return bezout(a, p)[0] % p
```

14.3 Binomial Coefficients

In the calculation of $\binom{n}{k}$, equal to $n!/(k!(n-k)!)$, it is risky to calculate $n(n-1)\cdots(n-k+1)$ and $k!$ separately, given the possibility of an overflow. We can exploit the fact that the product of i consecutive integers always contains a term divisible by i.

```python
def binom(n, k):
    prod = 1
    for i in range(k):
        prod = (prod * (n - i)) // (i + 1)
    return prod
```

For most of these problems, the calculation of binomial coefficients needs to be taken modulo a prime number p. The code then becomes as follows, with complexity $O(k(\log k + \log p))$, relying on the calculation of the Bézout coefficients.

```python
def binom_modulo(n, k, p):
    prod = 1
    for i in range(k):
        prod = (prod * (n - i) * inv(i + 1, p)) % p
    return prod
```

An alternative is to calculate Pascal's triangle by dynamic programming, which could be interesting if $\binom{n}{k}$ needs to be calculated for numerous pairs n, k.

14.4   Fast Exponentiation

Definition
Given a, b we wish to calculate a^b. Again, as the result risks being enormous, we are often asked to perform the calculation modulo a given integer p, but this does not change the nature of the problem.

Algorithm in $O(\log b)$
The naive approach performs $b - 1$ multiplications by a. However, we can rapidly calculate the powers of a of the form $a^1, a^2, a^4, a^8, \ldots$ using the relation $a^{2^k} \cdot a^{2^k} = a^{2^{k+1}}$. A trick consists of combining these values according to the binary decomposition of b. Example:

$$a^{13} = a^{8+4+1}$$
$$= a^8 \cdot a^4 \cdot a^1.$$

For this calculation, it suffices to generate $O(\log_2 b)$ powers of a. The implementation below is reproduced with the gracious permission of Louis Abraham. At the ith iteration, the variable a contains $a_0^{2^i}$ modulo p and the variable b contains $\lfloor b_0/2^i \rfloor$, where a_0, b_0 are the inputs to the function. Thus, it suffices to test the parity bit of b in the body of the loop to determine the binary decomposition of b. The operation b »= 1 is equivalent to performing an integer division of b by 2.

```python
def fast_exponentiation(a, b, q):
    assert a >= 0 and b >= 0 and q >= 1
    result = 1
    while b:
        if b % 2 == 1:
            result = (result * a) % q
        a = (a * a) % q
        b >>= 1
    return result
```

Variant
This technique can also be applied to matrix multiplications. Let A be a matrix and b a positive integer. Rapid exponentiation allows the calculation of A^b with only $O(\log b)$ matrix multiplications.

Problems
The last digit [spoj:LASTDIG]
Tiling a grid with dominoes [spoj:GNY07H]

14.5   Prime Numbers

The Sieve of Eratosthenes

Given n, we seek all prime numbers less than n. The Sieve of Eratosthenes is a simple method to execute this task. We begin with a list of all the integers less than n, with initially 0 and 1 marked. Then, for each $p = 2, 3, 4, \ldots, n - 1$, if p is not marked, then it is prime, and in this case we mark all the multiples of p. The complexity of this procedure is delicate to analyse; it is in fact $O(n \log \log n)$.

Implementation Details

The proposed implementation skips marking 0, 1 as well as the multiples of 2. This is why the iteration over p is done with a step of 2, in order to test only the odd numbers.

```python
def eratosthene(n):
    P = [True] * n
    answ = [2]
    for i in range(3, n, 2):
        if P[i]:
            answ.append(i)
            for j in range(2 * i, n, i):
                P[j] = False
    return answ
```

The Gries–Misra Sieve

A deficiency of the preceding algorithm is that it marks the same composite number several times. An improvement was proposed by David Gries and Jayadev Misra in 1978 that gets around this deficiency and has a theoretical complexity of $O(n)$. We thus gain a factor of $\log \log n$. Their algorithm is not much longer but the multiplicative constant in the complexity is a bit larger. Our experiments have shown an improvement in the execution time with, in general, a factor $1/2$ for the interpretor pypy, but a deterioration by a factor 3 for the interpretor python3.

Dexter Kozen showed that the algorithm could at the same time produce an array factor associating with every integer $2 \leq x < n$ the smallest non-trivial integer factor of x. This array is very useful in the generation of the decomposition in prime factors of a given integer.

The algorithm is based on the unique prime decomposition of a composite integer (fundamental theorem of arithmetic). Indeed, an integer y can be written in the form

$$y = \text{factor}[y] \cdot x$$

with $\text{factor}[y] \leq \text{factor}[x]$.

The algorithm enumerates all of the composite integers by looping first on $x = 2, \ldots, n - 1$, and then over all the prime numbers p, with $p \leq \text{factor}[x]$, where p

plays the role of factor[y] in the expression $y = p \cdot x$. The algorithm is correct, since at the time of processing x, all prime numbers less than or equal to x have been found, as well as the smallest factor of x. As every number y between 2 and $n-1$ is examined exactly once, the complexity of the algorithm is $O(n)$.

```
def gries_misra(n):
    primes = []
    factor = [0] * n
    for x in range(2, n):
        if not factor[x]:        # no factor found
            factor[x] = x        # meaning x is prime
            primes.append(x)
        for p in primes:         # loop over primes found so far
            if p > factor[x] or p * x >= n:
                break
            factor[p * x] = p    # p is the smallest factor of p * x
    return primes, factor
```

Problems
The Spiral of Primes [icpcarchive:2120]
Prime or Not [spoj:PON]
Bazinga! [spoj:DCEPC505]

14.6   Evaluate an Arithmetical Expression

Definition
Given an expression obeying a certain fixed syntax, we would like to construct the syntax (parse) tree or evaluate the value of the expression, see Figure 14.1.

Figure 14.1 The syntax tree associated with the expression $2 + (3 \times 4)/2$.

Approaches
In general, this problem is solved by decomposing the stream containing the expression into a series of lexical tokens, using a tool called a *scanner* or *lexical analyzer*.

Then, as a function of the lexical tokens identified, we construct the syntax tree according to a grammar, using a tool known as a *parser*.

However, if the syntax is similar to that of arithmetical expressions, an evaluation method using two stacks can be used, which is much simpler to implement. One stack contains the values and the other the operators. Each value encountered is pushed as-is onto the value stack. For each operator p encountered, before pushing it onto the operator stack, the following must be performed: as long as the top element q of the operator stack has priority at least as high as p, we pop q, as well as the last two a, b, and then push onto the value stack the result of the expression $a\ q\ b$ (the result of the operation q on the operands a, b).

In this manner, the evaluation of operators is delayed until the priority of the operators forces the evaluation, see Figure 14.2.

A special case is needed to distinguish the binary minus operator from the unary minus sign for integer constants. Usually, it suffices to test if the previous token was an operator or a closing parenthesis.

Spreadsheet Example

Consider a spreadsheet where each cell can contain either a value or an arithmetical expression. This expression can be composed of numerical constants and identifiers of cells, linked by the operators - + * / and parentheses.

We represent an expression by an integer, a character string or a triplet composed of an operator and two operands. The numerical evaluation of an expression is realised by the following recursive function, where cell is a dictionary, associating the names of cells to their contents.

token	value stack	operator stack
2	2	Ø
+	2	+
3	2,3	+
*	2,3	+,*
4	2,3,4	+,*
/	2,12	+
	2,12	+,/
2	2,12,2	+,/
;	2,6	+
	8	Ø

Figure 14.2 Example of the evaluation of the expression $2 + 3 \times 4/2$ with the marker ' ; ' as 'end of expression'.

```
def arithm_expr_eval(cell, expr):
    if isinstance(expr, tuple):
        (left, operand, right) = expr
        lval = arithm_expr_eval(cell, left)
        rval = arithm_expr_eval(cell, right)
        if operand == '+':
            return lval + rval
        if operand == '-':
            return lval - rval
        if operand == '*':
            return lval * rval
        if operand == '/':
            return lval // rval
    elif isinstance(expr, int):
        return expr
    else:
        cell[expr] = arithm_expr_eval(cell, cell[expr])
        return cell[expr]
```

The syntax tree is constructed following the method described above. Note the particular handling of the parentheses. A left parenthesis is always pushed onto the operator stack without doing anything else. Meeting a right parenthesis provokes the popping of the stack and the construction of the expressions, until the top of the operator stack corresponds to the matching left parenthesis; this is in turn popped. To completely empty the stacks at the end of the processing, we add to the stream a token ' ; ' as end of expression, and assign it the minimal priority.

```
PRIORITY = {';': 0, '(': 1, ')': 2, '-': 3, '+': 3, '*': 4, '/': 4}


def arithm_expr_parse(line_tokens):
    vals = []
    ops = []
    for tok in line_tokens + [';']:
        if tok in PRIORITY:  # tok is an operator
            while (tok != '(' and ops and
                    PRIORITY[ops[-1]] >= PRIORITY[tok]):
                right = vals.pop()
                left = vals.pop()
                vals.append((left, ops.pop(), right))
            if tok == ')':
                ops.pop()    # this is the corresponding '('
            else:
                ops.append(tok)
        elif tok.isdigit():  # tok is an integer
            vals.append(int(tok))
        else:                # tok is an identifier
            vals.append(tok)
    return vals.pop()
```

Beware of a Trap!
An error often committed during the implementation of this code is to write:

```
vals.append((vals.pop(), ops.pop(), vals.pop()))
```

which has the undesirable effect of inverting the left and right values of the expression, because of the order of evaluation of the arguments of the method append.

Problems
Boolean Logic [spoj:BOOLE]
Arithmetic Expressions [spoj:AREX]
Cells [spoj:IPCELLS]

14.7   System of Linear Equations

Definition
A system of linear equations is composed of n variables and m linear equations. Formally, a matrix A of dimension $n \times m$ is given, along with a column vector b of size m. The goal is to find a vector x such that $Ax = b$.

Application: Random Walk
Suppose we have a connected graph with the arcs labelled by probabilities, where the total weight of each outgoing arc is equal to 1. Such a graph is known as a *Markov chain*. A random walk is a walk that starts from a vertex u_0, then at the current vertex u an arc (u, v), chosen with the associated probability, is traversed. We want to know for each vertex v the expected time x_v for the walk to reach v. Then, by definition $x_{u_0} = 0$ and $x_v = \sum_u (x_u + 1) p_{uv}$, where p_{uv} is the probability associated with the arc (u, v) or 0 if it does not exist.

However, another application exists concerning random walks. After t steps, each vertex has a certain probability for the presence of the walker. In certain cases, this walk converges to a stationary distribution on the vertices. The calculation of this distribution boils down to solving a system of linear equations, where A essentially encodes the probabilities of the arcs, and the solution sought x is the stationary distribution.

Application: A System of Weights and Springs
Imagine a system composed of heavy balls linked by springs of negligible weight. Certain springs are hanging from the ceiling, and the springs can be compressed or stretched, see Figure 14.3. Given the position and weight of the balls, we would like to know if the system is stable or if it will start moving. The system will be stable if for each spring we have values, representing the force exercised on its ends, such that

the forces (including gravitational) cancel out for every ball. This is again a problem of resolution of a system of linear equations.

Application: Geometrical Intersection
In geometry, lines and hyperplanes are defined by linear equations. Determining their intersection reduces to the resolution of a system of linear equations.

Algorithm in $O(n^2m)$
If A were the identity matrix, then the solution of the system would be b. We are going to diagonalise A to obtain a form as close as possible to this ideal situation.

For this, we apply transformations that preserve the solutions of the system, such as changing the order of variables, exchanging two equations, multiplying one equation by a constant and adding one equation to another.

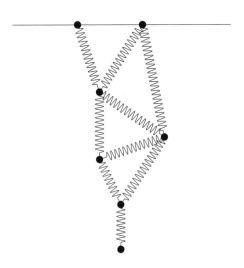

Figure 14.3 A system of balls and springs.

In order to simplify these manipulations and not modify the parameters A and b, we store the system of equations in a matrix S, which is composed of a copy of A along with an extra column containing b and an extra row containing the indices of the variables. Thus, when the columns are exchanged in S, it is possible to remember to which variable each column corresponds.

The invariant is the following: after k iterations, the first k columns of S are all zero, except on the diagonal where there are 1's, see Figure 14.4.

To obtain the invariant, we divide the kth row of S—hence the kth equation—by $S[k,k]$ if it is non-zero, which brings a 1 to the index (k,k). Then we subtract the kth equation from every equation $i \neq k$, but multiplied by the factor $S[i,k]$, bringing a 0 to all of the indices (i,k) for every $i \neq k$, as required by the invariant.

What can we do if $S[k,k]$ is nonetheless zero? We begin before these operations by looking for an element $S[i,j]$ of greatest absolute value in the rectangle between $S[k,k]$ and $S[m-1,n-1]$. This element is typically called the *pivot*; we choose the one of greatest absolute value in order to minimise rounding errors. Then we swap the columns k and j as well as the rows k and i. These operations preserve the solutions of the system.

But what if this rectangle contains nothing but zeros? In this case, the diagonalisation is terminated, and the solution must be extracted in the following manner.

If the diagonalisation terminates prematurely after k iterations, and the rows of S from k to $m-1$ are all zero, then the last column of these rows must be verified. If an element exists with a non-zero value v, then it represents the contradiction $0 = v$, and hence the system can be stated to be without a solution. Otherwise, the system admits at least one solution. Let k be the number of iterations executed by the diagonalisation. We have $k \leq \min\{n,m\}$. If $k < n$, then the system has several solutions. To choose one, we decide to set to 0 the variables corresponding to the columns k to $n-1$ in S. Then, the values of the other variables are given in the last column, forced by the diagonal of 1 in S. Finally, if $k = n$, then the solution is unique.

$$
A = \begin{pmatrix} 1 & 0 & 0 & \cdot & \cdot & \cdot \\ 0 & 1 & 0 & \cdot & \cdot & \cdot \\ 0 & 0 & 1 & \cdot & \cdot & \cdot \\ 0 & 0 & 0 & \cdot & \cdot & \cdot \\ 0 & 0 & 0 & \cdot & \cdot & \cdot \\ 0 & 0 & 0 & \cdot & \cdot & \cdot \end{pmatrix} \quad b = \begin{pmatrix} \cdot \\ \cdot \\ \cdot \\ \cdot \\ \cdot \\ \cdot \end{pmatrix}
$$

Figure 14.4 Structure of the invariant for $k = 3$.

Implementation Details

As we work here with floating point numbers, with rounding errors possible for each calculation, it is necessary to permit a slight tolerance when testing equality to zero. When subtracting the kth row from the ith row, we must assign the coefficient $S[i][k]$ to a variable `fact`, as the operation will change the value of $S[i][k]$. To calculate the solution exactly, we could work with fractions instead of floating point numbers. In this case, it is important to reduce the fractions at each iteration, otherwise the numerators and denominators of the solution could contain an exponential number of digits. Without the normalisation, the Gauss–Jordan algorithm is not polynomial, but happily the Python class `Fraction` reduces the fractions at each operation.

Variants

If the matrix is sparse, i.e. it contains only a small number of non-zero elements per row and column, then the execution time can be reduced from $O(n^2 m)$ to $O(n)$.

```python
def is_zero(x):                          # tolerance
    return -1e-6 < x and x < 1e-6
    # replace with x == 0 si we are handling Fraction elements


GJ_ZERO_SOLUTIONS = 0
GJ_SINGLE_SOLUTION = 1
GJ_SEVERAL_SOLUTIONS = 2


def gauss_jordan(A, x, b):
    n = len(x)
    m = len(b)
    assert len(A) == m and len(A[0]) == n
    S = []                               # put linear system in a single matrix S
    for i in range(m):
        S.append(A[i][:] + [b[i]])
    S.append(list(range(n)))             # indices in x
    k = diagonalize(S, n, m)
    if k < m:
        for i in range(k, m):
            if not is_zero(S[i][n]):
                return GJ_ZERO_SOLUTIONS
    for j in range(k):
        x[S[m][j]] = S[j][n]
    if k < n:
        for j in range(k, n):
            x[S[m][j]] = 0
        return GJ_SEVERAL_SOLUTIONS
    return GJ_SINGLE_SOLUTION


def diagonalize(S, n, m):
    for k in range(min(n, m)):
        val, i, j = max((abs(S[i][j]), i, j)
                        for i in range(k, m) for j in range(k, n))
        if is_zero(val):
            return k
        S[i], S[k] = S[k], S[i]      # swap lines k, i
        for r in range(m + 1):       # swap columns k, j
            S[r][j], S[r][k] = S[r][k], S[r][j]
        pivot = float(S[k][k])       # without float if Fraction elements
        for j in range(k, n + 1):
            S[k][j] /= pivot         # divide line k by pivot
        for i in range(m):           # remove line k scaled by line i
            if i != k:
                fact = S[i][k]
                for j in range(k, n + 1):
                    S[i][j] -= fact * S[k][j]
    return min(n, m)
```

Problems
Ars Longa [icpcarchive:3563]
Linear Equation Solver [spoj:LINQSOLV]

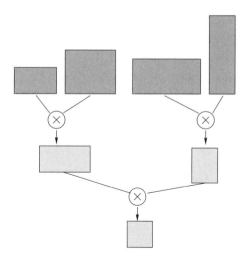

Figure 14.5 What parentheses should be added to multiply a sequence of matrices with the least total number of operations?

14.8   Multiplication of a Matrix Sequence

Definition
Given n matrices $M_1, \ldots, M_n$, where the ith matrix has r_i rows and c_i columns, with $c_i = r_{i+1}$ for every $1 \leq i < n$. We would like to calculate the product $M_1 M_2 \cdots M_n$ with as few operations as possible. By associativity, it is possible to place the parentheses in different ways. We have the following equality by associativity of the matrix product, but the number of operations could differ, based on the sizes of the various sub-products:

$$(((M_1 M_2)M_3)M_4 = M_1(M_2(M_3(M_4))) = (M_1 M_2)(M_3 M_4).$$

To multiply two matrices M_i and M_{i+1}, we use the standard algorithm which executes $r_i c_i c_{i+1}$ numerical multiplications. The goal is to find how to place the parentheses so as to multiply with least cost, see Figure 14.5.

Algorithm in $O(n^2)$
The recurrence formula[1] is simple. The last multiplication multiplies the result of $M_1 \cdots M_k$ with the result of $M_{k+1} \cdots M_n$ for a certain $1 \leq k < n$. Let opt(i, j) be the minimal cost for calculating $M_i \cdots M_j$. Then $opt(i, i) = 0$ and for $i < j$

$$\text{opt}(i, j) = \min_{i \leq k < j} (\text{opt}(i, k) + \text{opt}(k + 1, j) + r_i c_k c_j. \tag{14.1}$$

If we wish to compute both the cost of the optimal order and the order itself, we must store side by side with the matrix opt a matrix arg, containing the index k which realises the minimisation (14.1). This is done in the following implementation. The

---

[1] The complexity concerns only the computation of the optimal placement of parentheses, and not the operation of matrix multiplication itself.

function `opt_mult(M,opt,i,j)` then optimally multiplies $M_i \cdots M_j$ according to the information contained in `opt`.

Note the order in which the indices i, j are processed. By considering the increasing order of $j - i$, we can be sure that the values for the couples i, k and $k + 1, j$, necessary for the identification of the minimum in (14.1), will already have been computed.

```python
def matrix_mult_opt_order(M):
    n = len(M)
    r = [len(Mi) for Mi in M]
    c = [len(Mi[0]) for Mi in M]
    opt = [[0 for j in range(n)] for i in range(n)]
    arg = [[None for j in range(n)] for i in range(n)]
    for j_i in range(1, n):   # loop on i, j of increasing j - i = j_i
        for i in range(n - j_i):
            j = i + j_i
            opt[i][j] = float('inf')
            for k in range(i, j):
                alt = opt[i][k] + opt[k + 1][j] + r[i] * c[k] * c[j]
                if opt[i][j] > alt:
                    opt[i][j] = alt
                    arg[i][j] = k
    return opt, arg


def matrix_chain_mult(M):
    opt, arg = matrix_mult_opt_order(M)
    return _apply_order(M, arg, 0, len(M)-1)


def _apply_order(M, arg, i, j):
    # --- multiply matrices from M[i] to M[j] included
    if i == j:
        return M[i]
    k = arg[i][j]          # --- follow placement of parentheses
    A = _apply_order(M, arg, i, k)
    B = _apply_order(M, arg, k + 1, j)
    row_A = range(len(A))
    row_B = range(len(B))
    col_B = range(len(B[0]))
    return [[sum(A[a][b] * B[b][c] for b in row_B)
            for c in col_B] for a in row_A]
```

An even better algorithm exists in $O(n \log n)$, see (Hu and Shing, 1984), but we do not present it here.

Problems
Mixtures [spoj:Mixtures]
The Safe Secret [kattis:safesecret]
Sweet and Sour Rock [spoj:ROCK]

15 Exhaustive Search

For some combinatorial problems, no polynomial time algorithm is known. The usual last-gasp (desperate!) solution is then to exhaustively explore the space of potential solutions. The word *combinatorial* here refers to structures which are combined from simpler structures. Examples include the construction of trees by a combination of subtrees, or the assembly of tilings with small tiles. Exhaustive exploration then consists of exploring the implicit tree of possible constructions in order to detect a solution. The nodes of the tree represent partial constructions, and when they can no longer be extended to a solution, for example by the violation of some constraint, the exploration backs up and examines alternate branches. This technique is known as *backtracking*.

We will illustrate these principles with a simple example.

15.1   All Paths for a Laser

Definition
Suppose there is a rectangular grid, surrounded by a border with two openings in the top row, one on the left and one on the right. Certain cells of the grid contain double-faced mirrors, which can be oriented in two possible directions, diagonal or anti-diagonal, see Figure 15.1. The goal is to orient the mirrors in such a way that a laser beam entering by the left opening exits by the right opening. The laser beam traverses the empty cells horizontally or vertically, but when it hits a mirror, it is deflected by 90 degrees to the right or to the left, depending on the orientation of the mirror. If the beam hits the boundary of the grid, it is absorbed.

Reduction to a Problem of Maximum Matching
This reduction was constructed with Martin Hoefer and Lê Thánh Dũng Nguyễn in 2016, but was probably already known.

The problem can be modelled by a graph, see Figure 15.2, which admits a perfect matching (where all the vertices are matched) if and only if the laser problem has a solution. Each mirror generates up to four vertices, one for each direction, *top, left, bottom, right*. We assign (a, d) as the vertex corresponding to the mirror a and in the direction d. If a mirror b is accessible from the mirror a by the direction d, then the

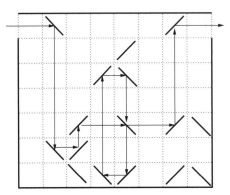

Figure 15.1 An orientation of the mirrors permitting the laser beam to traverse the grid.

vertices (a, d) and $(b, -d)$ are present in the graph and linked by an edge, where $-d$ denotes the opposite direction to d. However, if the direction d from a mirror a leads to the wall, then there is no vertex (a, d) present in the graph. The construction is completed with a vertex per opening, linked to the first accessible mirror, if such exists.

Figure 15.2 Reduction of the laser problem (left) to a perfect matching problem (right). The matching edges are shown with solid lines.

We can verify that every perfect matching in this graph corresponds to a solution of the laser problem and vice-versa. We distinguish the rectilinear edges linking the mirrors, and the diagonal edges linking different vertices associated with the same mirror. The interpretation is as follows. A rectilinear edge in the matching indicates that the beam will not follow this path, whereas a diagonal edge, say between vertices (a, d) and (a, e), indicates that the beam can be reflected from the mirror a by the directions d et e.

The graph thus produced is not bipartite. To compute a maximal matching we must thus resort to Jack Edmonds' 'flowers and petals' algorithm (1965), with a complexity of $O(n^2)$, where n is the number of mirrors. However, this is quite long and difficult to implement, which is why we propose in this section an alternative solution, which in contrast has exponential complexity in the worst case.

Algorithm

We propose a solution by exhaustive exploration. For each mirror, we store a state that can be one of three types: the two orientations and a type 'without orientation'. Initially, the mirrors are all without orientation. Then the route of the laser beam is simulated, from its entrance by the left opening.

- When an oriented mirror is hit, the beam is reflected as a function of the orientation.
- When the beam hits a mirror without orientation, two recursive calls are made, one for each possible orientation of the mirror. If one of these calls finds a solution, it is returned. If neither call finds a solution, the mirror is returned to the unoriented position and a failure code is returned.
- If the beam hits the boundary, the recursive procedure terminates with a failure code. The exploration then *backtracks* and considers other possible orientations.
- Finally, if ever the opening on the top right is reached, the solution is returned.

Implementation Details

The n mirrors whose positions are given as input are numbered from 0 to $n - 1$. Two dummy mirrors are placed at the openings and numbered n and $n + 1$. The program produces an array L with the coordinates and the indices of the mirrors.

The four possible directions of the beam are represented by the integers from 0 to 3, and the two orientations by 0, 1. An array reflex of dimension 4×2 indicates the change of direction made by the beam if it arrived in a given direction on a mirror with a given orientation.

In a pre-computation, the successive mirrors of a same row or a same column are linked together, with the help of the array next_. For a mirror i and a direction d, the element next_[i][d] indicates the index of the next mirror the beam will hit when it leaves i in the direction d. This entry is set to None if the beam is sent to the boundary. To populate the array next_, the array L is scanned first of all row by row and then column by column. Note the sort function that reverses the indices row and column for the lexicographic sort.

The variables last_i, last_r, last_c contain the information concerning the last mirror seen in the scan. If the last mirror is in the same row as the current mirror (for the scan row by row), then the two must be linked by the indications of their respective references in the array next_.

```
# directions
UP = 0
LEFT = 1
DOWN = 2
RIGHT = 3
# orientations None:? 0:/ 1:\

# destination UP            LEFT        DOWN            RIGHT
reflex = [[RIGHT, LEFT], [DOWN, UP], [LEFT, RIGHT], [UP, DOWN]]


def laser_mirrors(rows, cols, mir):
    # build structures
    n = len(mir)
    orien = [None] * (n + 2)
    orien[n] = 0       # arbitrary orientations
    orien[n + 1] = 0
    succ = [[None for direc in range(4)] for i in range(n + 2)]
    L = [(mir[i][0], mir[i][1], i) for i in range(n)]
    L.append((0, -1, n))                    # enter
    L.append((0, cols, n + 1))              # exit
    last_r, last_i = None, None
    for (r, c, i) in sorted(L):             # sweep by row
        if last_r == r:
            succ[i][LEFT] = last_i
            succ[last_i][RIGHT] = i
        last_r, last_i = r, i
    last_c = None
    for (r, c, i) in sorted(L, key=lambda rci: (rci[1], rci[0])):
        if last_c == c:                     # sweep by column
            succ[i][UP] = last_i
            succ[last_i][DOWN] = i
        last_c, last_i = c, i
    if solve(succ, orien, n, RIGHT):        # exploration
        return orien[:n]
    return None
```

The actual exploration is implemented recursively. For this kind of difficult problem, the instances are often quite small, so that there is little risk of overflowing the stack during the recursive calls. Note that after unsuccessfully exploring two subtrees corresponding to two possible orientations of the mirror j, the program sets back the contents of the variables to the correct state, i.e. to the position without orientation.

```
def solve(succ, orien, i, direc):
    assert orien[i] is not None
    j = succ[i][direc]
    if j is None:           # basic case
        return False
    if j == len(orien) - 1:
        return True
    if orien[j] is None:    # try both orientations
        for x in [0, 1]:
            orien[j] = x
            if solve(succ, orien, j, reflex[direc][x]):
                return True
        orien[j] = None
        return False
    return solve(succ, orien, j, reflex[direc][orien[j]])
```

15.2 The Exact Cover Problem

The Rolls-Royce of exhaustive search algorithms is the algorithm of *dancing links* (Knuth, 2000), which solves a quite general problem known as *exact cover*. Many problems can be reduced to it, hence mastering this technique can provide a real advantage in competitions.

Definition

The problem of exact cover concerns a set of points U, called the universe, and a collection of subsets of U, $\mathcal{S} \subseteq 2^U$, see Figure 15.3. A set $A \subseteq U$ is said to cover $x \in U$ if $x \in A$. The goal is to find a selection of sets of $\mathcal{S}$, i.e. a collection $\mathcal{S}^* \subseteq \mathcal{S}$, covering each element of the universe exactly once.

In terms of a characteristic matrix, the problem can be described as follows. On input, we are given a binary matrix M, the columns of which represent the elements of the universe, and the rows represent the sets of the collection $\mathcal{S}$. The element $\langle x, A \rangle$ of the matrix is 1 if and only if $x \in A$. On output, we must generate a set of rows $\mathcal{S}^*$ such that the matrix restricted to $\mathcal{S}^*$ contains exactly one 1 in each column.

Applications

The game Sudoku can be seen as an exact cover problem, see Section 15.4 on page 238. This is also the case for the *tiling problem*, wherein a set of tiles must be used to cover an $m \times n$ grid without overlap. Each tile must be used exactly once, and each cell of the grid must be covered by exactly one tile. The cells and the tiles thus form the elements of the universe, whereas the placements of individual tiles constitute the sets.

The 'Dancing Links' algorithm

This algorithm uses an exhaustive exploration as described in the preceding section. Its particularity resides in the choice of the data structures for its implementation.

First, the algorithm chooses an element e, ideally included in a minimum of sets of $\mathcal{S}$, hence the most constrained. This choice has a good chance to generate small exploration trees. As the solution must cover e, it necessarily contains one and only one of the sets $A \in \mathcal{S}$ with $e \in A$. The search space is thus divided by the choice of such a subset. For each set A with $e \in A$, a solution $\mathcal{S}^*$ is sought for the subproblem, and in the positive case, the solution $\mathcal{S}^* \cup \{A\}$ is returned as a solution to the initial problem.

The subproblem in question is constructed from $\langle U, \mathcal{S} \rangle$ by removing the elements of A from U, since each element $f \in A$ is already covered by A, and it must not be covered a second time. Moreover, all the sets B intersecting A are removed from $\mathcal{S}$, otherwise some elements of A would be covered several times, see Figure 15.3.

In terms of a characteristic matrix M, the general structure of the algorithm is as follows. If the matrix M is empty, then the empty set, which is a solution, is returned. Otherwise, look for the column c of M containing as few 1's as possible,[1] Loop over all rows r that could cover c, i.e. $M_{rc} = 1$. For each such r, perform the following: remove from M the row r as well as all the columns c' covered by r ($M_{rc'} = 1$). If the matrix thus obtained admits a solution S then return $S \cup \{r\}$. Otherwise restore M, and try again with another choice for r.

Compact Representation by Doubly Linked Lists

To compactly represent the sparse matrix M, we store only the cells of M containing a 1, and double-link them both vertically and horizontally, see Figure 15.4. Then, for a given c, we can easily find all rows r such that $M_{rc} = 1$ by using the vertical links, and for a given r, all the c' such that $M_{rc'} = 1$ by using the horizontal links. Each cell thus requires four fields L, R, U, D, standing for left, right, up and down, to code these double links.

---

[1] This choice reduces the number of branches at this point, and hopefully the size of the search tree.

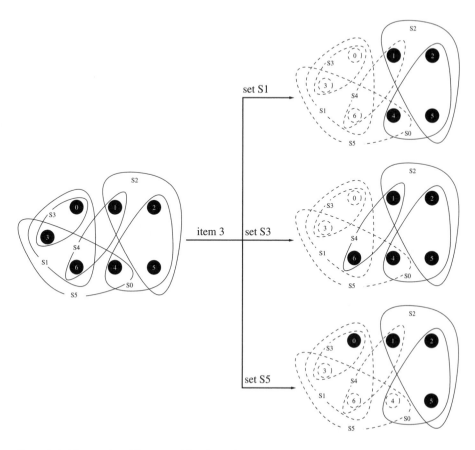

Figure 15.3 Three subproblems resulting from the choice of the element $e = 3$. Note that the third subproblem does not have a solution, as the element 0 cannot be covered.

For each column, we also require a header cell, which is included in the vertical linking, in order to gain access to the column. At the initialisation of the structure, the headers are stored in an array col indexed by the column numbers. Finally, we have a particular cell h, included in the horizontal linking of the column headers, in order to access them. This cell does not use the fields U,D.

Each cell possesses two additional fields S, C, the role of which depends on the type of cell. For the matrix cells, S contains the row number and C contains the column header. For the column header cells, S contains the number of 1's in the column, and the field C is ignored. The cell h ignores both of these fields.

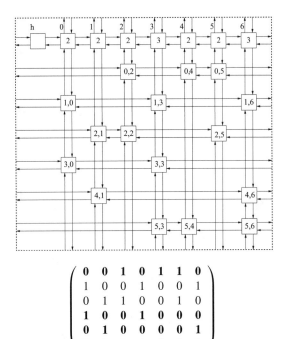

$$\begin{pmatrix} \mathbf{0} & \mathbf{0} & \mathbf{1} & \mathbf{0} & \mathbf{1} & \mathbf{1} & \mathbf{0} \\ 1 & 0 & 0 & 1 & 0 & 0 & 1 \\ 0 & 1 & 1 & 0 & 0 & 1 & 0 \\ \mathbf{1} & \mathbf{0} & \mathbf{0} & \mathbf{1} & \mathbf{0} & \mathbf{0} & \mathbf{0} \\ \mathbf{0} & \mathbf{1} & \mathbf{0} & \mathbf{0} & \mathbf{0} & \mathbf{0} & \mathbf{1} \\ 0 & 0 & 0 & 1 & 1 & 0 & 1 \end{pmatrix}$$

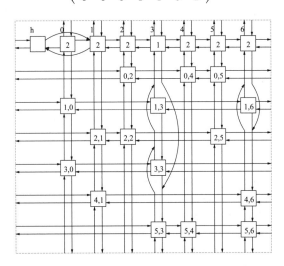

Figure 15.4 A binary matrix M, above its encoding and below the result of covering the column 0. The lists are circular, and the links leaving an edge of the image re-enter by the opposite edge.

```
class Cell:
    def __init__(self, horiz, verti, S, C):
        self.S = S
        self.C = C
        if horiz:
            self.L = horiz.L
            self.R = horiz
            self.L.R = self
            self.R.L = self
        else:
            self.L = self
            self.R = self
        if verti:
            self.U = verti.U
            self.D = verti
            self.U.D = self
            self.D.U = self
        else:
            self.U = self
            self.D = self

    def hide_verti(self):
        self.U.D = self.D
        self.D.U = self.U

    def unhide_verti(self):
        self.D.U = self
        self.U.D = self

    def hide_horiz(self):
        self.L.R = self.R
        self.R.L = self.L

    def unhide_horiz(self):
        self.R.L = self
        self.L.R = self
```

The Links

The idea of the algorithm of dancing links is due to Hitotsumatsu and Noshita in 1979 and was described by Donald Knuth (2000). To remove element c from a doubly linked list, it suffices to change the targets of the pointers of its neighbours, see Figure 15.5. To reinsert it in the list, it suffices to perform the reverse operations in the opposite order.

We use this observation to easily remove and restore a column of the matrix. The operation of *covering* a column c consists of removing it from the horizontal list of column headers, and for each row r with $M_{rc} = 1$, removing from the vertical lists all the cells corresponding to positions (r, c') in M with $M_{rc'} = 1$. We must make sure to keep up to date the counter S in the header of the cell c', decrementing it.

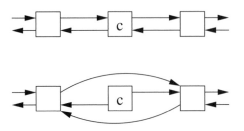

Figure 15.5 The operation hide removes element *c* from a doubly linked list. By preserving the pointers of *c*, it is then easy to reinsert it at its initial position.

```
def cover(c):           # c = heading cell of the column to cover
    assert c.C is None   # must be a heading cell
    c.hide_horiz()
    i = c.D
    while i != c:
        j = i.R
        while j != i:
            j.hide_verti()
            j.C.S -= 1    # one fewer entry in this column
            j = j.R
        i = i.D


def uncover(c):
    assert c.C is None
    i = c.U
    while i != c:
        j = i.L
        while j != i:
            j.C.S += 1    # one more entry in this column
            j.unhide_verti()
            j = j.L
        i = i.U
    c.unhide_horiz()
```

The Search

In the search procedure, we simply scan all the columns to find a column minimising the number of elements, hence with minimal counter *S*. We could accelerate this search by using a priority queue for the columns, but this would make the procedure of covering a column more costly. The following function writes the solution in an array sol if the function returns True.

```
def dancing_links(size_universe, sets):
    header = Cell(None, None, 0, None)  # building the cell structure
    col = []
    for j in range(size_universe):
        col.append(Cell(header, None, 0, None))
    for i, _ in enumerate(sets):
        row = None
        for j in sets[i]:
            col[j].S += 1                 # one more entry in this column
            row = Cell(row, col[j], i, col[j])
    sol = []
    if solve(header, sol):
        return sol
    return None
def solve(header, sol):
    if header.R == header:     # the instance is empty => solution found
        return True
    c = None                   # find the least covered column
    j = header.R
    while j != header:
        if c is None or j.S < c.S:
            c = j
        j = j.R
    cover(c)                    # cover this column
    r = c.D                     # try every row
    while r != c:
        sol.append(r.S)
        j = r.R                 # cover elements in set r
        while j != r:
            cover(j.C)
            j = j.R
        if solve(header, sol):
            return True
        j = r.L                 # uncover
        while j != r:
            uncover(j.C)
            j = j.L
        sol.pop()
        r = r.D
    uncover(c)
    return False
```

15.3   Problems

Sudoku [spoj:SUDOKU]
Making Jumps [spoj:MKJUMPS]

15.4   Sudoku

Several naive methods succeed in efficiently solving classic instances of Sudoku (see Figure 15.6). However, for Sudoku grids of size 16×16, the dancing links algorithm seems to be the right tool.

Figure 15.6 A Sudoku grid. The goal is to fill in the free squares so that each column, each row and each 3×3 block contains all the integers from 1 to 9.

Modelisation

How can we model the problem of Sudoku as an exact cover problem? There are four types of constraints. Each cell must contain a value. In each row of the Sudoku grid, every value must appear exactly once. The same holds for the columns and the blocks. There are thus four types of elements in the universe: the couples row-column, the couples row-value, the couples column-value and the couples block-value. These elements constitute the universe U of the instance $\langle U, S \rangle$ of the exact cover problem.

Then, the sets of S consist of assignments: triplets row-column-value, with each assignment covering exactly four elements of the universe.

The pleasant aspect of this representation is that it makes abstraction of the notions of rows, columns, blocks or values, giving a problem much easier to manipulate.

Sudoku grids typically come filled with a few predefined values. How can those be encoded? Our method consists of adding a new element e to the universe and a new set A to S that is the unique set containing e. Every solution must then include A. It then suffices to place in A all elements of the universe already covered by the initial assignments.

Encoding

The sets of the instance $\langle U, S \rangle$ of the exact cover correspond to assignments, and our implementation of the dancing links algorithm returns the solution in the form of an array with the indices of the selected sets. Hence, to recover the assignments corresponding to the indices, we must specify an encoding. We chose to encode the assignment of a value v to the square in row r and column c by the integer $81r + 9c + v$ (replace the coefficients by 256 and 16 for the case of a 16×16 Sudoku).

Similarly, the elements of the universe are encoded by integers. For example, the couple row-column r, c is encoded by $9r + c$, the couple row-value r, v by $81 + 9r + v$ and so on.

```
N = 3          # global constants
N2 = N * N
N4 = N2 * N2



# sets
def assignment(r, c, v): return r * N4 + c * N2 + v


def row(a): return a // N4


def col(a): return (a // N2) % N2


def val(a): return a % N2


def blk(a): return (row(a) // N) * N + col(a) // N
# elements to cover
def rc(a): return row(a) * N2 + col(a)


def rv(a): return row(a) * N2 + val(a) + N4


def cv(a): return col(a) * N2 + val(a) + 2 * N4


def bv(a): return blk(a) * N2 + val(a) + 3 * N4


def sudoku(G):
    global N, N2, N4
    if len(G) == 16:                # for a 16 x 16 sudoku grid
        N, N2, N4 = 4, 16, 256
    e = N * N4
    universe = e + 1
    S = [[rc(a), rv(a), cv(a), bv(a)] for a in range(N4 * N2)]
    A = [e]
    for r in range(N2):
        for c in range(N2):
            if G[r][c] != 0:
                a = assignment(r, c, G[r][c] - 1)
                A += S[a]
    sol = dancing_links(universe, S + [A])
    if sol:
        for a in sol:
            if a < len(S):
                G[row(a)][col(a)] = val(a) + 1
        return True
    return False
```

Problems
Easy sudoku [spoj:EASUDOKU]
Sudoku [spoj:SUDOKU]

15.5   Enumeration of Permutations

Applications
Certain problems, lacking structure, require a naive solution by testing one by one each element in the space of potential solutions. It is thus sometimes necessary to explore all permutations of a given array.

Example: Word Additions
Consider enigmas of the form

```
    S E N D
+   M O R E
= M O N E Y
```

where a distinct digit has to be assigned to each letter, in such a way that each word becomes a number without leading zero and the equation of the addition is correct. To solve this problem by naive enumeration, it suffices to construct an array tab = "@@DEMNORSY" composed of the letters of the problem, completed with enough @ as necessary to be of size 10. Then, there is a correspondence between the permutations of this array and the assignments of distinct digits to the letters, by assigning to each letter its rank in the array.

The interesting part is then the enumeration of all permutations of an array, and this is the subject of this section.

Definition
Given an array t of n elements, we want to determine the next permutation of t, in lexicographical order, or to signal that t is already maximal.

Key Observation
To permute t into the next lexicographical permutation, we need to preserve the longest possible prefix and exchange only elements in the suffix.

Algorithm in Linear Time
The algorithm consists of three steps. The first is to find the largest index p—called the *pivot*—such that $t[p] < t[p + 1]$. The idea is that the suffix of t begn inning at

$p + 1$ is a non-increasing sequence, and hence already lexicographically maximal. Hence, if such a pivot does not exist, the algorithm can terminate and announce the0. maximality of t.

Then, clearly $t[p]$ must be augmented, but in a minimal fashion. We thus seek within the suffix an index s such that $t[s]$ is minimal and $t[s] > t[p]$. As $p + 1$ is a candidate, such an index always exists. By swapping $t[p]$ with $t[s]$, we obtain an array that is lexicographically greater than the initial array. Finally, by sorting in increasing order the suffix of t starting at $p + 1$, we obtain the smallest permutation of t among those with prefix $t[1 \ldots p]$.

initial array	0	2	1	6	5	2	1
choice of pivot	0	2	[1]	6	5	2	1
swap	0	2	[2]	6	5	[1]	1
reverse suffix	0	2	2	[1	1	5	6]
final array	0	2	2	1	1	5	6

Figure 15.7 Computation of the next permutation.

Sorting the suffix in increasing order essentially comes down to reversing its elements since, initially, it was in decreasing order.

```
def next_permutation(tab):
    n = len(tab)
    pivot = None                          # find pivot
    for i in range(n - 1):
        if tab[i] < tab[i + 1]:
            pivot = i
    if pivot is None:                     # tab is already the last perm.
        return False
    for i in range(pivot + 1, n):         # find the element to swap
        if tab[i] > tab[pivot]:
            swap = i
    tab[swap], tab[pivot] = tab[pivot], tab[swap]
    i = pivot + 1
    j = n - 1                             # invert suffix
    while i < j:
        tab[i], tab[j] = tab[j], tab[i]
        i += 1
        j -= 1
    return True
```

The solution to the problem of word additions can then be coded as follows.

```python
def convert(word, ass):
    retval = 0
    for x in word:
        retval = 10 * retval + ass[x]
    return retval


def solve_word_addition(S):          # returns number of solutions
    n = len(S)
    letters = sorted(list(set(''.join(S))))
    not_zero = ''                    # letters that cannot be 0
    for word in S:
        not_zero += word[0]
    tab = ['@'] * (10 - len(letters)) + letters  # minimal lex permutation
    count = 0
    while True:
        ass = {tab[i]: i for i in range(10)}  # dict = associative array
        if tab[0] not in not_zero:
            difference = -convert(S[n - 1], ass)  # do the addition
            for word in S[:n - 1]:
                difference += convert(word, ass)
            if difference == 0:                  # does it add up?
                count += 1
        if not next_permutation(tab):
            break
    return count
```

Variant: Enumeration of Combinations and Permutations
A simple trick to enumerate the combinations of n elements taken k at a time, i.e. the subsets of $\{1, \ldots, n\}$ with k elements, consists of iterating over the permutations of the binary mask 'k taken, $n - k$ not taken', i.e. a list containing $n - k$ elements '0' followed by k elements '1'. Then, this mask allows us to select the elements forming the subset.

To enumerate the permutations of n taken k at a time, it suffices to enumerate the permutations of combinations of n taken k at a time, which comes down to using two nested iterations of next_permutation. This provides another solution to the problem of word additions, by selecting the permutations of k letters among 10 where k is the number of distinct letters.

We will next tackle a technique, already mentioned in Section 1.6.6 on page 34, to more cleverly iterate over the subsets of a set of n elements, in order to solve a great variety of problems of dynamic programming.

Problems
The Next Permutation [spoj:NEXT]
Great Swerc [spoj:SWERC14A]

15.6   Le Compte est Bon

This problem originated in a television game show 'Des chiffres et des lettres', broadcast in France since 1972. The UK version was known as 'Countdown' (1982).

Input
Integers $x_0, \ldots, x_{n-1}$ and b for n quite small, say $n \leq 20$.

Output
An arithmetical expression as close as possible to b, using each of the integers at most once, and using the operations +, -, *, / as often as necessary. Subtraction is allowed only if its result is positive, and division is allowed only if the result is without a remainder.

Algorithm
The algorithm uses exhaustive search and dynamic programming. In a dictionary E, we associate[2] with $S \subseteq \{0, \ldots, n-1\}$ all the values obtained by using each input x_i for $i \in S$ at most once. More precisely, $E[S]$ is in its turn a dictionary associating each obtained value with the corresponding expression.

For example, for $x = (3, 4, 1, 8)$ and $S = \{0, 1\}$, the dictionary $E[S]$ contains the pairs composed of a key x and a value e, where e is an expression formed from the inputs $x_0 = 3, x_1 = 4$ and x the value of e. Hence, $E[s]$ contains the mapping pairs $1 \mapsto 4 - 3, 3 \mapsto 3, 4 \mapsto 4, 7 \mapsto 3 + 4, 12 \mapsto 3 * 4$.

To compute $E[S]$, we loop over all of the partitions of S into two non-empty sets L and R. For each value v_L in $E[L]$ obtained by an expression e_L and each value v_R in $E[R]$ obtained by an expression e_R, we can form new values to be stored in $E[S]$. In particular, $v_L + v_R$ is attained by the expression $e_L + e_R$.

The complexity in the worst case is worse than exponential and is delicate to analyse. First of all, we must count the number of binary trees with at most n leaves, and then multiply by the number of possibilities to assign these operations to internal nodes of the trees. Nonetheless, with the restrictions on subtraction and division, in practice for values of n in the tens, the observed complexity remains acceptable.

Implementation Details
Particular attention must be paid to the order in which the sets S are processed. By respecting the increasing order of their size, we can ensure that the sets $E[L]$ and $E[R]$ have already been determined.

---

[2] With the exception of $S = \emptyset$, which is ignored.

```
def arithm_expr_target(x, target):
    n = len(x)
    expr = [{} for _ in range(1 << n)]
    # expr[S][val]
    # = string solely composed of values in set S that evaluates to val
    for i in range(n):
        expr[1 << i] = {x[i]: str(x[i])}   # store singletons
    all_ = (1 << n) - 1
    for S in range(3, all_ + 1):  # 3: first num that isn't a power of 2
        if expr[S] != {}:
            continue            # in that case S is a power of 2
        for L in range(1, S):   # decompose set S into non-empty sets L, R
            if L & S == L:
                R = S ^ L
                for vL in expr[L]:       # combine expressions from L
                    for vR in expr[R]:   # with expressions from R
                        eL = expr[L][vL]
                        eR = expr[R][vR]
                        expr[S][vL] = eL
                        if vL > vR:     # difference cannot become negative
                            expr[S][vL - vR] = "(%s-%s)" % (eL, eR)
                        if L < R:       # break symmetry
                            expr[S][vL + vR] = "(%s+%s)" % (eL, eR)
                            expr[S][vL * vR] = "(%s*%s)" % (eL, eR)
                        if vR != 0 and vL % vR == 0:  # only integer div
                            expr[S][vL // vR] = "(%s/%s)" % (eL, eR)
    # look for the closest expression from the target
    for dist in range(target + 1):
        for sign in [-1, +1]:
            val = target + sign * dist
            if val in expr[all_]:
                return "%s=%i" % (expr[all_][val], val)
    # never reaches here if x contains integers between 0 and target
    pass
```

16   Conclusion

In conclusion, here a few final remarks before we let you loose into the wilderness.

16.1   Combine Algorithms to Solve a Problem

At times, the problem may require you to find an optimal value. Can this value be found by dichotomy? If it lies between 0 and N and if the condition verifies a certain property, this adds only a factor $\log N$ to the complexity. This is why it is always profitable to know how to efficiently code a binary search, see Section 1.6.7 on page 35. Try your skills on this problem, one of the most difficult:

- It can be arranged [kattis:itcanbearranged].

Do you have to count the number of subsequences, or some other combinatorial structure, modulo some large prime number? Then, a recurrence relation by dynamic programming can be combined with replacing every division by a multiplication with the inverse modulo p, see Section 14 on page 214.

Is a greedy algorithm sufficient, or are we faced with a problem of dynamic programming? What is the recurrence? Is the recursive structure of the problem at hand a special case of some known problem? It is only by solving lots and lots of problems that you can build and hone these reflexes.

Finally, the size of the instances can sometimes provide a clue as to the expected complexity, see the table in Section 1.4 on page 18.

16.2   For Further Reading

Here is a selection of works completing the subjects treated in this book.

- An essential reference for fundamental algorithms is the substantial *Introduction to Algorithms* by T. H. Cormen, C. E. Leiserson, R. L. Rivest and C. Stein, MIT Press, 3rd ed., 2009.
- For a variety of more specialised algorithms, see *Encyclopedia of Algorithms*, a collective work edited by Ming-Yang Kao, Springer Verlag, 2nd ed., 2016.

- Flow algorithms are studied from top to bottom in *Network Flows: Theory, Algorithms, and Applications* by R. K. Ahuja, T. L. Magnanti and J. B. Orlin, Pearson, 2013.
- A good introduction to algorithms for problems in geometry is *Computational Geometry: Algorithms and Applications* by M. de Berg, O. Cheung, M. van Kreveld and M. Overmars, Springer Verlag 2008.
- If you would like to learn more about tricky manipulations with the binary representation of integers, the following is a delightful reference: *Hacker's Delight* by Henry S. Warren, Jr, Addison-Wesley, 2013.
- A very good introduction to programming in Python is *Think Python: How to Think Like a Computer Scientist* by Allen Downey, O'Reilly Media, 2015.
- Other highly appreciated books include *Python Essential Reference* by David M. Beazley, Pearson Education, 2009 and *Python Cookbook* by Brian K. Jones, O'Reilly Media, 2013.
- Two texts more adapted to the preparation for programming contests are *Competitive Programming* by Steven and Felix Halim, Lulu, 2013 and *The Algorithm Design Manual* by Steven S. Skiena, Springer Verlag, 2009.

Throughout this work, the references point to the bibliography at the end of the book. It includes books but also research articles, which are in general less accessible and destined for a public of specialists. Many of these articles can be accessed freely on the Internet, or found in a university Computer Science library.

16.3   Rendez-vous on tryalgo.org

This book is accompanied by a website, `tryalgo.org`, where the code of all the Python programs described here can be found, as well as test data, training exercises and solutions that, of course, must not be read before having attempted the problems. The package `tryalgo` is available on GitHub and PyPI under the MIT licence, and can be installed under Python 2 or 3 via `pip install tryalgo`.

```
>>> import tryalgo
>>> help(tryalgo)          # for the list of modules
>>> help(tryalgo.arithm)   # for a particular module
```

Happy hacking!

Debugging tool

If you are stymied when trying to solve a problem, speak to this rubber duck. Explain to it precisely and in detail your approach, go over and comment line-by-line your code, and you are guaranteed to find the mistake.

References

Ahuja, Ravindra K., Magnanti, Thomas L., and Orlin, James B. 1993. *Network Flows: Theory, Algorithms, and Applications*. Prentice Hall.

Alt, Helmut, Blum, Norbert, Mehlhorn, Kurt, and Paul, Markus. 1991. Computing a Maximum Cardinality Matching in a Bipartite Graph in Time $O(n^{1.5}\sqrt{m/\log n})$. *Information Processing Letters*, **37**(4), 237–240.

Andrew, Alex M. 1979. Another Efficient Algorithm for Convex Hulls in Two Dimensions. *Information Processing Letters*, **9**(5), 216–219.

Aspvall, Bengt, Plass, Michael F., and Tarjan, Robert Endre. 1979. A Linear-time Algorithm for Testing the Truth of Certain Quantified Boolean Formulas. *Information Processing Letters*, **8**(3), 121–123.

Bellman, Richard. 1958. On a Routing Problem. *Quarterly of Applied Mathematics*, **16**, 87–90.

Cormen, Thomas H., Leiserson, Charles E., Rivest, Ronald L., and Stein, Clifford. 2010. *Algorithmique*. Dunod.

Dilworth, R. P. 1950. A Decomposition Theorem for Partially Ordered Sets. *Annals of Mathematics*, **51**(1), 161–166.

Dinitz, Yefim. 2006. *Dinitz' Algorithm: The Original Version and Even's Version*. Berlin, Heidelberg: Springer Berlin Heidelberg. Pages 218–240.

Edmonds, Jack. 1965. Paths, Trees, and Flowers. *Canadian Journal of Mathematics*, **17**(3), 449–467.

Edmonds, Jack, and Johnson, Ellis L. 1973. Matching, Euler Tours and the Chinese Postman. *Mathematical Programming*, **5**(1), 88–124.

Edmonds, Jack, and Karp, Richard M. 1972. Theoretical Improvements in Algorithmic Efficiency for Network Flow Problems. *Journal of the ACM*, **19**(2), 248–264.

Elias, Peter, Feinstein, Amiel, and Shannon, Claude. 1956. A Note on the Maximum Flow through a Network. *IRE Transactions on Information Theory*, **2**(4), 117–119.

Fenwick, Peter M. 1994. A New Data Structure for Cumulative Frequency Tables. *Software: Practice and Experience*, **24**(3), 327–336.

Floyd, Robert W. 1962. Algorithm 97: Shortest Path. *Communications of the ACM*, **5**(6), 345–.

Ford, Lester Randolph. 1956. *Network Flow Theory*. Tech. rept. P-923. RAND Corporation.

Ford, L. R., and Fulkerson, D. R. 1956. Maximal Flow through a Network. *Canadian Journal of Mathematics*, **8**, 399–404.

Fredman, Michael L., and Tarjan, Robert Endre. 1987. Fibonacci Heaps and Their Uses in Improved Network Optimization Algorithms. *Journal of the ACM*, **34**(3), 596–615.

Freivalds, Rūsiņš. 1979. Fast Probabilistic Algorithms. Pages 57–69 of: *Mathematical Foundations of Computer Science 1979*. Springer.

Gabow, Harold N. 1976. An Efficient Implementation of Edmonds' Algorithm for Maximum Matching on Graphs. *Journal of the ACM*, **23**(2), 221–234.

Gajentaan, Anka, and Overmars, Mark H. 1995. On a Class of $O(n^2)$ Problems in Computational Geometry. *Computational Geometry*, **5**(3), 165–185.

Gale, David, and Shapley, Lloyd S. 1962. College Admissions and the Stability of Marriage. *American Mathematical Monthly*, 9–15.

Goldberg, Andrew V., and Rao, Satish. 1998. Beyond the Flow Decomposition Barrier. *Journal of the ACM*, **45**(5), 783–797.

Gries, David, and Misra, Jayadev. 1978. A Linear Sieve Algorithm for Finding Prime Numbers. *Communications of the ACM*, **21**(12), 999–1003.

Hierholzer, Carl, and Wiener, Chr. 1873. Über die Möglichkeit, einen Linienzug ohne Wiederholung und ohne Unterbrechung zu umfahren. *Mathematische Annalen*, **6**(1), 30–32.

Hitotumatu, Hirosi, and Noshita, Kohei. 1979. A Technique for Implementing Backtrack Algorithms and Its Application. *Information Processing Letters*, **8**(4), 174–175.

Hopcroft, John, and Karp, Richard. 1972. An $n^{5/2}$ Algorithm for Maximum Matchings in Bipartite Graphs. *SIAM Journal on Computing*, **2**(4), 225–231.

Hopcroft, John, and Tarjan, Robert. 1973. Algorithm 447: Efficient Algorithms for Graph Manipulation. *Communications of the ACM*, **16**(6), 372–378.

Hougardy, Stefan. 2010. The Floyd–Warshall Algorithm on Graphs with Negative Cycles. *Information Processing Letters*, **110**(8-9), 279–281.

Hu, T. C., and Shing, M. T. 1984. Computation of Matrix Chain Products. Part II. *SIAM Journal on Computing*, **13**(2), 228–251.

Huffman, David A. 1952. A Method for the Construction of Minimum-Redundancy Codes. *Proceedings of the IRE*, **40**(9), 1098–1101.

Karp, Richard M. 1978. A Characterization of the Minimum Cycle Mean in a Digraph. *Discrete Mathematics*, **23**(3), 309–311.

Karp, Richard M., and Rabin, M. O. 1987. Efficient Randomized Pattern-Matching Algorithms. *IBM Journal of Research and Development*, **31**(2), 249–260.

Knuth, Donald E. 2000. Dancing Links. *arXiv preprint cs/0011047*.

Knuth, Donald E., Morris, Jr, James H., and Pratt, Vaughan R. 1977. Fast Pattern Matching in Strings. *SIAM Journal on Computing*, **6**(2), 323–350.

Kosaraju, S. Rao. 1979. Fast Parallel Processing array Algorithms for Some Graph Problems (Preliminary Version). Pages 231–236 of: *Proceedings of the Eleventh Annual ACM Symposium on Theory of Computing*. ACM.

Kozen, Dexter C. 1992. *The Design and Analysis of Algorithms*. Springer Verlag.

Kruskal, Joseph B. 1956. On the Shortest Spanning Subtree of a Graph and the Traveling Salesman Problem. *Proceedings of the American Mathematical Society*, **7**(1), 48–50.

Kuhn, Harold W. 1955. The Hungarian Method for the Assignment Problem. *Naval Research Logistics Quarterly*, **2**, 83–97.

Lo, Chi-Yuan, Matoušek, Jiří, and Steiger, William. 1994. Algorithms for Ham-Sandwich Cuts. *Discrete & Computational Geometry*, **11**(1), 433–452.

Manacher, Glenn. 1975. A New Linear-Time On-Line Algorithm for Finding the Smallest Initial Palindrome of a String. *Journal of the ACM*, **22**(3), 346–351.

Moore, Edward F. 1959. The Shortest Path through a Maze. Pages 285–292 of: *Proceedings of the International Symposium on Switching Theory 1957, Part II*. Harvard Univ. Press, Cambridge, Mass.

Morrison, Donald R. 1968. PATRICIA - Practical Algorithm To Retrieve Information Coded in Alphanumeric. *Journal of the ACM*, **15**(4), 514–534.

Munkres, James. 1957. Algorithms for the Assignment and Transportation Problems. *Journal of the Society for Industrial and Applied Mathematics*, **5**(1), 32–38.

Ollivier, François. 2009a. Looking for the Order of a System of Arbitrary Ordinary Differential Equations. *Applicable Algebra in Engineering, Communication and Computing*, **20**(1), 7–32.

Ollivier, François. 2009b. The Reduction to Normal Form of a Non-normal System of Differential Equations. *Applicable Algebra in Engineering, Communication and Computing*, **20**(1), 33–64.

Papadimitriou, Christos H. 2003. *Computational Complexity*. John Wiley and Sons Ltd.

Roy, Bernard. 1959. Transitivité et connexité. *Comptes rendus de l'Académie des Sciences*, **249**, 216–218.

Schrijver, Alexander. 2002. On the History of the Transportation and Maximum Flow Problems. *Mathematical Programming*, **91**(3), 437–445.

Stoer, Mechthild, and Wagner, Frank. 1997. A Simple Min-Cut Algorithm. *Journal of the ACM*, **44**(4), 585–591.

Strassen, Volker. 1969. Gaussian Elimination Is Not Optimal. *Numerische Mathematik*, **13**(4), 354–356.

Tarjan, Robert. 1972. Depth-First Search and Linear Graph Algorithms. *SIAM Journal on Computing*, **1**(2), 146–160.

Ukkonen, Esko. 1985. Finding Approximate Patterns in Strings. *Journal of Algorithms*, **6**(1), 132–137.

Warshall, Stephen. 1962. A Theorem on Boolean Matrices. *Journal of the ACM*, **9**(1), 11–12.

Yang, I-Hsuan, Huang, Chien-Pin, and Chao, Kun-Mao. 2005. A Fast Algorithm for Computing a Longest Common Increasing Subsequence. *Information Processing Letters*, **93**(5), 249–253.

Index